"In *Adam and the Genome*, Denn[...]
us with a model of the kind of op[...]
between scientists and scholars of t[...]
plains complex scientific information in a way that nonscientists [...]
to understand, and Scot wrestles with ways we might understand what the
Scriptures say about Adam in light of both a high view of Scripture and an
openness to scientific discoveries. All who realize that we cannot ignore scientific discoveries as we think about the Christian faith will be grateful for
Dennis and Scot's partnership."

—**Roy E. Ciampa**, Nida Institute for Biblical Scholarship

"The dismal history of Christian opposition to the relatively assured results
of scientific discovery, and the impact on intelligent, scientifically savvy young
people of what may appear to them to be a failure by Christians to face facts,
should make us deeply grateful to faithful Christian scientists and biblical
scholars who seek to take both the Bible and the scientific data with full seriousness. Dennis Venema and Scot McKnight provide a fine model of such an
endeavor as they confront the compelling evidence for evolution in the human
line, involving a group of thousands of early hominins, and its meaning for
the biblical treatment of Adam and Eve. One may energetically disagree theologically or question aspects of the neo-Darwinian synthesis while still being
informed and stimulated by this ambitious, irenic, and engaging treatment."

—**Marguerite Shuster**, Fuller Theological Seminary

"Venema and McKnight offer a rare sort of work worthy of our attention,
combining Dennis's ability to give clear, cogent explanations of the strength
and motive force of the science behind biological evolution with Scot's winsome and coherent biblical, historical, and theological expositions. Their
honest appraisals help us see how they have managed the challenges and
opportunities of genomic science and presented a path for faithful commitment to biblical exposition. Even where the reader may disagree with some
particular aspect, their work challenges us to examine the traditions and
systems of exposition that have grown over time. In doing so, Venema and
McKnight help us see that exegesis that fully engages scientific discoveries
need not amount to a rejection of the Scriptures. They offer a viable way
forward, inviting a broader audience into the conversation."

—**Stanley P. Rosenberg**, University of Oxford

"Few topics generate greater passion among evangelical Christians today than
the question of the literal accuracy of the biblical creation story. With the
advances in science, we have two accounts of the origin of living beings—one
scientific, the other scriptural—and many believe that they are mutually exclusive. Choose science or choose the Bible, we are told, but we can't have it both
ways. This book, by two of evangelicalism's most articulate communicators—
one a scientist, the other a biblical scholar—carefully considers whether that
claim is true. The result is the most lucid and thorough discussion of the

topic I have ever read. Dennis Venema marvelously explains genetic concepts by using everyday illustrations. Scot McKnight's approach is pastoral. In an awe-inspiring manner, he sensitively leads us into an appreciation of the biblical issues and shows us how theologically rich and intellectually satisfying they are. Because it is so clearly and carefully written, this book will mark a watershed moment in the history of evangelical Christianity. The radical distinction between two seemingly disparate positions ought to disappear forever, these authors show, as each position melds with the other to form one harmonious whole."

—**Darrel Falk**, Point Loma Nazarene University

"This is an unlikely book. Who could imagine a geneticist and a New Testament scholar teaming up to write about Adam and Eve? We are fortunate that they did. Venema and McKnight address in a learned yet accessible way issues about which many of us have little understanding. We are indebted to them for giving us information and insights that enable us to think about human origins in ways that are both scientifically informed and grounded in a carefully nuanced interaction with the biblical text and early Jewish traditions. The church is well served by this sort of interdisciplinary collaboration, which assists us in both adapting and adopting Adam (and Eve) as interpreters have through the centuries."

—**John H. Walton**, Wheaton College

"This is a unique and valuable book: an expert geneticist and a leading New Testament scholar come together to address questions of Adam and Eve. Venema and McKnight guide readers in an in-depth look at the genetic evidence for human evolution and at the views of Adam in the ancient Jewish world. As these two Christian scholars listen to each other, share their personal journeys on origins, and address the questions of evangelicals, their pastoral concern for the church and for students shines through. Not all readers will agree with their conclusions, but the book is essential reading for all who seek an understanding of human origins that respects both Scripture and God's creation."

—**Deborah Haarsma**, president of BioLogos

"Anyone who doubts that Christian faith and evolutionary science can have a peaceful and fruitful relationship needs to read this remarkable book, a shining example of a complementary approach to science and religion in which both enhance, enrich, and complete each other. Dennis Venema offers indisputable scientific evidence for the evolution of living organisms, including humans, in a clear, accessible style. Scot McKnight deals with the challenging issue of whether Adam was a historical person. Drawing upon a wide range of creation accounts from the ancient Near East, and in particular ancient Jewish literature, he demonstrates that biblical passages on human origins and Adam must be read within their ancient milieu and context. I highly recommend this book."

—**Denis O. Lamoureux**, St. Joseph's College, University of Alberta

ADAM
AND THE
GENOME

*Reading Scripture
after Genetic Science*

DENNIS R. VENEMA
// AND //
SCOT McKNIGHT

BrazosPress

a division of Baker Publishing Group
Grand Rapids, Michigan

© 2017 by Dennis R. Venema and Scot McKnight

Published by Brazos Press
a division of Baker Publishing Group
P.O. Box 6287, Grand Rapids, MI 49516-6287
www.brazospress.com

Printed in the United States of America

Library of Congress Cataloging-in-Publication Data
Names: Venema, Dennis R., 1974– author.
Title: Adam and the genome : reading scripture after genetic science / Dennis R. Venema and Scot McKnight.
Description: Grand Rapids : Brazos Press, 2017. | Includes bibliographical references and index.
Identifiers: LCCN 2016042531 | ISBN 9781587433948 (pbk. : alk. paper)
Subjects: LCSH: Bible and evolution. | Creationism. | Human beings—Origin. | Genetic engineering—Religious aspects—Christianity. | Genomes. | Adam (Biblical figure)
Classification: LCC BS659 .V46 2017 | DDC 233/.1—dc23
LC record available at https://lccn.loc.gov/2016042531

In keeping with biblical principles of creation stewardship, Baker Publishing Group advocates the responsible use of our natural resources. As a member of the Green Press Initiative, our company uses recycled paper when possible. The text paper of this book is composed in part of post-consumer waste.

CONTENTS

FOREWORD

In 2009 the world commemorated the two hundredth birthday of Charles Darwin and the one hundred and fiftieth anniversary of the publication of his groundbreaking work *On the Origin of Species*. Many decades after the appearance of that book, evangelical Protestants find themselves once again in a bitter conflict over the theory of evolution. Though the controversy still rages with those outside our theological family, particularly the "New Atheists" such as Richard Dawkins, the most heated discussions are now taking place among evangelical Christians—between those who believe that one must make a choice between the Bible and evolution, and those who argue that the Bible and evolution are not in tension with each other.

Fuel for this intra-evangelical debate comes from the mapping of the human genome, which was completed in 2003 under the leadership of Francis Collins, who is not only a leading biologist but also a devout evangelical Christian. The evidence provided by the genome, added to the mounting evidence of hominid fossils, further testifies to the persuasiveness of the theory presented by Darwin in the mid-nineteenth century.

To compound the conundrum, the research of evolutionary biologists also points to another conclusion that disturbs many evangelical Christians—namely, that humanity begins not with a single couple but rather with an original population of some thousands of people. This evidence leads to the now-much-discussed question of the historical Adam. If Adam and Eve were not historical individuals, is the Bible true? Were humans originally innocent? Was there a fall? Is there such a thing as original sin? If so, how does original sin affect us today?

These are crucial questions that aren't easily answered. They are also questions that cannot be ignored by refusing to address them or by vilifying those who hold opinions that are different from the ones we are used to.

Further, the evidence is clear that the church has a credibility problem in the eyes of our youth when it unthinkingly rejects evolution. When presented with the choice of evolution or the Bible, many are choosing evolution. Those who choose the Bible and reject evolution often do so at the cost of their intellect.

As we will see in this book, to force such a choice on our youth (or anyone for that matter) misrepresents the Bible and has worked great harm.

To deal with these issues, we need to marshal our best theological and scientific thinking. With Dennis Venema and Scot McKnight, we are getting exactly that.

I have known Dennis for about five years and have come to appreciate him for his intelligence and his devotion to God. His knowledge of biology and, in particular, the genome is impressive, but so is his ability to explain complex research to laypeople like me. I have found him to be an incredible resource for understanding biological science, and I know that you will too.

I have known Scot for a long time as a fellow laborer in biblical studies and as a friend. Over the past three decades, he has taught New Testament in both college and seminary settings. He has established himself not only in the academy but also in the church. Scot is that rare academic who knows the scholarly material extremely well but is also able to communicate what is important to a broad audience in an understandable and winsome way. He is passionate about Jesus, and he wants Christians to love God with their whole selves, including their brains. Scot has devoted his life to the study of Scripture because he knows that it is the Word of God and it is in Scripture that we hear the voice of God.

I can't imagine a better combination of thinkers to help us navigate the difficult and controversial waters of questions surrounding evolution and the historical Adam. Dennis and Scot deserve our attention, and their arguments demand our careful consideration. I, for one, thank them for their lifelong work in elucidating God's "two books," Scripture and nature, for us.

Tremper Longman III
Robert H. Gundry Professor of Biblical Studies
Westmont College

INTRODUCTION

Like many evangelicals, I (Dennis) grew up in an environment that was suspicious of science in general, and openly hostile to evolution in particular. Yet I had a deep longing to be a scientist, even as a child. For a long time, I reconciled my two worlds by rejecting evolution—after all, evolution was "just a theory" pushed by atheists and supported by "evidence" so flimsy that even a child could see through it. Moreover, Jesus was the way, the truth, and the life, and "what the Bible said about creation" was good enough for me.

I almost didn't become a scientist; despite my childhood dreams, I intended to be a medical doctor, I think largely because I could see that role as having a place within Christendom. I was keen to use my mind and skills for the kingdom, and when I was a teenager, medical missions seemed to me the closest fit. I decided to use biology as a way to prepare for medical school, and along the way God rekindled my childhood interest in science. Looking back, I wonder if my path would have been less circuitous if the church had had a better relationship with science to begin with and "scientist" had been on the unofficial list of acceptable Christian careers. To be sure, "evolutionary biologist" is, at present, certainly *not* on that list.

Now I'm on the other side of the equation, teaching biology to undergraduates—many of whom, like me, come from an evangelical background. Like me, they've heard that evolution is evil and that they have to choose between the Bible and science. I wonder how many of their friends have already made that choice and aren't in my class. How many of them, I wonder, might have become the next Francis Collins? And how many of the students that do come to learn

biology, upon realizing that the Sunday-school flannel-board theology they
learned as kids just isn't up to the task, will abandon their faith, despite my
best efforts to walk them through it with love and pastoral sensitivity?

We as a community need to do better—for the future of the kingdom.

One way for us to do better is to learn—to learn what modern evolutionary
biology is really all about, not the caricature that I absorbed simply by being a
Christian. With that information on the table, then it's time to have a careful
look at Scripture, allow it to speak for itself without our cultural baggage,
and consider carefully what we teach our young people. Science has called
us back to the text before, and it is doing so again. That is what this book is
about, and it is a book I have wanted to write for a long time.

That said, I knew that I wasn't up to the entire task. I needed someone
with expertise in theology and exegesis—preferably someone with expertise
in the New Testament. For though Genesis was key, I was finding more and
more that the conversation was shifting from Genesis to Paul—specifically,
to what Paul says about Adam.

In March 2012, as I pondered these things, I attended a BioLogos meeting
in New York where Scot was one of the featured speakers. As he gave his
paper, I was startled to hear him mention my name and some of my work on
evolution, specifically referencing its implications for Adam and Eve. I had
no idea that a *theologian* was reading one of my papers—and considering
that paper's dense, technical language, it's a testament to his tenacity that he
got anything out of it at all. Like me, Scot had also been wrestling with these
questions from a theological angle, and he was more than willing to add his
voice to the conversation.

I (Scot) remember that meeting when I met Dennis, but what I remember
even more was reading Dennis's article the first time some months earlier.
It took me a good week to read it—so full of charts and information and
terms that were not part of my vocabulary and thinking patterns. Along with
Dennis's exceptional article I read the other articles in the magazine, and I
blogged about them—convinced that if Dennis was right about genetics,
then I had some work to do. It was time to do exactly what Dennis and so
many others were suggesting: take a new look at Adam and Eve in the light
of modern genetics.

It is undeniable in my circles that every time someone brings up evolution—
no matter how it is framed (old-fashioned Darwinian evolution, radical ma-
terialistic evolution, theistic evolution, evolutionary creation, or some forms

of intelligent design)—the question eventually comes to this: *How do I, Scot, believe in Adam and Eve if I embrace some form of evolution?* The perceived implications of embracing evolution haunt many: if evolution is true, the Bible can't be; if evolution is true, the historical Adam never existed; and thus, if evolution is true, there is no reason to preach the gospel to all. I call this theological construct the "historical" Adam and will discuss what that means at the end of chapter 5.

When Dennis contacted me to ask if I would participate with him in a BioLogos grant project on the genome and Adam, I knew the time was ripe. It was time for me to get after the problem and resolve the intellectual tensions in my head or to hide in the library behind my Bible and just do Bible studies. Here's what I did after agreeing to work on this project: I propped up Dennis's article on the genome and hominins next to my computer and proceeded to rewrite the whole thing in language I could understand. It was hard work for me, but I wanted to understand the science of genetics better so I could appreciate more deeply the conclusion of many geneticists today: the DNA in current humans could not have come from a pool of fewer than approximately 10,000 hominins. (These terms will be defined and Dennis's article will be noted in the chapters that follow.) Once I was done with that I sent it off to Dennis, and he informed me that I basically got it right—which was his kind way of saying that I'm a theologian and not a scientist, but that I understood the big picture.

What follows in *Adam and the Genome*, then, is a basic introduction to the science of evolution and genetics and how it impinges on the basic claim of many Christians: that you and I, and the rest of humans for all time, come from two solitary individuals, Adam and Eve. Genetics makes that claim impossible—as I understand it. But instead of leading me to hide behind the Bible or insult scientists, genetics sent me into the stacks of books in the library to investigate science with freedom and to ask yet again what Genesis 1–3 was all about in its original context and then how Jews and the earliest Christians understood "Adam" when they said that name. Did they, I will be asking, think the way we did about the so-called "historical" Adam and Eve? Did they somehow escape the "science" of their day to join hands with what we know today and write things that accord with modern science? Or, which I shall seek to explain in my chapters later in the book, did they think the way ancients thought and offer to their world a brilliant vision of the nature and mission of humans in the world—all captured in that golden expression, the "image of God"? Did they not counter the ancient world's views of God and humans with an alternative theology and anthropology that have become, even among many scientists, the widespread belief of the Western world?

Thus, the book has two parts: science and Bible. The second part (chaps. 5–8, by Scot) assumes the correctness of the first part and seeks to explain Adam and Eve as they were intended to be understood in the ancient world. The first part (chaps. 1–4, by Dennis) offers an accessible introduction to the major topics that have created intellectual tensions in the minds of many Christians.

Dennis R. Venema
Trinity Western University

Scot McKnight
Northern Seminary

Evolution as a Scientific Theory

I (Dennis) grew up in a small town in northern British Columbia, Canada. As a child, I spent a lot of time out in the woods with my father and older brother, hunting and fishing. It was there that I first developed a sense of wonder about the natural world and a desire to understand it better. When we cleaned a fish or a grouse, we examined its stomach contents to see what it had been feeding on. While my father fished for salmon, I puttered in the shallows and back eddies, catching minnows and aquatic insects with a net. At home, I concocted potions and brews from whatever household chemicals I could find. While other kids wanted to be policemen and firefighters, I wanted to be a scientist. Real science, as I understood it from my private-Christian-school workbooks, matched up perfectly with what God said about creation in his Word. "Darwin" and "evolution" were evil, of course—things that atheist scientists believed despite their overwhelming flaws, because those scientists had purposefully blinded their eyes to the truth. I distinctly remember that even hearing those words said out loud felt like hearing someone curse, and not mildly.

I am grateful to my colleagues at BioLogos for their support, encouragement, and shared wisdom over the years as I have worked on this volume. I am also grateful to my friend and brother Doug Chaffee, who read early drafts of my chapters and offered valuable suggestions. Lastly, I am deeply thankful for the love and support of my family as I wrote over many a late night.

My interest in science continued as I moved over to the local public high school, though, ironically, I found biology to be a dreadful bore compared with physics and chemistry. Those subjects required that I learn and apply principles, rather than slavishly memorize. Biology seemed to have no organizing principle behind it, whereas the others did: understand an atom, and you understand chemistry; understand how forces and matter work, and you understand physics. Biology? Here, memorize this laundry list of facts. No thanks.

Living in a small town also meant that I did not know any scientists beyond the ones I saw on TV. Thus I couldn't really picture science as a career, despite my youthful ambitions. My friends didn't want to be firemen or policemen anymore either, and "scientist" seemed to be as whimsical as those aspirations had been. I had, however, spent two summers on short-term missions trips, and I thought that perhaps becoming a doctor would be a good choice for a career that could be useful in the mission field. I had good grades, so medical school seemed like a viable option. So off to university I went to study biology, because a degree in biology seemed like a good way to prepare to be a doctor. My family explored the possibility of my attending a Christian university, but it was more than we could afford. So a secular university it was, and I braced myself for what would surely be a trial for my faith. One Sunday our church prayed for and "commissioned" us graduates as we went off to university or Bible college. Our pastor thanked God for those headed for the safe confines of further Christian training, and prayed that those of us headed to secular settings would not lose our faith in the process.

I must admit that I did not like my first two years of study. Again, memorization seemed to be the order of the day, and every so often the "evolution thing" would come up. Thankfully, evolution was mentioned only infrequently and easily ignored. Still, I wasn't doing that well, and biology seemed to be as boring as it had been in high school. I doubted my grades would be enough for the hypercompetitive medical school application process. But in my third year, I turned a corner. Having struggled through the basic introductory courses, I was finally getting into more interesting material where understanding principles was more important than memorizing details. Cell biology and genetics were especially interesting. I decided I wanted to earn an honors degree and write a research thesis. Why I thought this would be a good idea, given my lackluster performance to that point, I do not recall. Still, I found a professor willing to take me on, and I eagerly started working in her lab.

It changed everything. I was working on an open scientific question, one without a canned textbook answer. To address the question, I needed to understand the principles of developmental cell biology, genetics, and how gene products work at the molecular level. I was designing experiments to test hypotheses, and troubleshooting them to get them to work properly.

For the first time I was doing real science, and I was hooked.

Not surprisingly, my grades improved dramatically. At last I was being graded on my ability to think like a scientist, rather than regurgitate textbooks. While I had been worried that my average was too low for medical school, my last two years more than made up for my slow start. I had the grades for medical school now, but I had lost the desire. I didn't even bother applying, but rather signed up for a PhD program in genetics and cell biology directly out of my bachelor's degree. My childhood dreams were coming true, and I was as happy as a kid on a field trip to the fire hall.

Just a Theory

I later came to understand why biology suddenly came alive to me in the lab, and why up to that point it had seemed so dull. What had been missing was what I had glimpsed in high school chemistry and physics: underlying principles that gave order and cohesion to a body of facts. For me, it meant exploring biological theories of genetic inheritance and development, and understanding the details (facts) in light of those organizing structures (theories). Once I understood the theories, the facts were no longer unconnected details to be memorized: the facts made sense.

At this point we need to clarify some terminology: "theory" in common usage unfortunately means almost the opposite of what a scientist means by it. In common usage, it means something like "guess" or "conjecture." In science, however, it means anything but. In science, a theory is an explanatory framework for *why* the facts are the way they are. Theories are not developed overnight—on the contrary, they are the products of a long process of making observations, forming hypotheses, and testing those hypotheses with experiments.

Perhaps an analogy will help. When my children were younger, they liked to play a game called "Guess Who?" In this game, both players have a card with various characters on them, from whom they select one. The object of the game is to guess the character the other player has chosen. Each player takes turns asking questions to try to narrow down the options, questions such as "Is your character a boy or a girl?," "Does your character have glasses?," and so on. The initial guesses are just that, guesses. As the game proceeds, however, one begins to have a better-informed guess since some options have been eliminated. And once you've guessed correctly, every question you ask will be answered as you expect it to be.

A scientific theory is formed by a similar process. It starts with a guess of sorts—perhaps an educated guess, based on prior observations. It looks to the available facts and asks *why* the facts are the way they are. The result is a hypothesis—the technical term for "educated guess." A scientist can use that hypothesis to form a prediction: if this is why things are the way they are, then *such and such* should be the case. Then an experiment can be set up to test the prediction, and the result will either support or fail to support the hypothesis. If the prediction is not supported, a scientist will reject the hypothesis. If the prediction is supported by the experiment, the scientist will *fail to reject* the hypothesis. Note that this is not the same as "accepting" the hypothesis—an important distinction within science. *Accepting* a hypothesis would mean that no further tests would be required. This would make as much sense as deciding, on the basis of one or two correct guesses in the guessing game, that one had discovered the character one's opponent had selected. Not so—future tests may show that our hypothesis is not perfectly accurate. Sure, the character is female with a hat and glasses, but she *doesn't* have a purple scarf. Well, then, it's time to readjust the hypothesis in light of the new evidence.

In science, a hypothesis that is *not rejected* after many, many predictions and tests eventually becomes a broad explanatory framework that has withstood repeated experimentation and that makes accurate predictions about the natural world: in other words, a theory. The term "hypo" comes from the Greek for "less than," and "thesis" is another word for "theory." So "hypothesis" simply means "less than a theory." If a hypothesis withstands the trial of repeated experimentation, eventually it becomes a thesis—a theory.

Good theories, then, are close approximations of how the natural world actually works. Scientists don't ever fully "accept" them as "true" or "proven," but many theories in science are so well established that it is highly unlikely that new evidence will substantially modify them. The chromosomal theory of inheritance and the germ theory of disease are examples of such theories: the evidence supporting them is huge, and every new technology that scientists have developed to study either one continues to support them—though they have been revised and improved in the process. "Just a theory," then, is high praise from a scientific viewpoint—there is nothing better in science. A good theory, since it is a very close approximation of what is actually true, is very useful for making predictions about the natural world. Moreover, it provides a logical framework for making

sense of current data—something that my high school biology experience
lacked.

Science, Falsely So Called

Even though scientists know what they mean by the word "theory," nonscientists can be forgiven for thinking it means "relatively uninformed guess."
We've all read headlines about scientific discoveries that "overturn previous
theories" and "change everything we thought we knew." The truth is, these
headlines are misleading and are often more the result of journalists looking
for a catchy headline rather than accurately representing a new scientific finding. Often, the scientists themselves are eager to portray their work as novel
and exciting, and so aid and abet the journalists. "Incremental advancement
to a large body of prior knowledge!" just doesn't sell papers in the same way.

Another confounding issue is that often the topic is dietary science. One
day cholesterol is bad; the next day it's fine. One day tomatoes are linked to
cancer; the next day they've been shown to prevent cancer. (I'm not actually
making these claims, of course—the point is that we've all seen headlines
like these, many times over.) Why can't scientists make up their minds? It
looks, for all intents and purposes, like they're just guessing. This sort of
thing makes science look pretty wishy-washy—and leads many Christians
to think that they're better off sticking to the plain truth of the Bible. There
is a good reason why these news stories crop up so frequently: they naturally
have a strong interest for the average person in ways that many areas of science don't. You don't as often see news stories on genetics or particle physics,
unless something about a new finding is particularly interesting to average
people. Dietary research is naturally interesting to everyone, since we all want
to know how to lose weight and stay healthy.

Unfortunately, dietary science is one of the most challenging types of science to do well, and a lot of it is not performed to a high standard. Throw in
an overeager, self-promoting researcher and a journalist on a deadline, and it
is not surprising we get what we get in our Facebook feeds. One of the main
challenges for this type of research is that it is difficult to exclude potential
confounding variables: Are the two groups of research subjects as similar as
they can be? Not likely. Has the research been properly scrutinized by experts
in the field before being published? Perhaps not. Are the results shocking and
therefore newsworthy? Press release!

One study that beautifully reveals the challenges and problems with this
type of research and its subsequent news cycle came to light recently. It's not

surprising that this study gained international attention; after all, it showed that eating chocolate was a way to lose weight!

> "Slim by Chocolate!" the headlines blared. A team of German researchers had found that people on a low-carb diet lost weight 10 percent faster if they ate a chocolate bar every day. It made the front page of *Bild*, Europe's largest daily newspaper, just beneath their update about the Germanwings crash. From there, it ricocheted around the internet and beyond, making news in more than 20 countries and half a dozen languages. It was discussed on television news shows. It appeared in glossy print, most recently in the June issue of *Shape* magazine ("Why You Must Eat Chocolate Daily," page 128). Not only does chocolate accelerate weight loss, the study found, but it leads to healthier cholesterol levels and overall increased well-being. The *Bild* story quotes the study's lead author, Johannes Bohannon, Ph.D., research director of the Institute of Diet and Health: "The best part is you can buy chocolate everywhere."[1]

Before you get your hopes up and dash off to the store with a newly cleansed conscience, I've got some bad news: the study shows nothing of the kind. In fact, the real experiment was to see if a weak study with obvious flaws could be published and grab public attention. In other words, its actual purpose was to see how easy it was to game the "dietary science" news cycle, as the lead author of the study revealed after the fact:

> I am Johannes Bohannon, Ph.D. Well, actually my name is John, and I'm a journalist. I do have a Ph.D., but it's in the molecular biology of bacteria, not humans. The Institute of Diet and Health? That's nothing more than a website. Other than those fibs, the study was 100 percent authentic. My colleagues and I recruited actual human subjects in Germany. We ran an actual clinical trial, with subjects randomly assigned to different diet regimes. And the statistically significant benefits of chocolate that we reported are based on the actual data. It was, in fact, a fairly typical study for the field of diet research. Which is to say: It was terrible science. The results are meaningless, and the health claims that the media blasted out to millions of people around the world are utterly unfounded.[2]

Reading Dr. Bohannon's full account of this "study" is well worth your time, since it reveals just how easy it was to pull off this stunt. The secret to "success" in this case was using a small number of test subjects and examining them for a large number of traits (cholesterol levels, weight gain, general feelings of happiness, and so on). With this experimental design, it is highly probable that at least a few statistically significant differences between the two groups (groups on a low-carbohydrate diet either with or without a small serving of dark chocolate) would be found. Those differences, however, are due to chance alone. Every claim of statistical significance is based on rejecting the probability of it being a fluke. Test enough variables with a small number of subjects, however, and eventually you'll find, by chance alone, a few variables that show "significance." In this case, a small chance fluctuation in weight and cholesterol levels in the right group was what gave the needed results and led to the subsequent rapturous headlines. Now, the peer reviewers of a high-quality scientific journal would easily catch those flaws—but Dr. Bohannon didn't submit his paper to a good journal. Rather, he submitted it to one that any working scientist would immediately recognize as a poor one, even one likely to be a solely-for-profit publisher—the scientific equivalent of a vanity press. In fact, it seems the paper wasn't peer reviewed at all. But that didn't matter: the media fell for it anyway. What surprised Dr. Bohannon was just how readily the media lapped it up. He had suspected that the diet-science, news-hype cycle was uncritically pushing bad science, but even he wasn't prepared for just how easy the process was.

So it's not surprising that many people may have a low view of science; the "science" they see in the newspaper day to day is always changing and constantly contradicting itself. The reason for this unfortunate pattern is simple: it's not rigorous science, and it's being reported by gullible and un-informed journalists. That's not to say that there aren't scientists out there doing careful work in nutrition science and slowly advancing our knowledge base in this important area. Surely they must pull out their hair at the sorts of poor studies that hit the news cycle. Moreover, there are journalists out there who handle science well—such as Dr. Bohannon himself. Typically, they have advanced scientific training as well as a gift for writing for nonspecialists.[3] Unfortunately, they are few and far between.

So despite the diet-fad news cycle, good scientific theories are out there. They're the result of years of careful study, critical review by experts, and a large body of supporting evidence. They make accurate predictions with boring regularity, and Christians typically don't give them a second thought. Some theories do appear on the evangelical Christian radar, though—and evolution is surely one of them. Even as a child I knew from my early church experiences that evolution was bad—it was a way to explain where humans come from that excludes God. Science and God's actions, at least in this case, were placed in opposition to each other. If science could explain human origins as a natural phenomenon without recourse to God's miraculous, instanta-neous creation of our ancestors, then science was diametrically opposed to God and his Word. Everything science explained about our origins was one less reason to believe in God, and besides, we knew the science of evolution was full of holes. This reasoning made perfect sense to me as a child, and I accepted it uncritically.

One Book or Two?

Later, I would learn that this view sits in strong tension, to put it mildly, with centuries of Christian thought and practice. The long-standing tradition is one that views both nature and Scripture as "books" authored by God, and holds that science, properly done, is a way to understand the sustaining principles that God has built into the created order.[4] One of God's books is Scripture, and we interpret and apply its truths through interpretation (exegesis and hermeneutics). The second book is the natural world, which we interpret through the scientific method. Science flourished in Christian Europe in the Renaissance as it did because many scientists were Christians and thus felt that the universe would have logical, orderly underpinnings because it was the product of God's design. As Isaac Newton famously declared,

> This most beautiful system of the Sun, Planets, and Comets, could only proceed from the counsel and dominion of an intelligent and powerful being. . . . This Being governs all things, not as the soul of the world, but as Lord over all: And on account of his Dominion he is wont to be called Lord God.[5]

Thus science was seen as a praiseworthy activity for a Christian—the study of science *and* the study of nature revealed God's truth. Moreover, Newton was busy determining laws of motion and describing how they played out for planetary bodies. He viewed his discoveries as understanding the mind of his Creator and the laws that Creator had put in place. Regrettably, evangelical Christian communities seem largely to have lost these convictions for some areas of science.

If indeed nature and Scripture have the same author, as Christians affirm, then there cannot, ultimately, be any disagreement between what we "read" in one book and what we read in the other. The problem, of course, is that our "reading" of either book is not perfect. Science does not yet have a full picture of many aspects of the natural world. Similarly, our exegesis and hermeneutics are not infallible. As a result, there may *appear* to be conflict between science and Scripture, and it may take a long time to sort out apparent disagreements as we wait for improvements in science and theology.

Learning from History

Of course, the church has worked through apparent disagreements before—most notably, the disagreement over whether the earth is at the center of the known universe (i.e., geocentrism), or if the sun is (heliocentrism). Nowadays, we wonder what all the fuss was about. For those who lived through the process, however, it was as real and as pressing as the evolution issue is for us. The basic issues that were on the table for them are the same as they are now: the veracity of the new science, and its perceived threat to biblical authority. Then as now, there were plenty of apologists who thought the new science was wrong and that the Bible was clear in its endorsement of a geocentric universe. Take, for example, the following excerpts from a popular apologetics book from the late 1600s written by John Edwards. He mounts a case against the new science of Copernicus (i.e., heliocentrism) with, as he sees it, both Scripture and science firmly on his side:

> The Copernican Opinion seems to confront a higher Principle than that of Reason. If we will speak like Men of Religion, and such as own the Bible, we must acknowledge that their Assertion is against the plain History of the Holy Book; for there we read that the Sun stood still in Joshua's time, and went back in King Hezekiah's. Now this Relation is either true or false. If it be the latter then the Inspired Scripture is false, which I take to be as great an Absurdity as any Man can be reduced to: If it be the former, i.e., if the Relation is really true, then the Sun hath a Diurnal Motion about the Earth; for the Sun's standing still could not be a strange and wonderful thing (as it is here represented) unless its general course was to move. . . .
>
> Again, I argue thus, the Motion of the Earth can be felt, or it cannot: If they hold it cannot, they are confuted by Earth-quakes . . . I mean the gentler Tremblings of the Earth, of which there are abundant Instances in History, and we our selves have had one not long since; so that by too true an experiment we are taught that the Earth's Motion may be felt. If this were not a thing that had been frequently experienc'd, I confess they might have something to say, they put us off with this, that it is not possible to perceive the moving of the Earth: But now they cannot evade it thus; they must be forc'd to acknowlegd the motion of it is sensible. If then they hold this, I ask why this Motion also which they speak of is not perceived by us? Can a Man perswade himself that the light Trepidation of this Element can be felt, and yet the rapid Circumvolution of it cannot? Are we presently apprehensive of the Earth's shaking never so little under us? And yet have no apprehension at all of our continual capering about the Sun?[6]

The English language has shifted somewhat since the late 1600s, so some translation here might be helpful. (We will actually explore language change over time as a particularly apt analogy for evolution in the next chapter.) First and foremost, Edwards holds that when science and Scripture are in tension, it is science that must give way, since the Bible is a "higher Principle" than that of science ("Reason"). He goes on to argue that either the sun moves about the earth or Scripture is false, given the plain sense of Joshua 10 (Joshua's "long day") and the narrative of Hezekiah's miracle, both of which were common scriptural touchstones for anti-heliocentrists.

Edwards then shifts to a scientific argument: earthquakes can be felt (i.e., they are "sensible": they can be sensed). I recently had an experience of a small earthquake here in the Vancouver area, giving me a renewed appreciation of the force of this argument. When the earth moves, it moves, and you can feel it. In light of such experience, are we really to believe that we are careening around the sun at fantastic speeds and cannot feel it at all? Edwards drives the point home further:

> Nay, truly, if the earth were hurl'd about in a Circle (as these Persons assert) we should feel it to our sorrow, for we should not be able to keep our ground, but must necessarily be thrown off, and all Houses and other Buildings would be thrown down, being forcibly shaked off from the Circumference of the Earth, as things that are laid on a Wheel are flung off by it when it turns round.[7]

Game, set, match—at least in 1696.

Edwards cannot really be faulted for the stance he took at the time, even though there was good evidence, even in 1696, to support a heliocentric universe— evidence such as Galileo's observations, Kepler's laws of planetary motion, and Newton's work on gravitation. What was missing, however, was a key piece of evidence, and Edwards was keenly aware it was missing. One of the key predictions of a heliocentric universe was something called "stellar parallax." If indeed the earth circles the sun once per year, then as its position in space shifts, we should observe shifts in how stars are positioned relative to one another.

Perhaps a demonstration will help. Extend your hands in front of you and hold up one finger in each hand. Place the two fingers in line with each other, one about one foot from your face, and the other about two feet. Close one eye and move your head from side to side. Your fingers will appear to move relative to each other. This is what was expected for stars: if your head moving from side to side represents the earth as it revolves around the sun, then the expectation was that stars would appear to move relative to one another, just like your fingertips do.

What was not understood in the 1600s, however, was just how far stars are from the earth. They are so distant that observing parallax requires high-power telescopes that simply weren't available at the time, since the apparent shifts in position are tiny—imagine trying to detect parallax in closely spaced fingers from a distance of a few hundred yards. As a result, the church could bide its time and withhold its assent. In fact, it wasn't until the 1800s that the technology became available to detect stellar parallax, although other convincing lines of evidence were in place by that time. Since this progression in science played out over centuries, the church also enjoyed a slow pace in changing its stance on this issue. In the 1600s, pretty much all Christians were geocentrists, with only rare exceptions. From the 1900s through to the present day, the situation is reversed (yes, there are still Christian geocentrists out there, though they are extremely few in number). The shift, then, was a gradual one, with plenty of opportunity for gradual theological change within the church along the way. And what of Edwards's strong assertion that if heliocentrism is true, then Scripture is false? Well, it seems that few believers see it that way today.

Though the church has made its peace with a heliocentric solar system, many of us have yet to do so with evolutionary biology. My Christian grade-school books had no problem describing the solar system and gravity in ways that would have made the dear Mr. Edwards blanch, but they (and I) remained resolute on evolution. It was "science, falsely so called," to borrow the King James turn of phrase.[8]

Interestingly, I would remain an antievolutionist through the course of my PhD and on into my career as a professor, now teaching at the very same Christian university I was unable to afford as a student.[9] What would come as something of a shock to me as a young professor is that, contrary to the claims of my Christian grade-school workbooks, evolution is a theory in the scientific sense. Charles Darwin's original hypothesis—that modern species share common ancestors and are shaped by natural selection—has withstood over 150 years of vigorous scientific testing and remains a productive explanatory framework in the present. Make no mistake: there is not a biologist on the planet that would not dearly love to overthrow evolution and replace it with an even better theory. Doing so would be a sure path to research grants, likely a Nobel Prize, and to enduring scientific fame. Biologists have been trying to do just that for over 150 years; however, though we've improved on Darwin's ideas significantly, his core ideas remain intact. His original hypotheses have long since become a theory. Thus there is over 150 years of scientific evidence for evolution that we could discuss, and even a lengthy book could only scratch the surface. We'll turn to some of that evidence now, to illustrate how evolution has stood the test of time and remains our best explanation for biodiversity on earth.

Fish out of Water

One of the things I have come to love about the theory of evolution is how it often forces scientists to make counterintuitive predictions based on the available evidence. For example, evolutionary biology predicts that animals with backbones and four limbs (i.e., vertebrates and tetrapods, respectively, with tetrapods being a subset of vertebrates) are the descendants of fish. This is certainly not what one would intuitively predict apart from evolutionary theory. Fish are fish, and tetrapods are tetrapods; these groups seem very unlike each other. Fish, obviously, are aquatic, have gills, and lack limbs; conversely, tetrapods breathe air, have limbs, and are generally terrestrial. It would be hard to find two groups of animals so unlike each other in form and lifestyle.

Yet there are lines of evidence that somewhat force a biologist's hand in this case. The first clue is that all tetrapods are vertebrates, like fish are. Why might that be the case? Why are there not also *invertebrate* tetrapods? Secondly, as we go back in time in the fossil record, we observe a time when there are no tetrapods, but fish abound. When the first amphibians appear in the fossil record, they bear remarkable similarities to a certain group of fish that came before, some lineages of which persist to the present day—lungfish. Lungfish, as the name implies, have both gills and an air sac through which they can perform gas exchange (i.e., take in oxygen and expel carbon dioxide). These fish use their lung to survive in oxygen-depleted waters—often shallow waters. Even more interesting is that lungfish are lobe-finned fish, rather than ray-finned fish. Your standard aquarium goldfish is a good example of a ray-finned fish: these fish have fins that lack bones, instead being made of skin interspersed with thicker spine-like "rays." Lungfish, on the other hand, have fleshy limbs and bones within their fins; they are part of the group known as "lobe-finned fish." As it happens, early amphibians have a large number of features that are strongly reminiscent of lungfish. Curious, no?

It was these observations, and others, that prompted scientists to look for species in the fossil record that are intermediate in form between lungfish and early amphibians.[10] Knowing when the first amphibians appear in the fossil record helped, since any predecessor to amphibians would have to come before they appear. Now, it is important to understand that one will virtually never find remains of direct ancestors by looking in the fossil record. It is likely, however, that relatives might be found. This applies even to recent human populations. For example, I am of Dutch background, and there are surely individuals buried in the Netherlands who are my direct ancestors, perhaps stretching back hundreds or even thousands of years. The probability of finding one by digging up unmarked graves, even in close proximity to where my ancestors likely lived, is very small. On the other hand, it is likely that nearly any such remains are relatives of mine, to some degree. Examining their remains might be generally informative about my ancestors, even if they are not in my direct lineage. This same principle applies to species in the fossil record. Fossilization is a very infrequent event; nonetheless, careful work allows us to see what sorts of species lived at certain times in the past. If indeed amphibians descend from lobe-finned fish, then it is formally possible that the direct lineage connecting them could be found in the fossil record, however unlikely. There is a much better chance that at least some relatives of the direct lineage were preserved, however, even if those relatives lived before or after the transition took place. The types of species we observe in the fossil record thus could support the hypothesis that amphibians descend from fish, even if a direct transitional lineage remains elusive.

What is interesting is that paleontological work in this time period has found several species that have further blurred the distinction between "fish" and "tetrapod" over the past several years—one of which is informally (and affectionately) called a "fishapod"[11] because of its blend of amphibian-like and fish-like characteristics. These species are unlike any that persist to the present day, and while none of them are likely to be the direct ancestors of early amphibians, their characteristics are highly suggestive of an intermediate state. Thus it is now much harder to draw a definitive line between the categories "lungfish" and "amphibian." While such evidence is not "proof" of an evolutionary transition—recall that scientific hypotheses are not proven, after all—this evidence nonetheless supports one. Given this evidence, then, we *fail to reject* the hypothesis that early amphibians share common ancestors with lungfish. Indeed, on the basis of this successful prediction, it seems that this hypothesis is worth investigating further.

Of course, some might argue that it simply pleased God, as Creator, to create a series of unrelated species at this time in earth's history that happen to suggest an evolutionary relationship. Many Christians find this plausible; but note how this type of argument cannot ever be ruled out by additional evidence. Any additional such species we find in the fossil record would then merely be more separate species that God elected to create at this time. This explanation also leaves scientists bereft of a hypothesis to test with further research. If the species we observe in the fossil record are the direct, special creations of God, then we will not necessarily find a pattern in the fossil record. Faced with such an explanation, a scientist would not have the ability to make predictions about what should be found in the fossil record at certain times.

There and Back Again?

A second example of a counterintuitive prediction that evolution makes is that some tetrapods, after having adapted to a terrestrial environment, nonetheless returned to the sea. After tetrapods appear in the fossil record, we observe a proliferation of tetrapod forms—dinosaurs, birds, mammals, and so on—that are simply not to be found prior to the time suggested by the fish-fishapod-tetrapod transition. Indeed, such gradations of form are known that there are entire groups with names like "mammal-like reptiles" followed by "reptile-like mammals," with, as you might expect, creatures in between that could be reasonably included in either group. Mammals are tetrapods, it would seem, because mammalian characteristics arose in a lineage of tetrapods. Life comes to us in "nested sets," and "mammal" is a subset of "tetrapod." In other words, though all mammals are tetrapods, not all tetrapods are mammals. The probability of mammalian characteristics (such as having hair and feeding their young with milk, as well as a number of defining skeletal characteristics) arising in a separate, unrelated lineage is a pretty big stretch. Therefore, evolution predicts that all mammals are the descendants of terrestrial tetrapods: four-limbed animals that live on land, even fully aquatic mammals like whales, dolphins, and porpoises—even though these mammals have virtually no hair, and even though they have only front flippers and no hind limbs to speak of.

Darwin himself was driven to make this prediction, since the suite of mammalian characteristics is too improbable to assemble twice in unrelated lineages, and whales are clearly mammals. Darwin had no idea what terrestrial mammalian lineage led to whales, but he was convinced there was one. He speculated that the ancestor of modern whales may have been a carnivorous, bear-like mammal:

> In North America the black bear was seen by Hearne swimming for hours with widely open mouth, thus catching, like a whale, insects in the water. Even in so extreme a case as this, if the supply of insects were constant, and if better adapted competitors did not already exist in the country, I can see no difficulty in a race of bears being rendered, by natural selection, more and more aquatic in their structure and habits, with larger and larger mouths, till a creature was produced as monstrous as a whale.[12]

Not surprisingly, critics found the suggestion laughable. For example, R. Seeley wrote:

> Thus Mr. Darwin, while he finds it impossible to believe the plain words of Moses that on the fifth day, "God created whales"—"sees no difficulty" in

believing that a race of bears, by contracting a habit of swimming, gradually lost their legs, and were "developed" into whales of a hundred times their own bulk! And this sort of trash is called "science"! . . . Let us look, for a moment, at this whale, or bear, or bear-whale. What says Geological Science to it? Geology replies that she finds bears in the crust of the earth, and many of them; and that she also finds whales. But that the whale-bear, or creature which was developing from a bear into a whale, she never met with. And, not finding it, she no more believes in it than in a phoenix or a roc. In a word, Geology, which is really a science, declares Mr. Darwin's bear-whale to be a rank impostor.[13]

Indeed, the criticism and ridicule Darwin received on this point was seemingly enough for him to shorten this section as early as the second edition of *On the Origin of Species*.[14] And not surprisingly, since the suggestion that so great a change had been effected through natural selection was incredible to many. Present-day whales (together with dolphins and porpoises, a group collectively known as "cetaceans") have many differences relative to terrestrial mammals. As we have mentioned, one obvious difference is that cetaceans lack four limbs. They have no hind limbs at all, only forelimbs. Moreover, other mammals have two nostrils on the front of their faces. In contrast, cetaceans have a blowhole on the top of their heads. Hair is a defining feature of mammals, yet whales are almost hairless—and the list goes on. If any group of mammals seemed inexplicable to Darwin's critics, cetaceans certainly seemed to qualify. Darwin, however, was a man before his time on this point, though he would not live to see his eventual vindication. Cetaceans are now something of a poster child for evolution, and for good reason. Once again, despite much effort, scientists have not been able to reject this hypothesis.

Fossils documenting the cetacean progression from land to water was a long-standing scientific puzzle. Even though we expect the fossil record to at least preserve relatives if not the actual lineage, no fossils even mildly suggestive of such a transition were known. One ancient whale had already been discovered, though it was likely that Seeley, if he knew of it, would have considered it merely a whale. It was first described from its teeth and vertebrae in the 1830s and thought to be a reptile of grand proportions. Accordingly, it was named *Basilosaurus* or "king lizard."[15] Not long after, however, this classification was challenged and *Basilosaurus* was correctly redescribed as a cetacean, though the attempt to rename it as *Zeuglodon* ultimately failed.[16] Interestingly, this group of ancient whales (a few Basilosaurid species are now known) have small hind limbs unable to support their massive bulk. The presence of hind limbs in these species was not known until much later, however, when better-preserved fossils were found. Aside from these whales, however, no other species blurring the distinction between modern whales and their hypothesized terrestrial tetrapod ancestors were known. This dearth of evidence persisted up until the 1980s, to the delight of antievolutionary apologists.[17]

The issue, as it turned out, was that the Basilosaurids were widely dispersed on the planet, in part because they were completely committed to an aquatic lifestyle. This allowed them to disperse across oceans in ways their distant ancestors could not and, as a result, to be fossilized in many locations, which facilitated their discovery. Determining *where* the land-to-water transition had originally occurred was thus the key, and in the early 1980s it was finally worked out. The place to look for fossils was in present-day India and Pakistan. Once this was understood, a number of significant finds quickly appeared, and though they may not be the direct ancestors of modern cetaceans, these species make drawing a clear dividing line between "whale" and "terrestrial mammal" challenging.[18]

One characteristic of the modern cetacean skull is a distinctive thickened portion covering the middle ear, a structure known as the "involucrum." This characteristic feature was thought to occur only in cetaceans until it was also discovered in a diminutive hoofed mammal, *Indohyus*, an extinct species that lived in India approximately 48 million years ago.[19] *Indohyus* belongs to a group of mammals known as "artiodactyls": "even-toed" hoofed mammals, of which species like deer, cows, and hippos are present-day examples. The discovery that *Indohyus*, which is not a cetacean, nonetheless has a feature that was until that point considered unique to cetaceans, strongly suggests that it was at least a close relative of the ancestral cetacean lineage. Curiously, *Indohyus* was also found to have features consistent with a semiaquatic lifestyle. Its bones are thicker and heavier than one would expect for an artiodactyl of its size. Similar features are found in other aquatic artiodactyls such as hippos. Thick, heavy bones act as ballast when an animal is underwater bottom-walking, and *Indohyus* likely did this either to feed on aquatic plants or evade predators. This sort of behavior can be seen in a modern artiodactyl of comparable size, the African water chevrotain, supporting this hypothesis.[20]

One interesting feature of artiodactyls is that they have an ankle bone, the *astragalus*, that is readily distinguished from the astragalus of other mammals. A second group of ancient artiodactyl species from this region, the Pakicetids, also had this distinctive astragalus, as well as an involucrum and, like *Indohyus*, thickened, heavy bones. Analysis of the radioactive elements in Pakicetid bones indicates they were a group of semiaquatic freshwater predators. As their "cetid" name indicates, scientists include these extinct species within cetaceans because of the many skeletal features they share with modern whales. Relatives of Pakicetids, the larger Ambulocetids, also come from this region, except these extinct artiodactyls were semiaquatic marine predators. "Ambulo" means "walking," so their name literally means "walking whale." They probably would have appeared to us as gigantic otter-like creatures. They too have skeletal characteristics expected of both cetaceans and artiodactyls.

Later still we observe the Protocetids, a group of semiaquatic artiodactyls that have skeletal features indicative of a more fully aquatic lifestyle. The nostrils in Protocetids are not at the tip of the snout but are shifted back along the skull, and the hind-limb skeleton appears insufficient to bear the full weight of these mammals. Scientists believe these species behaved in a way analogous to modern sea lions: hunting and feeding in the ocean, but hauling themselves out to rest, mate, and bear young. Protocetids, like Basilosaurids, are widespread around the globe but were not discovered early like the Basilosaurids were. Basilosaurids, as we have already discussed, are fully aquatic with only tiny hind limbs unconnected to the rest of the skeleton that cannot possibly have been used for locomotion. Interestingly, when exceptionally well-preserved Basilosaurid fossils were discovered, they had the definitive artiodactyl ankle bones, despite their lack of locomotor function. While we cannot tell if any of these species are direct ancestors of modern cetaceans, these extinct forms support the hypothesis that modern cetacean lineage passes through something *Indohyus*-like, to something Pakicetid-like, and so on through Ambulocetid- and Basilosaurid-like forms. In other words, given this fossil evidence, we have *failed to reject* the hypothesis that whales, dolphins, and porpoises descend from terrestrial, tetrapod ancestors.[21]

Of course, this might be merely a series of coincidences—rather remarkable coincidences, to be sure, but coincidences nonetheless. Thus scientists seek corroborating evidence, even if a hypothesis has withstood some tests.

One way to continue to test a hypothesis that has made some successful predictions is to look to other areas of science. While paleontology supports the hypothesis that cetaceans are the highly modified descendants of terrestrial tetrapods, what about other scientific disciplines? Might there be other lines of inquiry that can be brought to bear on the question? In the case of modern cetaceans, certain details of their *embryology*, the study of their development in the womb, are informative. Modern cetaceans have two nostrils on the fronts of their faces as embryos, like all mammalian embryos do. Over the course of development, the nostrils migrate from this starting location to the top of the head and form a blowhole, with the process complete before birth. And strikingly, modern cetaceans are true tetrapods for a short period as embryos. Cetacean embryos develop forelimbs *and* hind limbs at the same stage that all mammals do, but later the hind limbs stop developing and regress back into the body wall. Studies have shown that the basic biological machinery for making a hind limb is properly activated in young cetacean embryos, but that a second set of instructions later causes the process to stop and regress.[22]

These features of cetacean embryology are very difficult to account for apart from an evolutionary explanation. They are strongly suggestive that modern cetaceans do indeed descend from terrestrial mammals, even if details remain to be discovered. Combined with the evidence from paleontology, the original hypothesis is supported by lines of evidence that converge on the same conclusion. Such convergence boosts our confidence that the hypothesis is at least close to the truth and suggests that it will continue to make accurate predictions.

Getting from Point A(mbulocetid) to Point B(asilosaurid)

It's common for people, upon seeing such evidence for the first time, to begin to reflect on the immense improbability of such large changes taking place repeatedly within a lineage. How could a mutation so large occur to change one animal from one form to another without killing it? How would such an animal breed with anything, unless these rare, massive mutations just happened to occur with a male and female in the same generation? Isn't this all wildly improbable?

Well, yes, such a process would be wildly improbable—so improbable, in fact, that no scientist thinks it could ever happen. This does not pose a problem for evolution, however, because *this is not how evolution works*. How it does, in fact, work is the topic we will turn to next.

Genomes as Language, Genomes as Books

When faced with compelling evidence for evolution, many nonbiologists assume that evolution requires substantial changes in multiple organisms in the same generation for a change to pass down over time. Therefore they conclude, reasonably enough, that evolution is too improbable to occur.

If indeed evolution worked that way, they would be right. But, in fact, that's not the way it works. Evolution works by incremental change within a population, shifting its average characteristics over long periods of time. To help us understand this idea better, let's explore an excellent analogy for evolution: how languages change over time.

Hearing the *Godspel*: Language Evolution as an Analogy of Biological Change

A useful analogy to help understand evolution as a population-level phenomenon is language change over time. Anyone who has read the Bible in King James English has at least some appreciation that languages change over time. Changes within a language take place over long timescales and do so within a population of speakers. Consider a familiar verse from John's Gospel:

> Jesus answered, "I am the way and the truth and the life. No one comes to the Father except through me." (John 14:6)

As we would expect from a modern translation, this verse reads easily for us. A mere thousand years ago, however, this verse in "English" is virtually unintelligible to us. The earliest known English Gospels, *Da Haglan Godspel on Englisc*, were written in Anglo-Saxon around the year 990. Anglo-Saxon from this period renders John 14:6 as follows:

> Se Hælend cwæð to him: Ic eom weg,
> and soðfæstnys, and líf: ne cymð nan
> to Fæder, buton þurh me.

FIGURE 2.1. John 14:6 from the Anglo-Saxon
Da Haglan Godspel on Englisc, ca. 990

Even with the advantage of knowing that we are reading John 14:6, we can barely make out the sense of the words. Beyond the marked differences in spelling and grammar, there are even letters that are no longer used in English today. It is something of a stretch to consider Anglo-Saxon and Modern English "the same language"—something that is true only in a technical sense. Yet Anglo-Saxon incrementally became Modern English over generations, within a continuous population of speakers. If we were to sample the "fossil record" for this transition, we can identify numerous "transitional forms" that show snapshots of what we know to be a continuous progression. A sampling of English translations of John 14:6 from the Middle Ages to the present will make the point:

> Jhesus seith to hym, Y am weie, treuthe, and lijf; no man cometh to the fadir, but bi me. (Wycliffe Bible, 1395)

> Iesus sayd vnto him: I am ye waye ye truthe and ye life. And no man cometh vnto the father but by me. (Tyndale Bible, 1525)

> Iesus saith vnto him, I am the Way, the Trueth, and the Life: no man commeth vnto the Father but by mee. (King James Version, 1611)

> Jesus saith unto him, I am the way, the truth, and the life: no man cometh unto the Father, but by me. (King James Version, Cambridge edition, 1769)

As we know, these various translations are not instantaneous changes from one to the next. Rather, they are samples drawn at intervals from a continuous process. All along the way they remained the "same language" in the sense that each generation could easily understand their parents and their offspring. Over time, however, changes accumulated that gradually shifted the language.

Word spellings, grammar, and pronunciations changed. Given enough time, it becomes more and more of a stretch to say the languages are the same—such as Anglo-Saxon and Modern English. Despite the striking differences we see now, the process that produced them was gradual. Additionally, there is no convenient point where we can say Anglo-Saxon "became" Modern English; the process was a continuum.

In the same way, the average characteristics of a species can shift over time. Now imagine a population with a genome—the total genetic instructions for building an organism. In humans, our genome resides on our 46 chromosomes: the 23 that we receive from our fathers, and 23 that we receive from our mothers. For women, the set of 46 includes two X chromosomes, and for males it includes an X and a Y. Each chromosome is a long string of DNA "letters," of which there are only four in the "alphabet." These "letters" are organic chemicals, of course—the chemicals called "adenine" (A), "cytosine" (C), "guanine" (G), and "thymidine" (T)—linked together in a long string. The human genome has about 3 billion of these letters in each set of 23 chromosomes (giving us around 6 billion letters in total). In our analogy, we can consider the human genome to be a "language" shared by a population of "speakers."

Just as no two speakers speak a language in exactly the same way, no two individuals in a population are genetically identical (even identical twins have subtle differences between them). These differences are not a barrier to being part of a species as long as they do not hinder reproduction with other members of the population. As with a language, one does not need uniformity to remain intelligible; slight differences are fine. Consider the word *truth* from the examples of John 14:6 above: from the 1300s on, this word shifts progressively between several very similar forms: *treuthe*, *truthe*, *trueth*, and finally the modern *truth*. Now, these changes would not have been instantaneous, but rather shifts in preference over time. For example, sometime between 1395 and 1525 there was a shift from *treuthe* to *truthe*. This did not, obviously, occur when all English speakers changed on a certain day from one form to the other. No, a much more likely scenario is that at some point along the way, *truthe* became a rare variant spelling of the proper *treuthe*. Over time, this alternative spelling became more and more common, until it too was seen as an acceptable variant spelling. Then, as time progressed, *treuthe* became less common than *truthe*, until *truthe* was seen as "correct" and *treuthe* was seen as "incorrect."

In a population of organisms, genetic change happens in much the same way. If we consider a gene—a section of DNA letters on a chromosome that acts as a unit of inheritance—as analogous to a word, then a new variant that arises through mutation—called an "allele" (pronounced "ah-leel")—is like a first misspelling. Most of the time, a misspelled word is simply eliminated as a mistake. Similarly, many alleles do not gain a foothold in a population because, at the beginning, they are rare and can easily be lost. By chance, however, some alleles increase in number in a population over many generations as they are inherited by numerous individuals. Sometimes the spread is favored because the new allele provides an advantage, but most of the time the spread is simply based on chance—for example, perhaps the first individual to have the mutation has a large family. In any population, how common an allele is can shift with every generation. Over time, an allele might go from rare to common, and then from common to being the only allele present in a population, just like the shift from *treuthe* to *truthe* to *truth*.

While the change in any one word is not that significant, the combined shifts of many words over generations is enough to radically change a language. Likewise for a population of organisms: a shift from one allele of a gene to another will not have a large effect. The combined action of many such shifts at many genes, however, can significantly shift the characteristics of a population over many generations. Like change within a language, changes within a population are incremental, and every generation remains the "same species" as their parents and offspring. Over time, however, genetic changes can accumulate to the point where generations far removed from each other would not reasonably be considered the same species. Anglo-Saxon and Modern English, then, are like *Indohyus* and a blue whale.

Language Evolution and Speciation

The ability of the characteristics of a language or genome to incrementally shift over time also means that an ancestral population (of speakers, or of organisms) might give rise to two or more distinct populations over time. Again, the evolution of language is a useful analogy here. With a last name like Venema, it will come as no surprise that I have ancestors that spoke West Frisian, a language most commonly found today in Friesland, a province of the Netherlands. My father's parents immigrated to Canada after World War II and learned English as a third language to complement their second language, Dutch, and their mother tongue, West Frisian. As a child I recall listening to them speak to each other primarily in West Frisian, but also with Dutch and English thrown in if either language offered a better word for the concept at hand. What was striking to me, even then, was how similar West Frisian was to English for many words—far too many correspondences for it to be a mere coincidence. What I didn't know at the time was that Modern

English and Modern West Frisian share a common ancestral population of speakers that lived in what is present-day northern Germany and Denmark around AD 400. A group from this population crossed the English Channel and settled in England, with the rest of the group remaining on the European continent. Once these two populations separated, changes in how they spoke their (once identical) language began to accumulate. Since the populations were geographically separated, the changes were independent of one another; the shifts in one group were not the same in the other. Over time, the two populations became more and more distinct. Moreover, there is no convenient point at which they "became different languages." Each generation in both populations spoke the "same language" as their parents and their children; the process by which the languages became distinct was incremental. Modern English and Modern West Frisian, as I heard them spoken by my grandparents, are of course "different languages" since they are mutually unintelligible to each other. Nevertheless, they retain numerous uncanny similarities that reflect their shared ancestry. A well-known sentence, pronounced essentially the same in both languages, will serve as an illustration:

Butter, bread, and green cheese is good English and good Frise.

Bûter, brea, en griene tsiis is goed Ingelsk en goed Frysk.

The analogy to biological speciation is straightforward. If a population is separated into two groups, the incremental process of allele shifting over time is now independent in the two groups. Thus the average characteristics of the two populations may now begin to diverge from each other. Given enough time, the characteristics of the two populations may become different enough that, even if the two groups were brought into contact with each other again, they would not recognize each other as members of the same species. Even though each generation in both populations is the "same species" as its parents and its offspring, gradual shifts in characteristics can, over long timescales, produce distinct species. And just as we have seen for languages, we can find related species by looking for shared similarities in their "texts" or, in genetic terms, in shared DNA letters in their genomes.

Genomes as Ancient Books

While the language analogy is an excellent one for evolution in that it forces us to think in terms of incremental change within a population, every analogy has its weak points. In a language, every word has meaning, and words tend to be relatively short. In contrast, genes—our genetic word equivalents—can be hundreds, thousands, or even tens of thousands of DNA letters long. Another surprising difference is that animal genomes have a lot of DNA letters that do not appear to have a specific function; they don't really seem to be "words," but rather just filler. If there is a function associated with them, it seems that almost any string of letters will do. Also, genomes are more like books than languages are. A genome has specific genes in a specific order, just as a book has specific words, paragraphs, and chapters arranged in a sequence. Another marked difference is that genomes take a long time to accumulate change. Languages change much more rapidly than genomes do. Every time chromosomes are copied, the process includes a careful proofreading step that minimizes errors. Since such errors—that is, mutations—are how new alleles arise, this proofreading slows down the rate at which populations change over time. Though we easily can document language "speciation" over a thousand years, biological speciation generally takes much, much longer.

In practice, these features of genomes mean that it is easy for scientists to identify related species through DNA sequencing. Since genome change is very slow, DNA letters that are inherited by two species from a common ancestral population will remain identical for a very long time, even if those letters do not have a sequence-specific function. If those letters are part of genes, then change will be even slower, since many changes will be eliminated if they alter the function of the gene. The length of genomes also assists here: we have millions, or in the case of humans, billions of DNA letters to compare with other genomes. Also, since genomes are like books, we can look for additional retained features when comparing them: things like chromosome structure and gene order on chromosomes in addition to DNA letters at the gene level. In other words, we can compare the genomes of two species to the texts of two books—at the chapter, paragraph, and word levels—even as we understand that a genome of any given individual is not absolutely identical to that of other members of that species. While the language analogy helps us understand how a population of genomes changes over time, the book analogy is useful for understanding how the genomes of two present-day species can be compared to test the hypothesis that they are descended from a common ancestral population.

Genetics 101

Though the book analogy is helpful, we should examine some differences between books and DNA sequences to better appreciate how geneticists compare

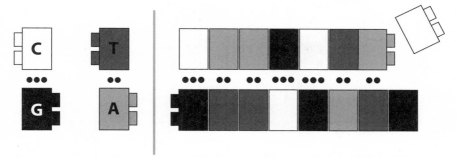

FIGURE 2.2. DNA is made of four possible building blocks that pair with one another. Cytosine (C) pairs with guanine (G) through three weak bonds called "hydrogen bonds." Adenine (A) and thymidine (T) pair with two hydrogen bonds. The bonding properties of these chemicals allow for precise DNA replication, since one strand can serve as a template to build a complementary strand.

two genomes to each other. Fair warning: it does get a bit technical—but the understanding gained will be worth it once we're ready to compare genomes with each other. As we have mentioned, each chromosome is a long string of DNA letters joined together. Each DNA letter has a partner that it pairs up with; in reality, one chromosome is made up of two long strings of letters. These two complementary strings twist around each other to form the DNA "double helix" structure that Watson and Crick famously solved in 1952. These two strings separate during chromosome replication, and each is used as a template to make a new complementary string. In this way, DNA can replicate with high fidelity, since the newly made DNA sequence is specified by the pairing properties of the letters on the template string.

One way I explain DNA replication to nonspecialists is to imagine a long stack of children's toy building bricks laid on its side. Since DNA has four letters, imagine four shades of bricks in the stack. Now imagine that each shade of bricks has magnets arranged in a specific pattern on its side. Let's say that the white bricks represent the "C" of DNA, and that they have three magnets in the right place to match up with the black "G" brick when it is facing the other way. Similarly, "A" and "T" match up with two magnets each (fig. 2.2).

From these simple rules, it would be easy to use one stack as a template to build a complementary stack. All that is needed is to allow the bricks to find their magnetic partners and snap in place. Now, the two stacks won't twist around each other into a double helix, and it would be unwieldy to show stacks millions of bricks long, but this simplistic model shows us the important properties of chromosomes: they are two separate strings of DNA letters (stacks of bricks) held together, which can be separated and used as a template to build a complementary string (stack) through the physical properties of

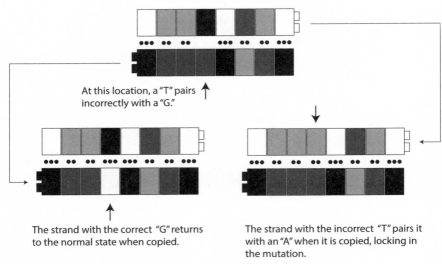

At this location, a "T" pairs incorrectly with a "G."

The strand with the correct "G" returns to the normal state when copied.

The strand with the incorrect "T" pairs it with an "A" when it is copied, locking in the mutation.

FIGURE 2.3. One mechanism for new mutations is rare, incorrect, nucleotide base pairing during chromosome replication. If the incorrectly paired bases are not repaired prior to the next round of replication, one of the new chromosome copies will lock in the error. A chemical that alters a nucleotide base and interferes with its ability to match up with its partner will increase the mutation rate, and thus is known as a "mutagen."

the letters (bricks). The sequence of the letters, of course, is what can be used to code for information—the genetic instructions for making the functional stuff of biological systems.

One key difference between DNA and a book, then, is that new DNA is copied using the physical properties of a template, whereas a book is typeset on a printing press. While every book in a print run will be identical, every time a genome is copied, the possibility of copying errors exists. Though DNA copying is highly accurate, chromosomes have millions of DNA letters in them; even a process that is over 99.9999 percent accurate is not likely to be perfect a billion times in a row. Copying errors arise through mismatched letter pairs—even though they don't fit together well, they can be forced to fit. The next time the chromosome is copied, however, each letter in the mismatched pair will correctly specify its proper partner. In this way, the mismatched pair—what we would call a "mutation event"—becomes locked in for one of the chromosome copies. For example, suppose a "G" brick inappropriately pairs with a "T" brick instead of a "C" one, and this mistake is not corrected (fig. 2.3). When this double helix is copied, one strand of the helix will have the correct white brick, which will most likely pair with its correct black partner when copied (the product on the left of the diagram). The strand that had the incorrect dark gray brick, on the other hand, will now specify a light gray brick and lock in the error (the product on the right of the diagram). The result is a new variant in the population.

Recent studies of the human mutation rate based on sequencing the entire genome for a set of parents and offspring reveal that of our 3 billion letter pairs, on average about one hundred are mutated every generation. These are the subtle changes, to recall the language metaphor, that enter a population and may become more common over time.

Another key difference between a book and a genome is that whereas every word in a book matters, not every (or even most) DNA letters do. It is often surprising to nonbiologists to find out that most of our genome is not genes. If we define a gene as a section of a chromosome that holds the information for a functional product (either an RNA or a protein, which we will discuss in detail later), genes make up only about 5 to 6 percent of our genome. Genes, as it turns out, are generally spread out on chromosomes with a lot of nongene sequences between them. There is strong evidence that most of this nongene sequence does not have a sequence-specific function. In other words, it could be any sequence of letters and do the same job, sort of like genetic spacers between genes. This is of course quite unlike a book, where pages of gibberish interspersed with short stretches of readable text would make no sense at all.

The last difference that matters for our discussion centers on how gene sequences work. The properties of DNA make it a great way to store and replicate genetic information but make it lousy at other jobs. DNA pretty much has only one shape—a long double helix—and living things need many molecules with a wide range of shapes to function. What is needed, then, is a way to convert the information in DNA into molecules that have a multitude of functional shapes. Proteins fit this requirement well. Proteins, like DNA, are strings of building blocks strung together, though they are much shorter than chromosomes. Unlike in DNA, however, there are twenty different building blocks to choose from instead of only four. The twenty building blocks, called "amino acids," are also much more diverse in their structure than are the building blocks of DNA. Because of this structural diversity, proteins fold up into a dizzying array of three-dimensional shapes—shapes that can act as enzymes, structural components of the cell, and signaling molecules, and perform a multitude of other tasks. Proteins are great at most biological functions, but they are lousy for information storage and replication, since the structure of a protein cannot be used as a template to make a copy of itself in the way that DNA can.

So living things use both DNA and protein to get the best of both worlds—DNA for information storage and transmission, and proteins to do the bulk of the day-to-day jobs a cell needs to do. The trick, of course, is transferring

FIGURE 2.4. The properties of DNA bases allow for a single-stranded "working copy" to be made in preparation for translation into a sequence of amino acids.

information from one system to the other: cells need to use gene sequences on chromosomes to specify the sequence of amino acids in proteins. Playing on the idea that DNA sequences and protein sequences are different "languages," biologists call the process of converting information from one to the other "translation." Before translation can take place, however, the cell makes a "working copy" of a gene it wishes to translate. This working copy, called "messenger RNA" or "mRNA," is made up of four building blocks very similar to the DNA building blocks (in fact, three of the four are identical, and the fourth one is only marginally different). The main difference, however, is that mRNA has only one strand. The process of copying a gene into a single-stranded mRNA copy is called "transcription"—again, making an allusion to copying a text in the same language. One of the two chromosome DNA strands is used as a template to make mRNA for a short region, spanning a gene (fig. 2.4).

Once a gene is transcribed, the next step is to *translate* the mRNA language into protein language—a sequence of amino acids that will fold up into a three-dimensional shape and do a job. Biologists use the analogy of translation for this process because the cell is converting information from one "language" (a sequence of DNA) into another "language" (a sequence of amino acids). How the translation process works was one of the key questions that arose after the double-helix structure of DNA was solved. One of the puzzles was this: How does a DNA sequence, with only four "letters," code for a sequence of amino acids when there are twenty different amino acids to choose from? One DNA letter specifying an amino acid wouldn't work unless there were only four amino acids.

What was eventually worked out, through much effort, was that *small groups* of DNA letters specified amino acids. Grouping DNA letters into pairs would provide only sixteen different options (four letters each with four pairing options = sixteen combinations), and thus not enough to account for all twenty amino acids. Grouping DNA letters into sets of three, on the other hand, would provide more than enough options—sixty-four combinations. As it turns out, DNA letters are indeed "read" in sets of three to specify amino acids, and biologists call the sixty-four possible combinations of DNA letters "codons." So there are sixty-four possible codons, but only twenty amino acids to code for. A few codons are used for other functions (such as "start adding amino acids from this point on in the mRNA sequence" and "stop adding amino acids to the chain, we're done"), but there are still many more codons than there are amino acids to code for. The way the cell deals with this is as follows: most amino acids can be specified by more than one codon. For example, the amino acid glycine (one of the twenty) can be coded for with the codons GGA, GGC, GGG, and GGT. All four codons are equivalent in that they specify the same amino acid. Other amino acids can be coded for by up to six different codons. In other words, the amino acid codon code is partially redundant.

A Real-World Example: Insulin

Let's examine a real example of a gene: the DNA sequence that codes for the insulin protein. Insulin is a short protein hormone that regulates blood glucose levels in animals. The "word" for insulin is very similar in all mammals. For example, when we compare the beginning of the insulin gene in humans with the same portion of the gene found in dogs (and wolves, since they are the same species), we observe many correspondences, and a few differences at the DNA level. Some of those DNA differences (shaded in black) result in different amino acids in the insulin protein, and some do not (fig. 2.5).

Now, in both species these "words" have the same "meaning"—both the human and canine genes produce a functional insulin hormone that regulates blood glucose levels. The fact that slightly different sequences can have the same

```
Human DNA:      atg gcc ctg tgg atg cgc ctc ctg ccc ctg ctg gcg ctg ctg gcc 45
Dog/Wolf DNA:   atg gcc ctc tgg atg cgc ctc ctg ccc ctg ctg gcc ctg ctg gcc

Human Protein:    Met Ala Leu Trp Met Arg Leu Leu Pro Leu Leu Ala Leu Leu Ala 15
Dog/Wolf Protein: Met Ala Leu Trp Met Arg Leu Leu Pro Leu Leu Ala Leu Leu Ala

Human DNA:      ctc tgg gga cct gac cca gcc gca gcc ttt gtg aac caa cac ctg 90
Dog/Wolf DNA:   ctc tgg gcg ccc gcg ccc acc cga gcc ttc gtt aac cag cac ctg

Human Protein:    Leu Trp Gly Pro Asp Pro Ala Ala Ala Phe Val Asn Gln His Leu 30
Dog/Wolf Protein: Leu Trp Ala Pro Ala Pro Thr Arg Ala Phe Val Asn Gln His Leu
```

FIGURE 2.5. An alignment of the first 90 DNA nucleotides (and 30 amino acids) of human and dog/wolf insulin. Differences between the two sequences are highlighted in black for the canine sequence. Numbers on the right indicate the nucleotide or amino acid number in this sequence.

function should not be a surprise; in many ways it is like the words *treuthe*, *truthe*, and *truth*, all of which carry the same meaning, despite their subtle differences. Protein hormones do their job by binding to a second protein, called a receptor, to signal to cells that the hormone is present. The hormone and the receptor simply need to work together, sort of like a lock and key. As long as the shapes of the two proteins match adequately, they will work together. Proteins are also not rigid like locks and keys are; they're floppy, and subtle shifts in shape are possible without losing a complementary fit. So these genes are free to change over time within those functional constraints, and changes in one (for example, insulin) open up a range of new possible changes for the other (the insulin receptor).

In looking at the sequences above, we can see that there is good evidence to support the hypothesis that these two present-day genes come from a common ancestral population in the distant past, just as "butter, bread, and green cheese" and "bûter, brea, en griene tsiis" do. The principle is the same: they are far more similar to each other than they are functionally required to be. In principle, any words could stand for these concepts in either English or West Frisian; similarly, any matched pair of hormone and receptor could function to regulate blood sugar levels in humans or dogs. Yet what we observe strongly suggests, in both cases, that the present-day sequences are the modified descendants of what was once a common sequence.

Now that we understand the redundancy of the codon code, we can see that for genes this rabbit hole goes even deeper. Many of the amino acids in insulin can be coded for by alternate codons. For example, "Leu" in the diagram indicates the amino acid leucine, for which there are six possible codons. This short snippet of the insulin gene codes for nine leucines, and eight of them use exactly the same codon in dogs and humans (and the ninth differs by only one letter). For these nine codons, there are 9^6 (= 531,441) possible combinations that will correctly code for just these nine leucines, to say nothing of the other 101 amino acids found in insulin, most of which can be encoded for by multiple codons. Is it merely by chance that what we observe in these two species is only one letter different for these nine codons? A simpler, more reasonable explanation (or what a scientist would call a more "parsimonious" explanation) is that these sequences come from a common ancestral population and have been slightly modified along the way.

Of course, scientists have sequenced the genomes of many other species, so we can test this hypothesis by looking at a larger data set. Humans are not thought to have shared a common ancestral population with dogs for a very long time; other species are thought to be our much closer relatives due to other shared features, such as anatomy. When the pre-Darwin biologist Carl

```
Human        atg gcc ctg tgg atg cgc ctc ctg ccc ctg ctg gcg ctg ctg gcc 45
Chimpanzee   atg gcc ctg tgg atg cgc ctc ctg ccc ctg ctg gtg ctg ctg gcc
Gorilla      atg gcc ctg tgg atg cgc ctc ctg ccc ctg ctg gcg ctg ctg gcc
Orangutan    atg gcc ctg tgg atg cgc ctc ctg ccc ctg ctg gcg ctg ctg gcc
Dog/Wolf     atg gcc ctc tgg atg cgc ctc ctg ccc ctg ctg gcc ctg ctg gcc

Human        ctc tgg gga cct gac cca gcc gca gcc ttt gtg aac caa cac ctg 90
Chimpanzee   ctc tgg gga cct gac cca gcc tcg gcc ttt gtg aac caa cac ctg
Gorilla      ctc tgg gga cct gac cca gcc gcg gcc ttt gtg aac caa cac ctg
Orangutan    ctc tgg gga cct gac ccg gcc cag gcc ttt gtg aac cag cac ctg
Dog/Wolf     ctc tgg gcg ccc gcg cct acc cga gcc ttc gtt aac cag cac ctg
```

FIGURE 2.6. An alignment of the first 90 DNA nucleotides of insulin for humans, chimpanzees, gorillas, orangutans, and canines. Sequences that differ from the human sequence are highlighted in black. Numbers on the right indicate the nucleotide or amino acid number in this sequence.

Linnaeus (1707–78) drew up his taxonomy of animal life (i.e., a system that organized life into categories), he famously placed humans and great apes in a category he called "primate," from the Latin indicating "prime" or "first." While he was certainly not thinking about common ancestry, he naturally recognized that these species (such as chimpanzees, gorillas, and orangutans) have a closer anatomical affinity to humans than other animals. In light of such an affinity, evolutionary theory predicts that these species share a more recent common ancestral population with humans than nonprimate species, such as dogs, do. Therefore, their gene sequences should be a closer match to human sequences than what we observe in dogs. Not surprisingly, this is exactly what we observe. Let's return to our example of the insulin gene and extend our comparison of the same short stretch to include three great apes (fig. 2.6).

What we observe for this short segment is that the gorilla sequence is identical to that of the human except for one letter; the chimpanzee is identical except for three; and the orangutan is identical except for five. As before, this level of identity far exceeds what is needed for functional insulin, and strongly supports the hypothesis that humans share a common ancestral population with great apes. Indeed, the similarities between these sequences make English and West Frisian look like very distant relatives by comparison.

Objection!

In the years that I've mulled over these data, I've encountered a number of objections to it from believers who are committed to the idea that humans were created directly, apart from an evolutionary process. While we will address common antievolutionary arguments in detail later, it's worth pausing at this point to consider a few in passing. Some are erroneously simplistic, such as the question, if humans evolved from apes, why are there still apes? (This is the equivalent of asking, if English evolved from other languages, why are there still other languages? Or, if American immigrants descend from Europeans, why are there still Europeans? Or, given one of our foregoing examples, if whales evolved from terrestrial mammals, why are there still terrestrial mammals?) This objection presupposes that evolution is like a ladder leading to a particular species. Rather, evolution is like a branching tree of related species. Other objections, at first blush, appear more compelling, such as the suggestion that the reason we see similarities between genes in different organisms is that they have the same Designer—namely, God. What we are observing, so the argument goes, is common *design*, not shared ancestry (common descent).

As we'll soon see, this argument doesn't hold up well in the face of other lines of DNA evidence. Yet even what we have discussed thus far is enough to evaluate this argument somewhat. Suppose you decided you wanted to design two languages. Would you design them in such a way that they appear to be closely related to each other, especially if your prowess as a designer is such that you can effortlessly design languages in any way you wish? Furthermore, as a designer, you understand that there are many possible ways to design words, grammar, syntax, and so on. Would you make it appear that your two languages are related to each other, if indeed you wanted to convince others that they were separate, independent creations?

Further Down the Rabbit Hole

The pattern we observed in the insulin gene sequence has now been confirmed to extend across the genomes of humans and great apes. Human and chimpanzee genes—and we have about 25,000 of them—are over 99 percent identical for the entire set at the DNA level. At the amino acid sequence level, 29 percent are absolutely identical, and the average difference for the entire set is only two amino acids.[1] Beyond genes, our entire genomes are either around 95 percent or around 98 percent identical, depending on how one counts the effect of deletions of small blocks of DNA. If you count every deleted block as a change for every missing letter (i.e., count a deletion of 10 letters as equivalent to 10 changes, even though the deletion was only one mutation event) then the identity value comes to 95 percent. No matter how you slice it, the human and chimpanzee genomes are nearly identical to one another.

To return to our "genome as book" metaphor, we also observe that humans and chimpanzees not only have nearly identical genomes, but that our genomes are organized in the same spatial pattern. At the sentence, paragraph, and chapter level, our two "books" are organized in the same way. As before, there is no biological reason why this needs to be the case. We, or chimpanzees, would be fine with our genes in very different spatial arrangements, and placing our genes into a different arrangement would be well within God's creative abilities. Yet what we observe, once again, is consistent with the hypothesis that the present-day human and chimpanzee genomes are slightly modified descendants of what was once the genome of a shared ancestral species.

Beyond these sweeping correspondences, there are more details that bolster the case for common ancestry, as well as provide information that biologists are curious about. For example, based on anatomy alone, there was a long-standing debate in the scientific community over whether chimpanzees or gorillas are our closest living relatives. As we saw with the gorilla and chimpanzee insulin sequences, when species are very similar to one another, it becomes more difficult to determine patterns of relatedness because there are fewer differences to compare. Genome sequence data resolved this question, and one way it did so provides further compelling evidence for our shared ancestry.

The Nose Knows (or at Least Knew)

Anyone who has owned a dog knows that some mammals have a much keener sense of smell than humans do. Mammals, on average, have about 1,000 genes devoted to the sense of smell—genes called "olfactory receptors"; and since mammals have only around 25,000 genes, this means a significant proportion of the mammalian genome is devoted to this type of function. These genes are *expressed* (i.e., transcribed and translated into proteins) in the cells that make up the surface of nasal passages. Olfactory receptors bind onto chemicals in the air as it is breathed in and transmit electrical signals to the brain that are perceived as odors. Mammals that hunt (such as wolves) have very keen senses of smell because their set of olfactory receptor genes is kept in good repair—mutations that remove the function of any one of these genes are weeded out of the population through selection. Dogs are the recipients of this genetic heritage, even though most breeds are not hunting or tracking dogs any longer. Our family's golden retriever "hunts" insofar as he finds food dropped in the kitchen, but his nose remains keen because his lineage has only recently arrived at such a coddled state, and mutations have not yet crept into his complement of olfactory receptor genes. Humans, on the other hand, have a diminished sense of smell relative to dogs, and the reason became clear after

Gene Name	Human	Chimpanzee	Gorilla	Orangutan
1 5AK4p	236-stop	236-stop	236-stop	236-stop
2 5H5p	212-deletion	212-deletion	212-deletion	+
3 7A8p	430-deletion	430-deletion	+	+
4 4L2p	249-insertion	+	+	+
5 1S1	+	+	96-deletion	+
6 10A3	+	824-stop	+	+
7 4A4	+	+	+	309-deletion

FIGURE 2.7. Shared mutations in seven olfactory receptor genes in great apes. A "+" indicates a functional, nonmutated gene. The number indicates the DNA nucleotide position within the gene where the mutation occurred. "Stop" = premature stop codon that halts translation and produces a short, nonfunctional protein; "deletion" = removal of one DNA nucleotide that renders the protein untranslatable; "insertion" = addition of one DNA nucleotide that renders the protein untranslatable.

we sequenced the human genome. Many of our olfactory receptor genes are damaged: they have numerous mutations in them that disrupt their ability to be transcribed or translated. The remains of these genes, however, persist in our genome because of the low error rate for copying chromosomes. Since the protein enzymes that copy DNA don't know that these genes are defective, they copy them as faithfully as possible, just like any other DNA sequence. As a result, these genes persist for a long time as genetic "fossils" in our DNA. The historical name for these damaged remains of genes is "pseudogenes" or "false genes." They earned the name because they have many of the features expected of genes but cannot be transcribed and translated as a gene should be in order to produce a protein product.

Interestingly, humans are not alone when it comes to having a reduced sense of smell: other primates share this reduction in olfactory acuity. Investigating this with their full genome sequences in hand reveals why: they too have lost many olfactory receptor genes due to mutation. Here's where things get interesting, and—if you're a biologist interested in the relationships between humans and other primates—informative. Not only do other primates have mutations in their olfactory receptor genes, but also in many cases the same genes are lost in other primates as in humans. Moreover, often the exact same mutation event, down to the exact DNA letter change, is seen in more than one species.

A sampling of real data from a paper investigating olfactory receptor genes in great apes[2] shows the categories of mutations we observe (fig. 2.7).

Some mutations, such as example 1 in the table, are shared among all four species. This gene, 5AK4p—a name based on its location in the genome—has a "stop" mutation at DNA letter 236 in humans, chimpanzees, gorillas, and orangutans. A "stop" mutation is a mutation that changes a codon intended to code for an amino acid into a codon that tells the translation enzymes to stop adding amino acids to the chain. The result is a protein that is too short, and likely no longer able to do its job. Since we see an identical mutation in all four species, we need to provide an explanation for this pattern. Once again parsimony comes into play. One option is that this mutation occurred four times, independently, in each species. The possibility of this occurring is very small but not impossible. A second possibility is that this mutation occurred once, in a common ancestral population of all four species, and was subsequently inherited by all four species. This is a much more parsimonious explanation, since it would require a rare event (the specific mutation in this gene) to occur only once. In the data set for this paper, the authors observe several mutated genes that fit this pattern—further boosting our confidence that this example is not a fluke or one-off event. Even if one gene might have this pattern by chance, it is extremely unlikely that numerous genes would have this same pattern by chance alone.

A second pattern we observe is shown by gene 2: in this case, a deletion mutation (i.e., one DNA letter missing) at position 212 in humans, chimpanzees, and gorillas. Deletion (or insertion) mutations mess up the codon code by shifting the codons after the deletion by one letter. Recall that codons are translated in groups of three. Deleting one letter means that every codon after the mutation will code for the wrong amino acid—something that will likely ruin the protein's function. Again, the simplest explanation is that this mutation occurred once, in the common ancestral population of humans, chimpanzees, and gorillas. Why did orangutans not inherit this mutation (as indicated by the "+" sign)? One explanation is that the orangutan lineage had already separated from the ancestral lineage of humans, chimpanzees, and gorillas by this time. Once again, the researchers found many examples that fit this pattern.

A third pattern (gene 3) shows a mutation shared by humans and chimpanzees alone (in this case, another deletion). Again, the likely explanation is that this mutation occurred in the common ancestral population of humans and chimpanzees after the lineage leading to gorillas separated from it. Once again, the researchers found many examples that fit this pattern.

Finally, we see mutations unique to a single species (examples 4–7). Such mutations are expected, since each species also has a period of unique history after its lineage separates from all the others.

Note, however, what we *don't* see: mutations shared by gorillas and chimpanzees, but not seen in the other species, for example; or mutations shared

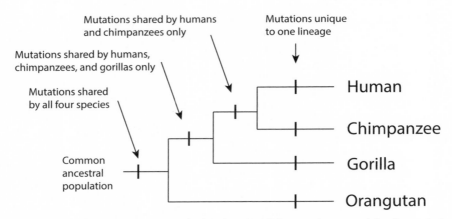

FIGURE 2.8. The phylogeny (tree of relatedness) of living great apes explains the nested hierarchy of mutations observed in olfactory receptor pseudogenes. Mutations that occur in a lineage prior to a speciation event will be inherited by all descendant species. Mutations that occur after all speciation events will be unique to one species.

by humans and orangutans that are not also seen in gorillas and chimpanzees. Why don't we see these categories? Well, if indeed these species are related in the manner suggested by the patterns we do see, we would not expect them.[3] Let's look at the "family tree" (or "phylogeny") of relatedness for humans and other great apes that the data support (fig. 2.8).

Here we see why the data form a "nested hierarchy": identical mutations seen in both humans and orangutans are present before these two lineages separate. Thus they must be present in the lineages leading to gorillas and chimpanzees, since those lineages have yet to separate from the lineage leading to humans. We don't see mutations shared between chimpanzees and gorillas but not humans because such mutations would have to be present in the human lineage as well. The data we observe, as well as the categories we don't observe, support the same conclusion: humans share a common ancestral population most recently with chimpanzees, then with gorillas, and then with orangutans. While this was worked out on the basis of partial genome sequencing, we now have full genome sequences for all four of these species. As you would expect, the genome-wide identity between humans and other apes follows the same pattern. We are most similar to chimpanzees, then to gorillas, and then to orangutans. These lines of genome evidence support the same pattern of relatedness among primates. So the long-standing question of who our closest relatives are has at last been settled, and that we have other species relatives is overwhelmingly supported. While these data are a small sample, they are representative. Thousands of examples that fit this pattern could be given.

Converging Lines, Once Again

Now that we have an understanding of how scientists can use mutated genes in nested hierarchies to determine relatedness, it will come as no surprise that biologists have applied this technique to cetaceans as well. Like primates, cetaceans have a reduced sense of smell relative to other mammals. One lineage of modern whales—toothed whales—appears to have no sense of smell at all, not even a nasal organ. This makes good sense: after all, mammalian olfactory receptor genes bind on to chemicals in air, and toothed whales hunt their prey in water, where such a system is not effective. Nonetheless, cetaceans, including toothed whales, have the defective remains of genes for air-based olfactory receptors. In fact, DNA evidence comparing a modern artiodactyl (hippos) and modern cetaceans was the first evidence that these species share a common ancestral population, before the key diagnostic fossilized ankle bones were found in ancient whales. Not surprisingly, paleontologists doubted the new DNA science until they found the fossils that confirmed its prediction.[4] DNA and fossils tell the same story; they are converging lines of evidence.

Something Old, Something New

But, you might ask, where does the *new* stuff that evolution requires come from? Sure, organisms can lose genes, or limbs, easily. How did whales gain their *new* features? Evolution might be able to explain loss, but what about *gain*?

One of the things evolution predicts is that seldom will any feature in an evolutionary lineage be truly "new." Would tetrapod limbs be considered "new" when they "first appeared"? Not really—there is evidence for a long series of incremental changes between "lobe fin" and "limb." So a limb is "nothing new" in that sense—it's a modified version of something that came before. Let's consider the distinctive cetacean features: the blowhole (not new: there is evidence for a gradual series connecting it to the standard mammalian nostril configuration); flippers (not new: there is evidence for a gradual series connecting them to the standard mammalian front limbs and hands in the same extinct species we have discussed); blubber (not new: other mammals store fat, just not in such vast quantities); aquatic lifestyle (not new: many other mammals are semiaquatic to one degree or another). In other words, what constitutes a cetacean is merely a remodeling of what was available in the standard mammalian body plan. A dramatic remodeling, yes, but a remodeling nonetheless.

Ah, the astute reader might object, what about echolocation? Modern cetaceans hunt for their food using the biological equivalent of sophisticated sonar. That's new. Checkmate, evolution! Well, not really—and the details are fascinating. Let's take a look.

If you've ever stumbled through a pitch-black room and pulled yourself up short just before colliding with a wall or other object, you have employed your (very rudimentary) sense of echolocation. What you detected (though you might not have even consciously perceived it) was that sound waves were reflecting off the object in your way. All mammals can do this, but most (like us) do it very poorly. We need to be very close to the object in question before it is even possible for us to notice reflected sound, and more likely than not we won't, and we'll stub our toe or worse.

As it turns out, cetacean echolocation is a specifically tuned sense of hearing that is based on the same genes used for hearing in other mammals. One key gene used for hearing in all mammals is called the "prestin" gene, a protein involved with the specialized structures in the mammalian ear that vibrate in response to sound waves. In whales, the prestin gene is tuned to the ultrasonic frequencies that are better suited to echolocation. This tuning required only a few amino acid changes within the protein—an amount of change easily within the reach of the sort of molecular tinkering we saw for the insulin gene in various mammals. This tinkering within the prestin gene to tune it for echolocation was so easy to achieve, it would seem, that nearly identical changes occurred independently in the lineage leading to modern bats, who also use a prestin tuned to ultrasonic frequencies for echolocation.[5] So even echolocation is not "new"—it too is remodeled from a standard mammalian sense of hearing. Along the way, as whales were losing their sense of smell, they were shifting over to another sense to replace it, one much better suited to hunting in water.

Unequally Yolked

While we might expect to see at least some olfactory receptor pseudogenes in mammals (especially mammals with reduced olfactory acuity like humans and whales), pseudogene remnants might persist in a lineage long enough that they can speak to a manner of life no longer relevant to the organism in question. One fascinating example is the presence of vitellogenin pseudogene fragments in placental mammals. Vitellogenins are proteins that egg-laying organisms use to transfer nutrients from the mother to the egg yolk before the eggshell is deposited. Vitellogenins are very large and thus can be broken down into many individual amino acids that can be used by the developing embryo to translate proteins of its own. The amino acids of vitellogenins are also covered with various sugars after translation, making these proteins a good source of carbohydrates. If that were not enough, the final three-dimensional shape of these proteins acts as a carrier for lipids as well. Thus these proteins are an excellent way for an egg-laying organism to store up a good supply of nutrients in the yolk before the eggshell hardens and cuts the mother off from the developing embryo. Placental mammals, on the other hand, retain a connection to their embryos throughout gestation, through the placenta. As a result, nutrient transfer can be accomplished directly from the bloodstream, and without the large carrier proteins that are stored in the yolk. There are many lines of evidence that placental mammals share a common ancestral population with marsupial mammals; before that, with egg-laying mammals; and before that, with other egg-laying vertebrates such as reptiles and birds. Thus evolution predicts that all placental mammals once had vitellogenin genes in their genome, even though such genes would no longer be useful. Might fragments of these genes persist in placental mammals in the present day? That was the research question a group of biologists decided to study in 2008.[6]

To start their research, this group examined the location of functional vitellogenin genes in the chicken genome. Chickens have three vitellogenin genes (VIT1, VIT2, and VIT3), and the researchers determined the local "neighborhood" around all three—what other genes flanked each chicken vitellogenin gene. For example, they noted that VIT2 and VIT3 sit side by side in the chicken genome, flanked by two other genes not involved in egg-yolk production: genes named SSX2IP and CTBS. Then they looked for these genes in the genome of a placental mammal—humans, in fact, since the human genome is the best-studied placental mammal genome to date. Interestingly, SSX2IP and CTBS are both found in the human genome, and like in the chicken genome, they are next to each other. Unlike in chickens, however, there is no functional gene between them in humans. By carefully analyzing the DNA between these two human genes, however, the researchers discovered tiny fragments of sequence that match the chicken VIT2 and VIT3 genes, as well as fragments that match chicken nongene sequences in this region (fig. 2.9, p. 40). These fragments, though very small, line up with the two chicken genes in the correct order. Encouraged by these findings, the group then examined the VIT1 region in the chicken genome. In chickens, the VIT1 gene sits quite close to another gene—again, not one involved in egg-yolk production (ELTD1). The ELTD1 gene is also found in the human genome, and next door to it, in the same relative location as in the chicken genome, there are numerous small fragments of sequence that match the chicken VIT1 gene, as well as sequences that match nongene sequences in this region of the chicken

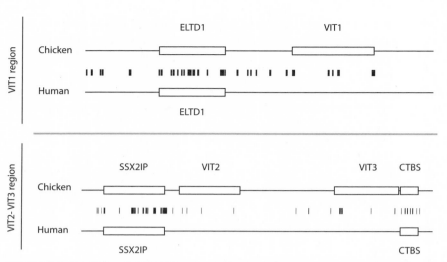

FIGURE 2.9. The VIT1 and VIT2-VIT3 regions in the chicken and human genomes. White boxes indicate functional genes. Black boxes indicate sequence matches between the two genomes. The ELTD1, SSX2IP, and CTBS genes in humans and chickens are highly similar and line up with one another when comparing these regions. Small fragments of matching sequence can be seen covering both regions, including fragments matching portions of the chicken VIT1, VIT2, and VIT3 genes, though the most extensive matching is seen in the fragmentary human VIT1 pseudogene.

genome. Once again, these small fragments are in the correct order and line up with the chicken region.

These results make perfect sense in light of evolution: placental mammals and birds share a common ancestral population in the distant past (about 310 million years ago, according to current estimates).[7] The lineage leading to modern birds retained vitellogenins because this lineage retained an egg-laying manner of life. Placental mammals, on the other hand, gradually left egg laying behind in favor of a modified form of reproduction (though some egg-laying mammal lineages persist into the present day, such as the platypus—and, not surprisingly, they retain a functional VIT gene). In this case, milk was gained before vitellogenin was lost. And in some mammalian lineages, this allowed for a shift away from vitellogenin and toward marsupial, and later placental, manners of life.[8]

Given the abundant lines of DNA evidence that support the hypothesis that humans are the product of evolution, it is no exaggeration to say that (the very, very few) trained biologists who reject common ancestry do so because of prior religious commitments, not for scientific reasons. One individual in this category—my friend and colleague Todd Wood,[9] who holds to a young-earth creationism perspective—nonetheless recognizes the success of evolution as a scientific theory:

I hope this doesn't turn into a rant, but it might. You have been warned.

Evolution is not a theory in crisis. It is not teetering on the verge of collapse. It has not failed as a scientific explanation. There is evidence for evolution, gobs and gobs of it. It is not just speculation or a faith choice or an assumption or a religion. It is a productive framework for lots of biological research, and it has amazing explanatory power. There is no conspiracy to hide the truth about the failure of evolution. There has really been no failure of evolution as a scientific theory. It works, and it works well.

I say these things not because I'm crazy or because I've "converted" to evolution. I say these things because they are true. I'm motivated this morning by reading yet another clueless, well-meaning person pompously declaring that evolution is a failure. People who say that are either unacquainted with the inner workings of science or unacquainted with the evidence for evolution. (Technically, they could also be deluded or lying, but that seems rather uncharitable to say. Oops.)

Creationist students, listen to me very carefully: There is evidence for evolution, and evolution is an extremely successful scientific theory. That doesn't make it ultimately true, and it doesn't mean that there could not possibly be viable alternatives. It is my own faith choice to reject evolution, because I believe the Bible reveals true information about the history of the earth that is fundamentally incompatible with evolution. I am motivated to understand God's creation from what I believe to be a biblical, creationist perspective.[10]

Not surprisingly, Todd soon had to defend himself against charges that he was a "closet evolutionist" pretending to be a young-earth creationist. He isn't—he's just being honest about the state of the evidence for evolution, despite his personal convictions otherwise. Needless to say, his approach hasn't won him too many friends among his antievolutionary peers, though he has my sincere respect for his stance.[11]

It was not in Darwin's wildest dreams that organisms would retain a text-like record of their evolutionary past in their hereditary material. Darwin, like all biologists of his day (save Gregor Mendel, who was working in isolation and essentially unknown) was confused about how heredity worked. Genetics, DNA sequencing, and comparing whole genomes between species have thus been a great boon to evolutionary science, but they have also been, potentially, a great threat. Evolution, as a theory, could have been completely upended by these scientific advances. In actuality, these new technologies have provided some of the most detailed and convincing evidence that our current understanding of evolution is close to the actual truth. Humans do share common ancestors with other apes; apes share common ancestors with other mammals; mammals share ancestors with other tetrapod vertebrates;

tetrapod vertebrates, as we have seen, share ancestors with fish; and ultimately all life on earth shares common ancestors dating back over 3 billion years.

But wait, you say: If humans are the product of evolution, what about Adam and Eve? How do they fit in to the story? Are they the sole parents of humanity, even if they had an evolutionary past? When did they live? Were they *Homo sapiens*, like we are, or some other species? We will address these questions—at least from a biological perspective—next.

3

Adam's Last Stand?

In the summer of 2011, my wife and I were in the process of adopting our youngest son. As part of that process, we packed up our family and for a few weeks moved in with the foster family that had cared for him since birth, in a city several hours away from our home. It was a wonderful process, but understandably stressful: Would the transition from a family of four to a family of five go well? Would our new son bond with us as his parents? Would he come to see our biological children as his siblings, and vice versa?[1]

It was in the midst of this process that a controversy rocked the evangelical community and set the phones of my administrators ringing. Earlier that summer, *Christianity Today* had run a cover article titled "The Search for the Historical Adam," replete with art depicting Adam and Eve as Neanderthal-like individuals.[2] The article summary said it all: "The center of the evolution debate has shifted from asking whether we came from earlier animals to whether we could have come from one man and one woman."

The reason my administrators were fielding phone calls was that one of my academic papers, published in the journal of the American Scientific Affiliation (ASA)[3] and featured on the BioLogos website,[4] was prominently discussed in the *Christianity Today* article. Moreover, I had given an extensive interview to National Public Radio (NPR) on the topic, after they caught wind of the *Christianity Today* article. NPR would edit that interview down to a few sound bites, and the resulting discussion of "my views" led off with this:

> But now some conservative scholars are saying publicly that they can no longer believe the Genesis account. Asked how likely it is that we all descended from Adam and Eve, Dennis Venema, a biologist at Trinity Western University, replies: "That would be against all the genomic evidence that we've assembled over the last 20 years, so not likely at all."[5]

No wonder my administrators were fielding angry calls—according to NPR, I no longer believed the Genesis account. Sigh.

In contrast to the NPR piece, the *Christianity Today* article provided a much more nuanced and accurate presentation of my views. After discussing evidence I had presented supporting common ancestry for humans and apes, the author turns to the primary focus of his article:

> The second—and perhaps more troublesome—issue treated by Venema involves "population genomics." Over the past decade, researchers have attempted to use the genetic diversity within modern humans to estimate primordial population sizes. According to a consensus drawn from three independent avenues of research, he states, the history of human ancestry involved a population "bottleneck" around 150,000 years ago—and from this tiny group of hominids came everyone living today. But the size of the group was far larger than a lonely couple: it consisted of several thousand individuals at minimum, say the geneticists. Had humanity begun with only two individuals, without millions of years for development, says an ASA paper, it would have required God's miraculous intervention to increase the genetic diversity to what is observable today. A BioLogos paper by Venema and Falk declares it more flatly: The human population, they say, "was definitely never as small as two. . . . Our species diverged as a population. The data are absolutely clear on that."

I must admit that the furor over this issue caught me somewhat by surprise—and not merely because of the shock that conservative American evangelicals apparently listen to NPR. Naively I had assumed that people understood that evolution was a population-level phenomenon. If humans evolved, then we did so as a population. Doesn't everyone know that? As I was about to learn, the population genetics data that indicate we descend from a population of about 10,000 individuals rather than a pair in many ways were more inflammatory than the data supporting common ancestry. Our son's foster parents likely didn't know what to make of it all, with me on the phone with my administrators and constituents calling for my job. What kind of crazy family were we, anyway?

Speciation and Populations

One of the reasons that language change over time is such an apt analogy for evolution is that it clearly illustrates how speciation takes place by incremental changes of average characteristics after two populations separate. No one expects a new language to start because two speakers suddenly start speaking in radically new ways that separate them from their prior population of speakers. Yet this is how many people think speciation works. They assume that *all* species are founded by an ancestral breeding pair that is suddenly and markedly different than the population it arose from. Thus I've encountered many folks who, upon understanding the evidence that humans and other apes share common ancestors, assume that humans—like all other species, in their thinking—got their start when a founding couple "mutated away" in tandem from their ape-like ancestors. These folks then wonder if the Genesis narratives may be portraying this radical shift, with perhaps God intervening to create the necessary, large-scale mutations that made us a biologically distinct species.

While I'll leave the theological questions for Scot,[6] this picture is not based on an accurate understanding of how speciation works. Rather, the process starts when populations are genetically separated in some way, usually through physical separation (though other mechanisms are known). What matters is that two subgroups of what was formerly a continuous population cease interbreeding. This means that as mutations occur in either group, they are not shared across the divide. The incremental process of change is now un-coupled, and the two populations may begin to drift apart in terms of their form and behavior. Eventually, enough change may occur to make the rift permanent, but the process is a gradient over time. Attempting to draw a line on a biological gradient is as nonsensical as deciding what day Old English became Modern English. Any such lines of demarcation are for convenience only, since the processes of language and species formation are continuums.

Lo(o)sing It

To better understand how genetic variability works within a species, let's return to the language analogy for evolution in more detail. As we have seen, languages change over time either through gain or loss of words, meanings, spellings, and so on. The key is how common such variants are within a language, and their "commonness" is a function of how many individuals employ them. For example, while discussing this analogy with one of my genetics classes recently, I asked them how to spell the English word "lose." A few of the brighter students immediately cracked a smile as they saw what I was up to, and pretty soon the class as a whole had a good laugh. The reason, of course, is that it is depressingly common to see the word "lose" misspelled as "loose," especially on social media. This is a relatively recent "innovation." Ten years ago it was not nearly so common, and (God forbid) ten years from now it may be more common still. Thirty years from now it might be viewed as an acceptable variant spelling, and fifty years from now employing "lose" might be the sure sign of an aging grammarian, comparable to calling a car an "automobile." For better or worse, languages change. (That said, if the words "their," "there," and "they're" ever collapse into a single word determined solely by context, I pray I won't be there to see it. Even evolutionary biologists have their limits.)

Here's where the analogy is once again helpful: the ability of a language to simultaneously "hold" spelling or grammatical variants is dependent on the number of the speakers of that language. Dying languages (for example, the sad case of many indigenous languages of North America) have almost no variation at all since they have so few speakers. Endangered species have the equivalent problem. Languages with large populations of speakers, on the other hand, can hold a large number of variants. Modern English is a prime example; as it increasingly becomes a global language, the opportunity for variation within it increases. The same occurs with species: a large population size allows for maintaining a large number of variants, since each member of a species is able to hold up to two distinct variants (alleles) of any given DNA sequence in its genome.[7] Thus there is a connection between the number of variants present in a population and the size of the population—a connection that scientists can use to estimate one from the other. And since the rate of change over time is slow, it is straightforward to extrapolate backward from the present into the past.

So the baseline expectation *should* be that if humans are the product of an evolutionary process, we arrived at our current state as a population. Now it is technically possible that a species could be founded by a single ancestral breeding pair, just as it is technically possible that a new language could be founded by two speakers. This is not what one would usually expect, however—in fact, it would be highly unusual. If a species were formed through such an event, or if a species were reduced in numbers to a single breeding pair at some point in its history, it would leave a telltale mark on its genome that would persist for hundreds of thousands of years—a severe reduction in genetic variability for the species as a whole.

Poor Devils

One such species with a profound lack of genetic variability is the Tasmanian devil, a carnivorous marsupial once found across Australia, but now solely on the island of Tasmania off the Australian coast. Tasmanian devils have had very little genetic variability for the last few hundred years: most of them have exactly the same alleles with only rare differences. This suggests that at one point in their past they experienced a severe population "bottleneck."[8] This term derives from imagining a population as marbles in a bottle, with marbles of different color representing gene variants within the population. The bottleneck event occurs when there is a severe reduction in population size; that is, the bottle is tipped over, and only a few marbles escape. The genetic variation of the new population, then, is dependent on which variants happen to pass through the bottleneck. So at some point in their history, Tasmanian devils seem to have suffered a significant reduction in numbers, and they lost a large amount of genetic variation in the process. This has now become a serious issue for conserving this species in light of a new threat: a lethal, transmissible facial cancer. This cancer started in only one devil but was transmissible to others through biting. After a bite, a few cancerous cells take up residence in the new host. Normally, a recipient animal would fight off the cancerous cells, since they would be recognized as foreign. Here's the problem: all devils are so genetically similar to one another that the cancer cells do not trigger an immune response. As a result, this cancer threatens the devil population as a whole, and conservationists are working to save a cancer-free population in captivity that carries as much of remaining devil variation as possible. Should the population in the wild go extinct, they hope to replace it with the captive one.

In humans, on the other hand, tissues transferred between individuals almost invariably produce a strong immune reaction and subsequent rejection, to the point that organ donors and recipients must be carefully screened and matched to each other to minimize their differences. Even when a close match is found, drugs that suppress the immune system must be employed, because no match will be perfect, unless sourced from an identical twin. The reason for this is that humans are genetically highly diverse. In contrast, almost any devil could be an organ donor (or, sadly, a tumor donor) for any other in the population, without drugs. This example also illustrates just how long it takes a population to rebuild its genetic variation after a bottleneck event occurs. New alleles have to be supplied by new mutations, and as we have seen, the mutation rate is very low. As a result, after a bottleneck event, a species will have reduced genetic diversity for thousands of generations to come. The implications are clear: Tasmanian devils experienced a severe bottleneck in the distant past, but humans did not.

All in the Family

One of the challenges of discussing the data relevant to measuring human ancestral population sizes is that the data are quantitative in nature. It's one thing to describe the remnants of the vitellogenin pseudogenes in humans, and another to start discussing mathematical methods for estimating population size from genetic diversity. Still, given the importance of this question for many Christians—and the strong insistence of many apologists that the science is completely wrong[9]—it is worth at least sketching out a few of the methods geneticists use that support the conclusion that we descend from a population that has never dipped below about 10,000 individuals.

While the story of the beleaguered Tasmanian devil provides a nice way to "see" the sort of thing we would expect if in fact the human race began with just two individuals, scientists have many other methods at their disposal to measure just how large our population has been over time. One simple way is to select a few genes and measure how many alleles of that gene are present in present-day humans. Now that the Human Genome Project has been completed and we have sequenced the DNA of thousands of humans, this sort of study can be done simply using a computer. Taking into account the human mutation rate, and the mathematical probability of new mutations spreading in a population or being lost, these methods indicate an ancestral population size for humans right around that 10,000 figure. In fact, to generate the number of alleles we see in the present day from a starting point of just two individuals, one would have to postulate mutation rates far in excess of what we observe for any animal.

Ah, you might say, these studies require an estimate of mutation frequencies from the distant past. What if the mutation frequency once was much higher than it is now? Couldn't that explain the data we see now and still preserve an original founding couple?[10] Aside from the problems this sort of mutation rate would present to any species, we have other ways of measuring ancestral population sizes that do not depend on mutation frequency. These methods thus provide an independent way to check our results using allele diversity

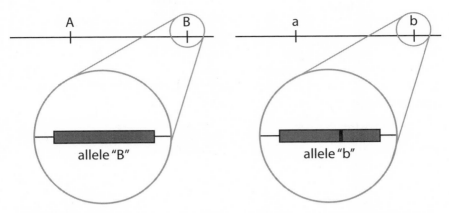

FIGURE 3.1. Geneticists use line diagrams to represent the location of genes and combinations of alleles present on the same chromosome.

alone. Let's tackle one of these methods next: estimating ancestral population sizes using something known as "linkage disequilibrium."

I've often joked with my students that no scientist will choose a simple name when a complicated one will do, and "linkage disequilibrium" ranks right up there as an example of this habit. Despite the name, it is not a difficult concept to grasp. The basic idea is that if two genes are located close to each other on the same chromosome, the alleles present at both locations tend to be inherited together. For example, suppose "gene aye" with possible alleles "A" or "a" and "gene bee" with alleles "B" or "b" are close together.

In figure 3.1, the long line represents a chromosome, and the hash marks across it show us where the two genes in question are located. Geneticists even use the Latin word for "location" (*locus*, pronounced "low-cuss") as a synonym for "gene." (Latin makes us sound smarter, I guess.) If we could zoom in on the diagram, we would see a long DNA molecule with two re-gions that are translated into proteins (the two genes). The different alleles at either locus would have slight sequence differences, giving us four possible combinations for these two *loci* (plural for "locus," pronounced "low-sigh"). The four possible combinations are "AB," "Ab," "aB," and "ab."

During the cell divisions that make gametes (i.e., eggs or sperm), there is a process of mixing and matching of alleles to make new combinations. For example, suppose an individual had one chromosome with the "A" and "B" alleles, and the other with "a" and "b." During gamete formation, it is possible to produce gametes that are "recombinant"—in this case, ones that have either an "Ab" or "aB" combination. Recombination requires a process of precise

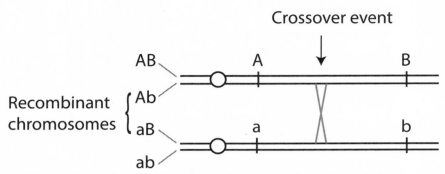

FIGURE 3.2. During the cell divisions that produce gametes (eggs or sperm), chromosomes are replicated and held together at special sequences called "centromeres" (open circles). Replicated chromosomes then pair up with their partner chromosomes, and physical breakage and rejoining occurs along their length at random. If a crossover falls between two loci that have alternate alleles present, a crossover will produce chromosomes with new combinations of alleles. Chromosomes with new combinations of alleles are said to be "recombinant."

chromosome breakage and rejoining called "crossing over"—something you might recall from high school biology (fig. 3.2).

The key point to understand is that the closer together two loci are on a chromosome, the less likely it is that a crossover event will happen between them. The further apart two loci are, the more likely it is that a crossover will recombine them. What this means is that alleles of loci close together tend to be inherited as sets.

Let's work through an example of how this plays out in practice. Consider an extended family represented by a *pedigree*. This is the type of diagram geneticists use to trace alleles through large families. Females are represented by circles, and males by squares. Horizontal lines connecting males and females indicate that they are the parents of the offspring below them (connected with a vertical line). Generations are labeled with Roman numerals (I, II, III, and so on); individuals are labeled with Arabic numerals (1, 2, 3, and so on). In this way we can refer to any individual in the pedigree (fig. 3.3).

Now consider a larger pedigree where we know the allele combinations of everyone represented (fig. 3.4, p. 52). For example, individual I-4 has one chromosome with the "AB" alleles linked together, and one chromosome with the "ab" alleles as a set. We can represent her chromosome set, then, as "AB/ab"—the shorthand that geneticists use. We can then use this convention for other individuals in the pedigree. For example, the daughter of I-1 and I-2 might have an "AB/aB" combination. If these two loci are very closely linked together, it is highly unlikely that crossing over will occur. Thus she would have inherited her "aB" set from her mother, and the "AB" set from her father. Likewise, her husband, II-3, would have inherited "Ab" from his dad, and "ab" from his mom. Their children (generation III) similarly would inherit these sets without crossing over. Looking at the combinations carried by these children, then, allows us to infer things about their ancestors. If these two loci are very close to each other, we might not expect them to recombine over hundreds of generations or more. Thus it's reasonable to infer that these four combinations come from four distant ancestors. Not exactly rocket science.

The trick is that we can now do this for tens of thousands of loci across the whole human genome. As we have sequenced the DNA of more and more individuals in different people groups around the globe, we've simply been asking the question: Based on the number of allele combinations that we observe in this population, how many ancestors do we need to invoke in order to explain what we observe? In this case, rather than estimating mutation frequency, the calculations require knowing how often crossing over happens between two loci. This is also something we can measure directly in humans and other animals, and there is a well-characterized relationship between chromosome distance between two loci and crossing-over frequency. We've now done this sort of analysis for millions of pairs of loci (yes, millions) for each chromosome pair in our genome (all 23 pairs). And what is the final tally after crunching all that data and counting up ancestors? The results indicate that we come from an ancestral population of about 10,000 individuals—the same result we obtained when using allele diversity alone.[11]

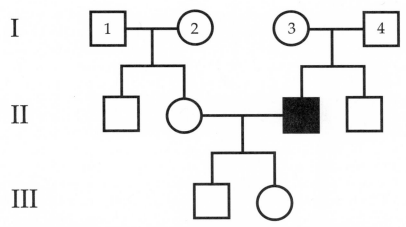

FIGURE 3.3. A pedigree is a diagram showing family relationships. Males are represented with squares, females with circles. Lines connecting individuals represent family groups. Each generation is labeled with a Roman numeral, and each individual within a generation is labeled with an Arabic numeral. Individuals affected with a genetic condition may be represented with a filled-in symbol. In this example, individual II-3 is affected with a genetic condition, though his wife (II-2) and two children (III-1 and III-2) are not affected.

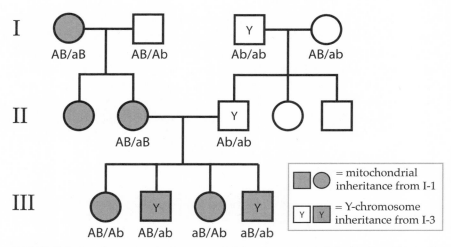

FIGURE 3.4. A pedigree showing how sets of alleles of two closely linked loci are inherited in an extended family. Each set of alleles is called a "haplotype." In the most recent generation, we observe four different haplotypes: AB, ab, aB, and Ab. Since these loci are linked closely to each other, recombination between them is rare.

One interesting feature of this approach is that it allows us to scale how far back in time we want to do the tallying. If we want to examine our distant ancestors, we can pick pairs of loci that are very, very close together. Alleles at these loci require thousands of generations, on average, before a crossover event recombines them. If we're interested in our more recent history, we can select pairs of loci that are further apart from each other. In this way, this approach provides a population "snapshot" at various times in our prehistory. One study using this approach scaled its analysis to investigate our lineage from the present dating back to approximately 200,000 years ago, which, as we will discuss later, is when our species first appears in the fossil record. The researchers found that, during this period, humans living in sub-Saharan Africa maintained a minimum population of about 7,000 individuals, and that the ancestors of all other humans maintained a minimum population of about 3,000—once again, adding up to the same value other methods arrive at.[12]

A more recent and sophisticated model that uses a similar approach but also incorporates mutation frequency has recently been published. This paper was significant because the model allows for determining ancestral population sizes over time using the genome of only one individual.[13] This method is feasible since even one individual, with two copies of each chromosome, will have many regions of her genome where she has allele pairs inherited from different ancestors (just like the children in our example pedigree did). Instead of looking at a given pair of loci in many individuals, this method looks at many pairs of loci within one individual. Since this was a new method, the authors tested it by creating artificial data sets where they knew the actual population history (since they designed it into the data) and seeing how well their mathematical model would predict what they already knew to be true. The model performed well, and so they applied it to real data from fully sequenced individual human genomes. For sub-Saharan Africans, they observed a population bottleneck down to a minimum of about 5,700 individuals 50,000 years ago. For non-sub-Saharan Africans, they observed a bottleneck down to a minimum population size of about 1,200 between 40,000 and 20,000 years ago. Taken together, this is in good agreement with previous, less powerful methods, with a combined minimum size of around 6,900 individuals. These numbers may shift upward, however, as we sequence more and more individuals from both groups. The authors also extended their analysis back approximately 3 million years and found that the population size of our lineage increases the further one goes back in time, with a prior, less severe bottleneck about 500,000 years ago.

Getting Sorted

One last method to estimate ancestral population sizes that we will discuss has the ability to look back further than 3 million years—back to the common ancestral population we shared with chimpanzees about 4–6 million years ago, as well as back to other common ancestral populations with other great apes. This method, like linkage disequilibrium analysis, is virtually unaffected by varying estimates of mutation rates.

This method exploits the fact that we expect the relatedness pattern of certain genes to sit at odds with what we expect on the basis of species relatedness. While humans and chimpanzees are the closest living relatives of each other as species, we expect that some human genes will be closer matches to those of other great apes, such as gorillas. The reason for this arises out of something called "incomplete lineage sorting," or "ILS."

When a population is undergoing a speciation event, some of the genes/loci in that population will have two or more alleles within the population as a whole. As the population separates, the two new populations will likely both inherit that diversity. We can represent two alleles as shaded boxes on a phylogeny and show how the history of these two alleles may play out within a larger tree of species relatedness (fig. 3.5, p. 54).

In this phylogeny, or "species tree," we see that the common ancestral population of gorillas, chimpanzees, and humans has two alleles of one gene

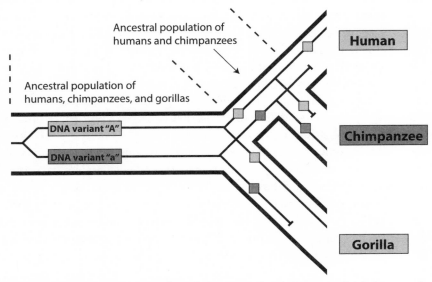

FIGURE 3.5. Alleles in an ancestral population may not sort down completely to every descendant species. In some cases, the sorting pattern produces a "gene tree" at odds with the overall "species tree."

(DNA variant "A" and "a") within the population. As this population separates into the common ancestral population of humans and chimpanzees and the population leading to gorillas, both populations inherit both alleles. In the gorilla lineage, however, variant "a" is later lost, leaving only variant "A" in the present-day gorilla population. The common ancestral population of humans and chimpanzees maintains both variants until after this lineage divides into two, one leading to humans and the other to chimpanzees. In the lineage leading to chimpanzees, the "A" variant is lost, leaving it only with "a" in the present day. Conversely, in the lineage leading to humans, the "a" variant is lost, with only "A" remaining. The final pattern is as follows: humans and gorillas have "A," and chimpanzees have "a." Gorillas and humans, then, have more closely related alleles than either does with chimpanzees. This "gene tree" for the "aye" gene sits at odds with the overall "species tree."

Here's the interesting part: this pattern lets us know that the common ancestral population of humans and chimpanzees had both "A" and "a." It also lets us know that the common ancestral population of humans, chimpanzees, and gorillas had both variants. If you have a way to infer what genetic variants were present in a population, you have a way to estimate its population size. The data here show us that both the common ancestral population of humans and chimpanzees and the common ancestral population of humans, chimpanzees, and gorillas were large—about 50,000 individuals (effective population size). In fact, based on prior work, scientists predicted in advance how much ILS we should observe with the gorilla genome (estimated at around 25 percent) before we had the gorilla genome sequence to measure it. We observe 30 percent ILS, which is an excellent match to the predicted value. We later made a similar prediction for ILS with the orangutan genome, and once again the predicted value (1 percent) matched the observed value (0.8 percent) very well. These results provide good evidence that our estimates of the ancestral population size leading to humans over the last several million years are accurate. It seems our smallest effective population size over the last 18 million years was when we were already human, at around the time some of our ancestors left Africa.[14]

As our methodology becomes more sophisticated and more data are examined, we will likely further refine our estimates in the future. That said, we can be confident that finding evidence that we were created independently of other animals or that we descend from only two people just isn't going to happen. Some ideas in science are so well supported that it is highly unlikely new evidence will substantially modify them, and these are among them. The sun is at the center of our solar system, humans evolved, and we evolved as a population.

Put most simply, DNA evidence indicates that humans descend from a large population because we, as a species, are so genetically diverse in the present day that a large ancestral population is needed to transmit that diversity to us. To date, every genetic analysis estimating ancestral population sizes has agreed that we descend from a population of thousands, not a single ancestral couple. Even though many of these methods are independent of one another, all methods employed to date agree that the human lineage has not dipped below several thousand individuals for the last 3 million years or more—long before our lineage was even remotely close to what we would call "human." Thus the hypothesis that humans descend solely from one ancestral couple has not yet found any experimental support, and it is therefore not one that geneticists view as viable.[15]

Bones and Contention

While genetics is an excellent way to address the question, How many of us were there at various stages of our evolution?, it is not as well suited to the question, And what were we like? For evidence of physical form and behavior, we must turn to the fossil record. Once again, we are confronted with the challenge that the fossil record cannot conclusively reveal who our direct ancestors might be, though it will likely be possible to find remains of our close relatives.[16] Just as with whales, however, finding our relatives in the fossil record can give us a good sense of the general trajectory of our evolutionary past.

Though Charles Darwin largely avoided the issue of human ancestry in *On the Origin of Species*, except to briefly muse that "light would be thrown on the origin of Man and his history,"[17] the idea of human descent from ape-like ancestors was obviously a topic of much scientific debate and theological concern following the publication of *Origin* in 1859. Darwin predicted, from the distribution of living great apes, that human origins would be found in Africa; but in the 1860s there were no fossils known that seemed to be intermediate between living apes and humans. A few Neanderthal remains were known, but these were too few and not yet studied well enough to be fully appreciated by the scientific community. They were also so very similar to modern humans that it was thought by many that they were merely ancient human remains.[18]

At this time there was also a widespread expectation within the scientific community that an evolutionary lineage would be a ladder-like progression from one species to the next, culminating in the present-day species. The famous "ape to human" images that look like a police lineup are an example of this expectation. Yes, for any species there should be a lineage that resembles a ladder leading to it, if indeed we had a perfect fossil record to draw from. In reality, fossilization is such an infrequent process that it cannot capture every subtle shift along the way. What the fossil record does capture are common species—species with large population sizes. Thus, when looking in the fossil record, what one will find is biased toward widespread species with large populations. Most of those species will not be direct ancestors of living species, but their relatives. The understanding that evolution was more like a branching bush of related species than an ascent up a linear ladder leading to present-day species would have to be worked out on the basis of paleontological evidence, and much of that work remained to be done in Darwin's time. From Darwin's ideas, scientists and the public expected there to be a series of "missing links" connecting humans and apes that could be found in the fossil record, and that any such species *would* be direct ancestors of humans. Since the most obvious difference between living great apes (for example, chimpanzees and gorillas) and humans was brain capacity and cognitive function, the "ladder" was expected to show a progression from ape, to ape with a bigger brain, to human. In other words, early expectations were that our lineage first evolved from the chin up, and only then from the chin down.

Unfortunately this expectation would hamper research into human evolution for decades. In the 1880s, when the first remains of *Homo erectus* were discovered in Indonesia, they showed a humanlike skeleton with a small, ape-like skull. This, of course, was the complete opposite of the expectations, and so many scientists doubted that the find was in fact a single species. Rather, they suspected, human skeletal remains had been mixed together with an ancient ape skull. Though the discoverer, Eugene Dubois, championed his find as a transitional form linking humans and apes—his original name for the species was *Pithecanthropus erectus*, the "ape-man that stands upright," a choice that was anything but subtle—he was a voice in the scientific wilderness.[19]

Any traction that Dubois did gain would soon be lost in light of a stunning find in the United Kingdom, of all places—a find that fit precisely what was expected of a "missing link" between ape and human. This species had an ape-like jaw and a human-sized skull, suggesting that it had an ape-like skeleton wedded to a human-sized brain. A second find shortly after confirmed that these results were not merely a chance association of ape and human remains. It would be decades before the skulls, belonging to the now-infamous Piltdown Man, would be revealed as frauds. They were constructed using a human skull and the jaw of an orangutan, with the teeth filed to shape them to the expected form for a transitional species. The perpetrator of the fraud has never been discovered, but his handiwork threw scientists off the scent for a long time to come.

Fortunately, paleontological research continued, and data continued to accumulate. These data increasingly showed that Piltdown Man did not, in fact, fit the expected pattern, which was very much pointing to our lineage evolving from the chin down before the chin up, vindicating Dubois. Scientific suspicion of the veracity of Piltdown Man grew, and eventually the remains were carefully reexamined. The evidence of filing on the teeth was uncovered, and the jig was up.

As we have seen for cetaceans, eventually a picture emerged that gives us a good idea of how our lineage changed after we parted ways with the lineage leading to chimpanzees. Though chimpanzees are our closest *living* relatives, a host of species in the fossil record are more closely related to us than chimps. These species are collectively known as "hominins," and we are now aware that there were a lot of hominin species out there.[20] As you might expect, there are different classifications of fossil hominins, and the boundaries between them are fuzzy (fig. 3.6, p. 58). The earliest hominin fossils, grouped together as "probable hominins," include species like *Ardipithecus ramidus*, a species that lived in Africa about 4 million years ago. This species has skeletal characteristics that are intermediate between upright (i.e., bipedal) walking and

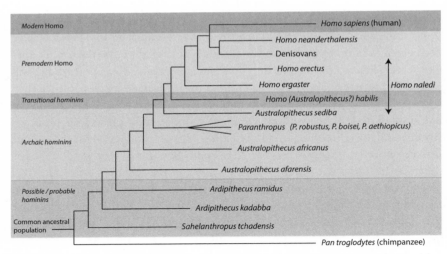

FIGURE 3.6. A phylogeny of hominins—species more closely related to humans than to chimpanzees. The phylogeny is constructed from morphological data, and in some cases genome sequence data. *Ardipithecus kadabba* and *Sahelanthropus tchadensis* may not be hominin species (as indicated by the shaded area at the bottom of the figure). *Homo naledi* has not yet been placed precisely into the phylogeny, though its characteristics place it within *Homo*.

the climbing of trees,[21] and a small cranial capacity of only 300–350 cubic centimeters (cc), or about the volume of a can of soda,[22] whereas modern humans have a cranial capacity of about 1,300 cubic centimeters. Later in the fossil record, we observe various Australopithecine species, of which the famous fossil called "Lucy" is the best known. Lucy's species, *Australopithecus afarensis*, is found in the fossil record between about 4 and 3 million years ago and shows further shifts to bipedal walking,[23] and a larger cranium (between 400 and 550 cc).[24] Later still we observe the earliest members of the genus *Homo*, in a group named "transitional hominins." These hominins have a cranial volume that ranges between 500 and 700 cubic centimeters, and are thought by some paleontologists to be Australopithecines rather than within *Homo*, highlighting their "transitional" features, such as a lack of full bipedalism.[25] Later still we see species within "premodern *Homo*" such as Dubois's renamed *Homo erectus*, a widespread species dating to about 1.8 million years ago with an essentially modern human skeleton but a reduced cranial capacity compared to modern humans. The earliest premodern *Homo* cranial capacities begin at about 700 cubic centimeters and, moving toward the present, eventually reach the present-day human volume of about 1,400 cubic centimeters, and even exceed it in the Neanderthal lineage (Neanderthal skulls with a cranial capacity of 1,600 cc are known). In this group of species we also observe skeletal features indicative of full bipedalism.[26] A recent fossil find, *Homo naledi*, has been placed within *Homo* but nonetheless has a cranial capacity below that of *Homo erectus* and *Homo habilis* at about 450–550 cubic centimeters. The relationship of this species to other hominins is not yet known, but it has attracted widespread attention because of the evidence suggesting it deliberately placed its dead into the cave in which the remains were found.[27]

Similar to what we discussed regarding whales, we cannot be certain that any of these species is in fact a direct ancestor of present-day humans. What these species can show us, however, is the probable path of our actual lineage, since these species are at least close relatives of our ancestral line. The evidence thus suggests that our lineage over the past 4 million years passed through an Ardipithecine-like species, on to an Australopithecine-like species, and then through various shades of *Homo* until our species is first preserved in the fossil record 200,000 years ago. And as we have seen for languages, the process was a continuous one of average change within a population over time. What we see in the fossil record matches up with what we see in our DNA. Recall just how similar humans and chimpanzees are at the DNA level. These fossil species, then, would have DNA even more similar to us than to modern chimpanzees. In this sense, humans are, biologically speaking, not new—we are the modified descendants of similar species that lived in the past.

National Enquirer, Paleogene Edition

One of the frustrating things about science is that while it is well suited to answer certain questions (and even better at raising questions in the first place), it is not suited to answer others. It's very common, for example, for Christians, when they come to understand this evidence, to naturally wonder where Adam fits in. I sometimes think of this as "pin the Adam on the phylogeny," alluding to the children's game. The main point of such an allusion is that the child is blindfolded, and so are we in this case, so to speak. Science can tell us a few things—we descend from a population rather than a pair; our ancestors likely passed through these sorts of forms; and so on—but it is simply unable to weigh in on the historicity of Adam and Eve as individuals. What we can conclude, however, is that if they were in fact historical, they were not the sole parents of all humanity but part of a larger population. Beyond this, science cannot say.

It should come as no surprise that Christian antievolutionary apologists do feel a need to fit Adam into the fossil record, despite the myriad difficulties—and we will examine some of those attempts in the next chapter.

This task, however, has recently become even more challenging with the advent of *paleogenomics*—the ability to recover and sequence the DNA of extinct organisms. While scientists have been able to recover DNA from the remains of a 700,000-year-old horse that had the good sense to die in the Canadian arctic and be preserved in permafrost,[28] we have yet to stretch the sequencing hominin DNA back that far. The range of hominins does not appear to have included arctic regions until fully modern *Homo sapiens* arrives on the scene, alas—though I hold out hope that one day we will locate a particularly adventurous (and well-preserved) member of *Homo erectus* or a similar species. That said, we have now been able to sequence the DNA of hominins stretching back to about 80,000 years ago, and the results have proved fascinating.

When modern humans first arose in Africa 200,000 years ago, there were other hominin species alive on the planet, some of whom had migrated out of Africa prior to our species coming into being. *Homo erectus*, for example, was already widespread in Africa and outside it. Similarly, the ancestors of Neanderthals had left Africa at least 100,000 years prior to our species evolving, going on to colonize the Middle East and parts of Asia and Europe. Humans left Africa in significant numbers about 50,000 years ago, roughly coinciding with the reduction to our minimum population size; some stayed behind, becoming the ancestors of present-day sub-Saharan Africans, and the rest of us derive from that smaller population that left. As we have seen, the minimum population size within Africa was about 6,000, compared with approximately 1,200 for the emigrating group. As humans left Africa, then, we encountered other hominin species that had left previously.

Scientists have long wondered what the nature of those encounters was like. Some fossils, for example, have long been thought to suggest that Neanderthals and humans had interbred with each other, given their characteristics intermediate between the two species. With the advent of paleogenomics, the opportunity arose to test this hypothesis directly by sequencing Neanderthal DNA. Not surprisingly, Neanderthal DNA is nearly identical to our own, yet it falls (just) outside the range of present-day human variation.[29] This was expected, since Neanderthals are our closest known relatives according to their skeletal morphology. What was noteworthy, however, is that some modern humans do indeed have Neanderthal DNA in their genomes. When our two species encountered each other, there was a limited amount of interbreeding. Some of the offspring of those unions were raised as human, and some of those individuals have passed their DNA down to us in the present day. In part because the group of humans that left Africa was so small, this Neanderthal DNA is present in every present-day human who is not a sub-Saharan African by ancestry. These individuals derive between 1 and 4 percent of their genomes from Neanderthal ancestors.

Of course, this raises the whole "species question" again: If humans and Neanderthals interbred, then aren't we just members of the same species? Recall that attempting to demarcate species is an attempt to draw a line on what is in fact a continuous gradient. So we "sort of" are the same species, because we did interbreed to a limited extent, and some present-day members of our species, yours truly included, descend in part from Neanderthal stock. Are dogs, coyotes, and wolves the same species, or distinct? What about lions and tigers?[30] It's a similar question. As a species, then, we had to shift our Facebook relationship status to "it's complicated" when it comes to Neanderthals. Not long after, however, a second discovery would complicate things even further.

From Russia, with Love

Once it was worked out that ancient DNA could be recovered and sequenced from hominin remains, researchers have been busy sequencing DNA from an increasing number of samples. One such sample turned out to have exceptionally preserved DNA, though it was not previously noted as especially remarkable. The DNA work, however, was a bombshell: this was a previously unknown species of hominin, neither human nor Neanderthal. Found in Denisova Cave in the Altai Mountains of Siberia, the remains would be called the Denisova hominin or, when referring to the species as a whole, Denisovans.[31] Denisovans share a more recent ancestor with Neanderthals than they do with any other known species. We have little sense of their skeletal form, since all that has been found to date are finger bones and teeth—though, in this day and age, that was enough to determine their complete genome sequence. Even more surprising was the finding that we interbred with this species as well. Present-day humans of Asian and Oceanic descent inherit about 3–5 percent of their DNA from this extinct species. A further finding of note was that the Denisovan genome seems to contain stretches of DNA from yet another hominin species. It's tempting to speculate that this DNA comes from *Homo erectus*, since this species was widespread in Asia prior to the Denisovans, or their ancestors, arriving there. There is still no way to test that hypothesis, since we have not (yet) found *Homo erectus* remains that have yielded DNA, though the temporal range of this species in the fossil record (*Homo erectus* persists up until about 100,000 years ago) suggests such a find might be possible given the right conditions.

62 Adam and the Genome

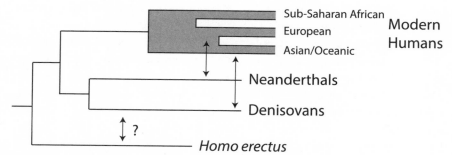

FIGURE 3.7. A phylogeny of modern humans and our closest known relatives. Double-headed arrows indicate interbreeding. Modern humans have diverged from one another slightly as we spread across the globe (gray shading in the expanded human branch). As humans left Africa in large numbers approximately 50,000 years ago, they encountered and interbred with Neanderthals in the Middle East. Humans from this population subsequently expanded into Asia and interbred with the Denisovans, a species related to Neanderthals. Genome sequence data from Denisovans suggests they may have interbred with another hominin species, perhaps *Homo erectus*.

As it stands, then, not only is hominin evolution a branching bush, but there are connections between some of the branches (fig. 3.7). Humans, Denisovans, and Neanderthals share a common ancestral population in Africa dating to around 800,000 years ago.[32] Sometime between 500,000 and 300,000 years ago, the common ancestral population of Neanderthals and Denisovans leaves Africa, later splitting into two species. As humans leave Africa about 50,000 years ago, they encounter Neanderthals in the Middle East and interbreed with them. As this human population expands into Asia, they encounter the Denisovans and further interbreed with them. The result is that present-day sub-Saharan Africans lack Neanderthal or Denisovan DNA, Europeans have Neanderthal but not Denisovan DNA, and Asian and Oceanic peoples have both.[33] Thus there are now even more human ancestors to account for, though they themselves were not members of our species.

The Curious Case of Mitochondrial Eve

When presenting these data to evangelical audiences, I commonly get questions about Mitochondrial Eve (and occasionally Y-Chromosome Adam, her male equivalent). Mitochondrial Eve is an ancestor to every living human, hence the name chosen by the scientific community. Likewise, Y-Chromosome Adam is an ancestor to every living male.

Wait just a minute, you might say. If we all descend from one man and one woman, how is it that scientists can claim we descend from a population of thousands? Well, *both* are true, though it will take a bit of effort to understand why.[34] It has to do with how mitochondrial and Y-chromosome DNA are inherited, so we'll start there.

Most people are familiar with how the Y chromosome is passed down from father to son, so we need not belabor that here. Mitochondrial DNA, on the other hand, is not generally so well understood. Mitochondria are subcellular compartments that do energy conversion for animals, and they have their own genomes distinct from the usual chromosome set (the so-called nuclear genome, because it is found in the nucleus, another subcellular compartment). In humans, then, we have a nuclear genome consisting of 23 chromosome pairs (thus 46 in all) and the mitochondrial genome. The mitochondrial genome is tiny compared with the nuclear genome, and it is circular (whereas nuclear chromosomes are linear).[35] Mitochondria are passed down only through eggs, not through sperm, since the part of the sperm that fuses with the egg to release its contents does not carry mitochondria. As a result, this tiny circular snippet of DNA is passed down only from mothers to their children, and not from fathers. Mitochondria in males have thus hit a dead end.

Similarly, the Y chromosome has its unique pattern of inheritance: from father to son, and only to sons, since inheriting a Y chromosome determines that the offspring will be male. These two forms of DNA, then, have a pattern of inheritance that is different from that of regular chromosomes, which can be passed on by either mothers or fathers to offspring of either gender. Y chromosomes hit a dead end if a male has only female offspring, and

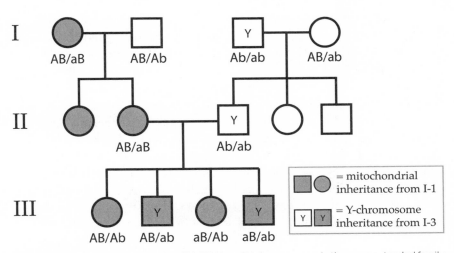

FIGURE 3.8. Inheritance of mitochondrial DNA and Y chromosomes in the same extended family discussed previously. Though the children in generation III must have at least four ancestors for their regular chromosomal DNA, they have only one ancestor for their mitochondrial DNA and their Y-chromosome DNA, respectively.

mitochondria hit a dead end if females have only male offspring. With these two inheritance patterns in mind, let's consider how this might play out in a population over time. Once again, we'll use a pedigree to help us see what may happen—the same pedigree we used to look at inheritance of closely linked alleles previously, but now with a view to tracing mitochondrial and Y-chromosome variation as well (fig. 3.8, p. 63).

With our knowledge of mitochondrial inheritance in hand, we can see that the four children in generation III will inherit the mitochondrial DNA of their mother, who in turn inherited it from her mother (individual I-1). The four children, then, have only one ancestor from generation I for their mitochondrial DNA: their maternal grandmother. Neither their maternal grandfather (I-2), paternal grandfather (I-3), nor paternal grandmother (I-4) contributes mitochondrial DNA to generation III. Similarly, the two boys in generation III have only one ancestor in generation I for their Y-chromosome DNA: their paternal grandfather. The Y chromosome of their maternal grandfather (I-2) has not been transmitted to generation III (nor II, since this man had only daughters).

In contrast, you will recall that all four grandparents contributed regular chromosomal DNA to generation III, and that the DNA diversity in this generation requires that we infer that they have at least four ancestors. These children descend uniquely from one man (for their Y-chromosome DNA), one woman (for their mitochondrial DNA), but from at least four ancestors for their regular chromosomal DNA. This, in microcosm, is exactly the reason why all humans can descend from one Mitochondrial Eve for our mitochondrial DNA, one Y-Chromosome Adam for our Y chromosomes, and 10,000 other ancestors for our regular chromosomal DNA.[36] Both mitochondrial DNA and Y-chromosome DNA are prone to being lost in a lineage over time because of their gender-specific inheritance patterns. The population bottlenecks that we passed through as a species also likely contributed to the loss of many mitochondrial and Y-chromosome lineages. Regular chromosomal DNA, on the other hand, is much more resistant to loss because it can be passed down to offspring of either gender by parents of either gender. Y chromosomes require an unbroken line of male ancestors; mitochondrial DNA requires an unbroken line of female ancestors; but regular chromosomes simply require an unbroken line of ancestors to be passed on.

Now, the elimination of a mitochondrial or Y-chromosome lineage happens not overnight but incrementally over time. Mitochondrial variants and Y-chromosome variants are like any other DNA variation in the sense that they can become more common within a population over time, or less common. Typically, variants that are eliminated have become progressively less and less common over time, thereby becoming more susceptible to loss. The gender-specific inheritance pattern of these types of DNA does increase the possibility that they will be lost merely by chance, however, once they become rare enough.

Unfortunately, many antievolutionary organizations like to promote Mitochondrial Eve and Y-Chromosome Adam without explaining these issues. Typically, it is enough for them to state that they are respectively the common female ancestor for all women and the common male ancestor for all men, to claim (or merely imply) that these data are consistent with Adam and Eve being the *sole* parents of all humans, and to leave it at that.[37] Thus, for their case to seem plausible, they count on their audience not completely understanding how these types of DNA are inherited—or perhaps they misunderstand it themselves.

Responding to the Evidence

Following that 2011 cover article in *Christianity Today*, a few Christian apologists have attempted to rebut the scientific evidence that humans descend from a population rather than a pair, though without success.[38] Others have merely cast the entire field as "speculative," such as some within the intelligent-design movement.[39]

> Stephen Meyer, a Discovery Institute leader of the intelligent design movement, [claims that] BioLogos leaders are using "an unsubstantiated and controversial claim to urge pastors and theologians to jettison a straightforward reading of Genesis about the human race arising from one man and one woman. They think 'the science' requires such a reinterpretation, but apart from speculative models that make numerous question-begging assumptions, the science does no such thing."[40]

The claim may be controversial to Christians, but it is certainly not controversial to scientists, who are aware of the multiple, independent, converging lines of evidence that support and substantiate the conclusion. Meyer's confident assertions aside, antievolutionary scholars have not yet mounted a convincing response to population genetics evidence, nor is it clear that they will be able to do so, since there does not appear to be anyone in the antievolutionary camp at present with the necessary training to properly understand the evidence, much less offer a compelling case against it. In his critique of one attempt to rebut the evidence, young-earth creationist scholar Todd Wood states the problem clearly:

The population reconstructions are complex and not easily understood by lay-people right now. So creationist responses lag behind the current science, and the best your typical creationist can do is cast aspersion on the science. Until we have a creationist well-trained in modern theoretical population genetics, I think we will continue to have only unsatisfactory answers to these ancestral population reconstructions.[41]

Several scholars have expended considerable effort on attempting to rebut the evidence for evolution in general, however—and their claims are widely accepted among Christians. In the next chapter, we'll examine two of their key claims: that evolution is unable to produce certain complex biochemical structures, and that it cannot produce the high level of information we observe in DNA.

What about Intelligent Design?

Although I am fully convinced of the truth of the views given in this volume under the form of an abstract, I by no means expect to convince experienced naturalists whose minds are stocked with a multitude of facts all viewed, during a long course of years, from a point of view directly opposite to mine. It is so easy to hide our ignorance under such expressions as the "plan of creation," "unity of design," &c., and to think that we give an explanation when we only restate a fact. Any one whose disposition leads him to attach more weight to unexplained difficulties than to the explanation of a certain number of facts will certainly reject my theory.

Charles Darwin[1]

Weizsäcker's book *The World-View of Physics* is still keeping me very busy. It has again brought home to me quite clearly how wrong it is to use God as a stop-gap for the incompleteness of our knowledge. If in fact the frontiers of knowledge are being pushed further and further back (and that is bound to be the case), then God is being pushed back with them, and is therefore continually in retreat. We are to find God in what we know, not in what we don't know; God wants us to realize his presence, not in unsolved problems but in those that are solved.

Dietrich Bonhoeffer[2]

In the late 1990s I was a PhD student at the University of British Columbia in Vancouver, studying genetics and development. I had weathered my bachelor's degree with my faith and antievolutionary views intact, and my area of study did not require me to think about evolution much at all.[3] Evolution was not completely avoidable, however: one very proevolution professor down the hall from my lab maintained a bulletin board called "Crackpot's Corner," where antievolutionary views were held up as objects of ridicule. It was here, on this bulletin board, that I first became aware of biochemist Michael Behe, a leader in the intelligent-design (ID) movement.[4] A little digging indicated that he had recently published a book, *Darwin's Black Box*. In that book, which I eagerly devoured, Behe makes the case for what he calls "irreducible complexity":

> Darwin knew that his theory of gradual evolution by natural selection carried a heavy burden: "If it could be demonstrated that any complex organ existed which could not possibly have been formed by numerous, successive, slight modifications, my theory would absolutely break down."
>
> It is safe to say that most of the scientific skepticism about Darwinism in the past century has centered on this requirement. . . . Critics of Darwin have suspected that his criterion of failure had been met. But how can we be confident? What type of biological system could not be formed by "numerous, successive, slight modifications"?
>
> Well, for starters, a system that is irreducibly complex. By *irreducibly complex* I mean a single system composed of several well-matched, interacting parts that contribute to the basic function, wherein the removal of any one of the parts causes the system to effectively cease functioning. An irreducibly complex system cannot be produced directly (that is, by continuously improving the initial function, which continues to work by the same mechanism) by slight, successive modifications of a precursor system, because any precursor to an irreducibly complex system that is missing a part is by definition nonfunctional. An irreducibly complex biological system, if there is such a thing, would be a powerful challenge to Darwinian evolution.[5]

Behe's argument was straightforward, and I found it compelling. There are many biochemical features of cells where numerous components are required to work together to perform a function. Take away one part, and the system no longer works. Therefore, I reasoned along with Behe, such features would be beyond the reach of evolution to produce in the first place. They must have been directly created. Behe did include one caveat, however:

> Even if a system is irreducibly complex (and thus cannot have been produced directly), however, one can not definitively rule out the possibility of an indirect, circuitous route. As the complexity of an interacting system increases, though, the likelihood of such an indirect route drops precipitously. And as the number of unexplained, irreducibly complex biological systems increases, our

confidence that Darwin's criterion of failure has been met skyrockets toward the maximum that science allows.[6]

Still, I felt that Behe had a strong case. Science has yet to provide a detailed account of the origins of many biochemical features of cells. Many of those systems are highly complex and comprise numerous interdependent parts. Evolution, I reasoned, was not capable of building them.

One way to understand Behe's argument is to envision a stone arch. All the stones, when properly arranged, have a function. (Behe calls this the "purposeful arrangement of parts.")[7] If any stone is removed, the arch falls. The arch, then, is irreducibly complex: all of the parts are needed, and the function does not exist until all of the parts are in place. Humans can build arches because they employ an "indirect, circuitous route" with a scaffold to support it until it is complete. None of the stones are essential, then, until the scaffold is removed.

Behe would publish a second book in 2007, *The Edge of Evolution: The Search for the Limits of Darwinism*. In it he would refine his argument and define a limit for what evolutionary mechanisms could achieve in the construction of new biochemical complexes. First, he argued, new irreducibly complex biochemical structures would require new binding sites to form between proteins, which certainly is the case. However, he argues that forming new binding sites between proteins requires multiple mutations to occur simultaneously—something that would be highly improbable. Since new irreducibly complex biochemical structures would require several new binding sites between proteins, and these mutations would have to occur simultaneously—so his argument goes—we can be confident that irreducibly complex systems are beyond the reach of evolutionary mechanisms. As such, Behe claims, they are examples of structures that cannot be produced by "successive, slight modifications"; they must arise as a unit, and thus are a hallmark of ID—that is, direct manufacture, or special creation.

Behe's argument for design, then, is based on probabilities.[8] Biochemical complexes form through proteins binding to one another; getting new proteins to bind to one another requires numerous mutations; and these mutations must occur simultaneously. Since several mutations occurring simultaneously is far too improbable, Behe argues, we can infer when we see protein complexes composed of several proteins that bind to one another that they are the product not of evolution but rather of design.

While Behe restricts himself to biochemistry in his books, he has also used an illustration from paleontology to illustrate his ideas. Interestingly this illustration, from the early 1990s, touches on cetacean evolution. At that time it was not known that cetaceans were artiodactyls, and the evidence then available suggested that they descended from a carnivorous group called Mesonychids. In a conference presentation where Behe would go on to discuss his ideas about biochemistry, he cites the paucity of evidence linking whales and their supposed terrestrial ancestors as a typical case for evolutionary explanations:

> Finally, most glaringly obvious, if random evolution is true, there must have been a large number of transitional forms between the Mesonychid and the ancient whale. Where are they? It seems like quite a coincidence that of all the intermediate species that must have existed between the Mesonychid and whale, only species that are very similar to the end species have been found. . . .
>
>   I have started my contribution to this symposium with a discussion of the Zeuglodon whale because it is a paradigmatic example of evolutionary argumentation: a small change in a preexisting structure is used to argue to massive changes involving completely new structures or functions. It is like arguing that because a man can jump over a fissure five-feet wide, then given enough time he could jump over the Grand Canyon. Now, a believer in the unabating rule of natural law would argue that the man could jump over the Grand Canyon if there were ledges and buttes for him to use as steppingstones. The skeptic would ask to be shown the steppingstones.[9]

We can see similarities between these biochemical and paleontological arguments, and Behe intends us to. Behe argues that evolution, though capable of small changes, is incapable of generating the sort of change required to shift a terrestrial tetrapod to a whale. Similarly, he doubts that "stepping-stones" exist on the path to new biochemical structures or functions. Though for obvious reasons Behe no longer uses whale evolution as "a paradigmatic example of evolutionary argumentation," his biochemical arguments remain essentially unchanged. Yet they too are vulnerable to advances in scientific knowledge.

Make Mine a Double

So, do biochemical equivalents of "stepping-stones" exist? It's a more challenging question to address than looking for ancient whale relatives, since genes, proteins, and the biochemical structures they make do not fossilize. There are lines of evidence, however, that forming new protein binding sites, structures, and functions includes processes readily accessible to evolution—even if numerous mutations are necessary—without invoking miraculous intervention. Let's explore a few examples.

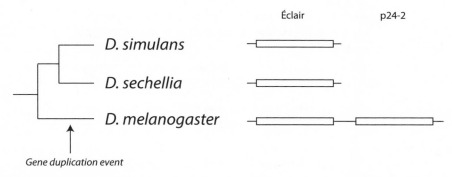

FIGURE 4.1. A phylogeny of three fruit fly (Drosophilid) species, and the status of the Éclair and p24-2 loci in each. After the lineage leading to *D. melanogaster* separates from the others, a duplication event produces an Éclair paralog, p24-2.

In chapter 2 we saw how examining the pattern of shared mutations in humans and other apes allowed us to place these species into a phylogeny—a tree of relatedness. The same approach has been used for many other organisms, including a number of fruit fly species. Scientists have been studying fruit flies for over one hundred years: the first evidence that chromosomes were the vehicle of hereditary information was worked out in flies, for example. Once scientists started sequencing genomes, that of the standard lab fly (*Drosophila melanogaster*) was one of the first to be done. Scientists have now fully sequenced the genomes of many fruit fly species, and how they are related to one another is well understood. The two closest living relatives to *D. melanogaster* are *D. sechellia* and *D. simulans*, and these latter two species share a more recent common ancestral population with each other than either does with *D. melanogaster*. As you would expect, the genomes of these three species are highly similar to one another. There are differences between their genomes, however, and one area of interest to biologists is to look for new genes. One example that has been studied is the p24-2 gene of *D. melanogaster*—a gene not found in any other species of the genus *Drosophila*.[10] This gene is highly similar to another gene, however: a gene called Éclair. This gene is found in other species and happens to sit next door to the p24-2 gene in *D. melanogaster* (fig. 4.1).

Thus it's no mystery where p24-2 came from: it's a duplication of the Éclair gene. At some point in the lineage leading to *D. melanogaster*, the enzymes that do chromosome copying were accidentally bumped back after copying Éclair, and then copied it again, producing two nearly identical genes side by side. (The new copy happens to be fused together with some sequences of another neighboring gene, causing the new copy to be translated in cells

Amino acid divergence between the paralogous
genes Éclair and p24-2 of *D. melanogaster*

```
Éclair  MRDQFISLALILCVLHSACGLYFHISQTERKCFIEEVPDETTVIVNYKVELYDPRSNGFM  60
p24-2   MRDQFISLALILCVLHSACGLYFHISETERKCFIEEVPDETTVIVNYKVELYDPRSNGFM  60


Éclair  PSSPGIGMHVEVRDSDDKIVLSRVYSSQGRISFTSHTPGEHVICMFSNSTAWFSGAQLRV  120
p24-2   PSSPGIGMHVEVRDSDDKIVLSRVYSSQGRISFTSHTPGEHVICMFSNSTAWFSGAQLRV  120


Éclair  HLDIQVGEHAIDYAHVAQKEKLTELQLRIRQLLDQVEQITKEQNYQRYREERFRHTSEST  180
p24-2   HLDIQVGEHAIDYAHVAQKEKLTELQLRIRQLLDQVEQITKEQNYQRYREERFRHTSEST  180


Éclair  NSRVLWWSLAQTVVLVCMGFWHLFNL  206
p24-2   NSRVLWWSLAQTVVLVCMGFWQMRHL  206
```

FIGURE 4.2. The amino acid sequences of Éclair and p24-2 in *D. melanogaster*. There are five amino acid differences (underlined); four of these cluster at the end of the protein, where they likely form a new protein binding site. Numbers on the right indicate the nucleotide or amino acid number in this sequence.

that do not translate the original Éclair gene into protein.) This new "double Éclair" variant then gradually became more common within this population, until the single gene variant was lost. Gene duplication through this process is well documented in many organisms, and the resulting genes are known as "paralogs," genes that share a common ancestral gene sequence but arose from duplication events within one organism. While recently diverged paralogs tend to retain a very high similarity to one another, paralogs that resulted from ancient duplication events may be much more dissimilar.

Not surprisingly, given their recent divergence, the amino acid sequences of Éclair and p24-2 are nearly identical to one another: they differ by only five amino acids out of a total of 206. Amino acids can be represented by single letters in order for us to compare these two proteins more compactly (fig. 4.2).

What we observe is that of the five differences, four are clustered together at one end of the protein. Work on Éclair has shown it to be required for transporting other proteins around the cell, and we know that p24-2 cannot step in to do Éclair's function when it is missing. Similarly, Éclair cannot replace p24-2, suggesting that it is transporting something distinct from Éclair, and in different cell types. Interestingly, p24-2 is an essential gene—if it is removed, the fly dies.

The evidence we have, then, supports the following scenario. Éclair is duplicated to form an Éclair / Éclair arrangement of neighboring paralogs. At this stage, the second copy cannot be essential, since it did not exist prior to the duplication event. Over time, the two copies diverge from each other. As this divergence takes place, one of the copies begins to be able to transport another protein cargo. Eventually, with other changes, this new transport becomes essential to the organism. Thus a new gene and new function have been added to an existing system and have now become essential to that system.

Now, this does not necessarily demonstrate that an entirely new irreducibly complex system, by Behe's definition, has been formed. It does, however, provide evidence that new protein binding sites can form readily through evolutionary processes, and that is the key issue for Behe's claims. The p24-2 protein is doing *something*, since it is essential, and it cannot be doing its function without interacting with other proteins. The amino acid differences we observe strongly suggest it is binding a new cargo of some kind.

Of course, one of the problems with this evidence is that no one was there to observe it happening, and re-creating the last 3 million years of *Drosophila* evolution is not feasible. Thus it may well be that the five amino acid changes we observe between Éclair and p24-2 are in fact the result of design, not evolution. This is in fact what Behe has argued in response to this evidence:

> There are five specific amino acid differences between Éclair and p24-2. Professor Venema seems not to comprehend that they may not have arisen by random mutation. Once one gets beyond one or two random mutations, one can't assume that multiple further mutations arose by chance. In other words, as far as anyone knows, those five point mutations may have required guidance or design in their appearance.[11]

This is formally possible, if somewhat strained—and there is no way to definitively settle the matter short of a time machine. This option, however, raises interesting questions about the designer involved. Why did the designer do this for *D. melanogaster* and not for any other Drosophilid species? Why did the designer do this at all? Since every other Drosophilid gets by just fine with only one copy of Éclair, and no p24-2 at all, why does one species need a duplicated and (slightly) engineered copy? If a new function was needed, why design the required gene to appear as a slightly modified version of a gene right next to it in the genome? Wouldn't that potentially fool researchers into thinking they were observing the results of natural processes? Aside from these questions, the important point to note is Behe's claim: anything more than one or two random mutations means that design must be considered. By that measure, the designer may have independently designed insulin proteins many times over in separate species, yet with uncannily similar sequences.

Behe's designer seems oddly constrained to designs that have the strong appearance of having evolved.[12]

Make Mine a *Double* Double?

But, one might contend, duplicating a few genes here and there might generate
some new information, but not *enough* to do the heavy lifting that large-scale
evolutionary change requires. Interestingly, geneticists have long suspected
that the lineage leading to present-day vertebrates (i.e., all animals with a
skull and backbone) experienced gene duplication en masse, through what
is known as a "whole-genome duplication (WGD) event"—and that this type
of event occurred not once but twice. WGD events sometimes occur when
reproductive cells fail to divide after they have replicated their chromosomes
in preparation for cell division. For example, the cell divisions that make
gametes (i.e., eggs or sperm) in sexually reproducing organisms are supposed
to reduce the chromosome count by half, so that the new embryo has the normal chromosome number after two gametes fuse together. Sometimes the cell
divisions that produce an egg fail to perform chromosome segregation, and
all the chromosomes end up in the egg, giving it a doubled set. And as crazy
as it sounds, this does not always make the egg defective. If a normal sperm
fertilizes it, the result is an offspring with three copies of every chromosome,
rather than the normal two copies. These organisms can make gametes with
the proper single chromosome set or a doubled set—and if two "doubled"
gametes fuse, the result is an organism with four chromosome sets rather
than the normal two. Breeding between two such organisms may then start
a new lineage that has four chromosome sets as the new "normal" instead
of the previous two sets—a complete doubling of the entire genome. As far-
fetched as it sounds, scientists have documented these sorts of WGD events
in present-day vertebrates such as fish and frogs.[13] So the idea that this may
have happened to the ancestral vertebrate lineage deep in the past is not out
of the question; and as long as there is adequate temporal separation between
the events, there is no reason to think it could not happen twice.

One early piece of evidence for two rounds of WGD in the vertebrate lineage was the observation that some key genes in vertebrates seem to come in
sets of four highly similar, but not identical, copies. Could these sets of four
be the result of two WGDs? Or might they merely be the result of smaller
duplications of chromosome regions?

One way to distinguish between these options is to examine the pattern of
where paralogs are in present-day vertebrate genomes. While small duplications

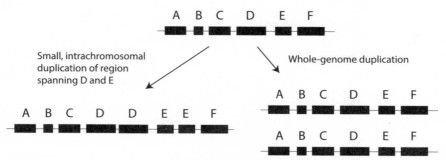

FIGURE 4.3. A small intrachromosomal duplication event (left) produces a few paralogs within one chromosome. A WGD event (right) produces copies of all chromosomes, with a full set of paralogs for every gene in the genome (only one chromosome is shown).

produce a small number of paralogs on one chromosome, a WGD event will produce full copies of every chromosome (fig. 4.3).

After a WGD event, we would expect many paralogs to be lost, since they cannot have been necessary when they first appear. Some, however, may remain and shift their function slightly (as we saw for Éclair and p24-2). Over time, we would expect a pattern similar to part B in figure 4.4 (p. 76). If a second WGD event occurred thousands of generations later, it too would produce copies of all chromosomes, with paralogs arranged in order on each duplicated chromosome (part C). After this event, we would again expect some loss and some retention of paralogs, with those retained shifting their functions over time.

With the advent of whole-genome sequencing, it is now possible to examine the distribution of paralogs within vertebrate genomes to see if the data support small intrachromosomal duplications or WGD events.[14] The human genome is the best-studied vertebrate genome at present, so it was chosen as a representative vertebrate genome for this analysis. Of course, for this work, researchers needed to identify the subset of genes in present-day vertebrates that would have been present long ago, before the first hypothesized WGD event. Only these genes would have gone through the two WGD events, if they indeed had occurred. Other genes may have arisen through small intrachromosomal duplications later on, and such genes needed to be excluded from the study.

To identify this set of ancient genes that would have been present prior to any WGD event, the researchers used a straightforward approach using known relationships between vertebrates and related groups. Vertebrates are nested within the chordates; in other words, all vertebrates are chordates, but not all chordates are vertebrates. The complete genome sequence of a nonvertebrate

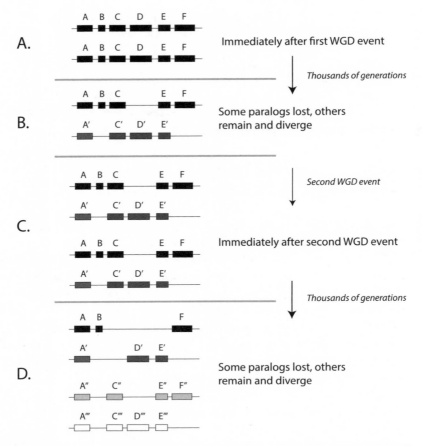

FIGURE 4.4. A WGD event produces chromosome copies with ordered paralogs (A). Over time, some paralogs will be lost, and others diverge to new functions (B). A second round of WGD repeats the process (C), and again paralogs are lost or diverge (D). The final pattern of paralogs for a lineage that has experienced two rounds of WGD would be expected to match (D); even though many paralogs have been lost, the remaining paralogs retain the spatial organization indicative of WGD.

chordate (a sea squirt named *Ciona intestinalis*) is now available, as is a genome of a bony fish (the puffer fish *Takifugu rubripes*). Humans, puffer fish, and sea squirts share a common ancestral population deep in the past, prior to the hypothesized WGD events (fig. 4.5). Thus the genes present in this last common ancestral population would be the ones that would have been present for any WGD events that occurred.

This known relationship (based on many lines of evidence, including genome sequences) allowed the researchers to identify the genes in present-day

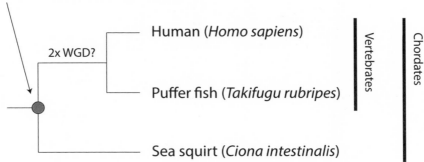

FIGURE 4.5. A phylogeny of humans, puffer fish, and sea squirts. Genes present in the last common ancestral population of these three species (gray circle) would have gone through any WGD events on the lineage leading to present-day vertebrates.

vertebrates that were present in the last common ancestral population that vertebrates share with sea squirts. Any genes that vertebrates and sea squirts share in the present day, they most likely inherited from their common ancestral population. The alternative hypothesis (that thousands of genes arose de novo in two independent lineages, which nonetheless happen to be highly similar) is far too unlikely. So they restricted their analysis to the genes that humans and sea squirts share.

The results of this study were dramatic: this subset of human genes is arranged in four groupings in the pattern predicted by two WGD events.[15] In contrast, when the researchers looked at duplicated human genes not shared with sea squirts, they found that these paralogs were adjacent to each other on chromosomes, consistent with small duplications. Therefore, the evidence strongly supports the hypothesis that many human paralogs are the result of two WGD events deep in our lineage's past, but that some are the result of more recent, small duplications within chromosomes.

And here's the rub: we know that these paralogs, whether recent or ancient, have greatly diverged from each other and acquired new functions. Moreover, many of those functions are now absolutely essential for vertebrates. If Behe's argument is correct, none of this should have been possible.

Show Me the Mutations

Despite this evidence, those in the ID community remain skeptical. Rerunning the last several hundred million years of vertebrate evolution is of course no more possible than a few million years of fruit fly evolution. In an ideal world, scientists would have the ability to track a population of organisms over time and note the sort of changes that occurred within it, with a full record of the DNA variation of every generation along the way. Indeed, to truly refute Behe's claims, such an experiment would need to be done. When Behe testified during the 2005 *Kitzmiller v. Dover* case, which tested the constitutionality of teaching ID in the US public school system,[16] he was questioned during cross-examination on what he would consider adequate evidence for the evolution of an ancient, irreducibly complex system (in this case, the vertebrate immune system):

> Q. And I'm correct when I asked you, you would need to see a step-by-step description of how the immune system, vertebrate immune system developed?
> A. Not only would I need a step-by-step, mutation by mutation analysis, I would also want to see relevant information such as what is the population size of the organism in which these mutations are occurring, what is the selective value for the mutation, are there any detrimental effects of the mutation, and many other such questions.
> Q. And you haven't undertaken to try and figure out those?
> A. I am not confident that the immune system arose through Darwinian processes, and so I do not think that such a study would be fruitful.[17]

Of course, it is not possible to provide the level of detail Behe requires for the development of this system, since the relevant events occurred in the deep past. Behe's criteria are a tall order, even for experiments done in the present. Despite the challenges, however, a handful of ambitious experiments have provided the level of detail Behe requires. Not surprisingly, they use organisms that reproduce very quickly, to allow many generations to be examined in a reasonable time frame.

One such experiment examined the ability of a population of viruses to infect bacterial hosts.[18] The virus is called "lambda phage," and it infects *E. coli*, the common human intestinal bacterium. In order to infect its host, lambda phage uses one of its proteins, called "protein J," to bind on to a receptor protein on the surface of its *E. coli* victim. After this binding, other protein-binding interactions take place in a sequence that allows the virus to inject its DNA into the host cell, followed by a number of further interactions that result in virus replication within the host and that break the host open to release new viruses and continue the cycle. Not a pleasant way to go, to be sure, but the point is that the process requires a defined sequence of many specific protein-binding events to occur. If any of the proteins is missing, virus replication cannot proceed. Thus we see "a purposeful arrangement of parts" to accomplish virus replication, and each part is essential to the process—an irreducibly complex system according to Behe's definition.

The researchers were curious to know whether the virus could evolve to use a different host protein for entering *E. coli*. Lambda phage uses a protein on *E. coli* called LamB for this purpose. The researchers set up a system where only a tiny fraction of their *E. coli* population had LamB on their surfaces. Most of their culture of *E. coli* was thus resistant to the virus, but the few susceptible bacteria in the culture allowed for enough Lambda phage replication that it would not die out. In this system, any virus that gained an ability to infect *E. coli* without using LamB would have access to millions of previously resistant hosts. What might happen?

One key feature of this experiment was that the researchers frequently saved and froze samples of the virus population. So if anything interesting happened later, they would have a perfect "fossil record" of the virus population in the freezer, ready to be revived and examined.

Interestingly, the virus did evolve to use a second host protein, one called OmpF. Not only did this happen once, but it happened repeatedly in the experiment. Sequencing the DNA of the viruses able to use OmpF instead of LamB revealed that one of the virus proteins—the one that normally binds to LamB, called "protein J"—had accumulated four amino acid changes. By looking at the preserved samples, the researchers showed that the new binding requires all four mutations to be present. They also showed that these mutations did not happen simultaneously, but rather sequentially. As it turns out, these single mutations allowed the protein J to bind more tightly to LamB, which was a significant advantage since hosts with LamB were so scarce in the experiment. Once three single mutations were in place, the virus was only one mutation away from the ability to bind and use OmpF. Interestingly, viruses capable of using OmpF retained their ability to bind LamB—the virus could now use either host protein.

Two key aspects of this experiment are problematic for Behe's thesis. First and foremost, this experiment documents the addition of a protein to an irreducibly complex system. The original system was composed of virus protein J binding to LamB, plus numerous other protein-binding events. The modified system lacks LamB and has a modified virus protein J that binds to OmpF instead. The intermediate system has the modified virus protein J and LamB, as well as OmpF, but now only one of LamB or OmpF is required. The transition from one irreducibly complex system to another has an intermediate state between them that acts as a scaffold, or to use Behe's term, a stepping-stone.

The second major problem for Behe is that the transition from one system to another required no less than four mutation events. Behe bases his entire argument on the assumption that these mutations must occur simultaneously. The probability of these four changes happening at once in one virus is about one in a thousand trillion trillion—far, far beyond anything that is remotely possible, and far beyond what Behe sets as his "limit" for what evolution can accomplish. The reason that the virus could repeatedly skip past Behe's so-called limit was that the mutations happened *sequentially*, not simultaneously. Not only were the four mutations possible, but they also were probable enough to happen again and again, all under the watchful eye of science.

Thus Behe is now faced with a concrete example of a new protein-binding site arising through multiple mutations, with that new binding event replacing a previously essential part of a complex system—and all documented to a level of detail that cannot be disputed. Indeed, without a demonstration of the intermediate forms (the variants with one, two, or three mutations), Behe would conclude that design was likely involved, as he does for p24-2. While we cannot catch Éclair and p24-2 in the act, as it were, we have done so here in a way that even the staunchest critic cannot dispute. Thus it is difficult to argue that millions of years of evolution are incapable of doing the equivalent of what we can directly observe in the lab in a matter of days.

Information and Design

A second major argument proffered by the ID movement is that new biological information cannot be produced by evolutionary mechanisms. A leading proponent of this view in ID circles is philosopher and historian of science Stephen Meyer; the argument from information forms a significant part of his two major books.[19] Briefly, Meyer's argument is that evolution cannot account for "specified, complex information" that we observe in living systems, and that ID is the only known cause for information. As such, he argues, ID is the best explanation for the information we observe in DNA. Meyer argues that design is needed to explain both the ultimate origin of DNA information (i.e., at the origin of life) and the information needed to develop new features after the origin of life, such as the diverse body plans we observe in the fossil record. For this latter observation, Meyer argues, we need new genes encoding for proteins providing new functions, and for new proteins we need to generate what are called "protein folds." In order for proteins to do their jobs, they need to twist and bend up into stable three-dimensional shapes. Unsurprisingly, these stable shapes are referred to as "protein folds" by biologists. One major argument within ID in general, and Meyer's works in particular, is that stable, functional protein folds are exceedingly rare—so rare, the argument goes, that evolution is incapable of producing new ones. As a result, Meyer claims, ID is needed to explain the origin of new functional proteins, and thus the genes that code for them. Since new genes, or even new protein folds, are beyond the reach of evolution to produce, Meyer claims, we can be confident that the biological information we observe is the product of design rather than evolution.

In spite of Meyer's objections, geneticists have determined numerous mechanisms by which new genes and new functions come into being. As we have seen with Éclair and p24-2, gene duplication and mutation can create a new gene with a new function. Also, we now have evidence that the base of the vertebrate lineage had two rounds of WGD, greatly increasing the number of genes available to be converted into modified functions—something that Meyer, to my knowledge, has not acknowledged or responded to. Of course, it is always possible to claim that such duplication and divergence are "not new"—and Meyer does make this argument for individual genes. Of course, recall that evolution seldom makes things that are truly "new": evolution is all about descent *with modification*.

Beyond these obvious flaws in Meyer's thesis, other mechanisms are known where gene sequences can be duplicated, broken apart, and rejoined into new combinations, making chimeric genes (genes with parts of previously separate genes fused together) with functions not present in any of the contributing genes. Even more dramatic are cases when a sequence that was not a gene at all becomes one, something called "de novo" gene origination. In considering these mechanisms, however, Meyer also finds them inadequate, claiming that they "either (1) beg the question as to the origin of the specified information contained in genes or parts of genes, or (2) invoke completely unexplained de novo jumps—essentially evolutionary creation ex nihilo ('from nothing')."[20]

Meyer goes on to claim that even if evolution can explain some new genes (through duplication events), these genes have the same protein folds. As such, he argues, they are not "truly novel."

> [Biologists cite] numerous scenarios of this type—scenarios attempting to explain the evolution of slight gene variants (and their similar proteins), not the origin of new protein folds. This is an important distinction, because . . . new protein folds represent the smallest unit of selectable structural innovation, and much larger innovations in the history of life depend on them. Explaining the origin of structural innovation requires more than just explaining the origin of the same gene and protein or even the origin of new genes capable of coding for

new protein functions. It requires producing enough genetic information—truly novel genes—to produce new protein folds.[21]

So Meyer claims both that evolution cannot deliver the goods when it comes to generating information needed for new protein folds, and that gene-duplication-based mechanisms beg the question, since they do not explain where information ultimately comes from (i.e., at the origin of life). Let's examine Meyer's arguments in detail before we evaluate them in light of the biological evidence. We'll start with his claim that evolution is incapable of producing new genes with new protein folds before tackling the issue of the origin of life. Since the scientific support for this claim is based on only one paper—published by ID advocate Douglas Axe in 2004[22]—it's worth understanding how the experiment was done.

Taking an Axe to the Tree?

Axe was interested in studying the function of a bacterial enzyme that breaks down penicillin-class antibiotics, specifically a "beta-lactamase." Penicillin-class antibiotics have a chemical bond structure called a "beta-lactam ring," and beta-lactamases cut this ring open and so destroy the antibiotic. This sort of enzyme is easy to use in these sorts of experiments, since if it is functional it will allow the bacteria that harbor it to survive exposure to antibiotics. Axe was interested in seeing how much the folded structure of the beta-lactamase could be changed without removing its function.

You might think that the way to do this would be to take a normal, functional beta-lactamase, begin changing amino acids one at a time, and test the mutant proteins for function. While this in principle could work, it is well known that doing so nearly always results in functional proteins. Protein folds are usually very stable, and single mutations seldom have a detectable effect on protein shape or function unless an absolutely critical amino acid is changed. So Axe designed his experiment around a modified beta-lactamase instead; he engineered one that was barely functional to begin with. Starting with this weakly functional enzyme (which was about 150 amino acids in length), he then changed groups of ten amino acids at a time to see if such a change would remove the tiny amount of function left. Not surprisingly, the vast majority of mutations of this sort did destroy the small amount of function the enzyme had left. From this experiment, as well as using sequence comparisons with beta-lactamases in other bacteria, Axe estimated that only 1 in 10^{77} sequences would allow his engineered beta-lactamase to retain its function.

Now these results are not controversial for Axe's engineered beta-lactamase. What is controversial, however, is Meyer's claim that these results apply to the evolution of proteins in general. If functional protein folds are so exceedingly rare, Meyer claims, then we cannot expect that evolution would be able to find the needles (functional, folded proteins) in the staggeringly vast haystack (the nonfunctional, unfolded protein sequences).

> All this requires searching for a functional needle in a vast haystack of combinatorial possibilities. Recall that Douglas Axe estimated the ratio of needles (functional sequences) to strands of straw in the haystack (non-functional sequences) to be 1 in 10^{77} for sequences of modest length (150 amino acids).
>
> Of course, in naturally occurring proteins, the interactions between side chains in units of secondary structure do maintain stable folds. But these proteins, with their stable three-dimensional folded structures, depend upon exceedingly rare and precisely arranged sequences of amino acids. The question is not whether the combinatorial search problem necessary to produce stable protein folds has ever been solved, but whether a neo-Darwinian mechanism relying on random mutations . . . provides a plausible explanation for how it might have been solved.[23]

The answer, for Meyer, is a resounding *no*, since he goes on to claim that no known mutational mechanism can overcome this problem. If functional protein folds are so rare, he argues, then there is no way for evolution to find them. Even converting one type of fold to another is impossible, since a huge gulf of nonfunctional sequences separates the functional ones; there is no way to get there from here. So the information we see in genes—or even in the protein folds within genes—is simply too improbable for natural processes to generate. To put Meyer's claim in perspective, there are thought to be about 10^{78}–10^{82} atoms in the known universe. If only one in every 10^{77} proteins is functional, then evolution finding one is far, far less probable than finding one special atom among all the atoms in our galaxy, or even numerous galaxies. That just isn't going to happen, and evolution simply cannot proceed under such constraints. So, Meyer argues, ID is needed to explain new protein folds and the genes that contain them. We know that intelligence can do this, even against the odds—and so Meyer claims that a designing intelligence is the best explanation.

Using Axe's work to extrapolate to the formation of functional proteins in general obviously requires some caveats.[24] First off, recall that Axe's experiment used a mutated, barely functional protein because it is well known that natural proteins are able to tolerate many mutations without losing their function. It's not controversial to state that had Axe used a normal, stable protein, he would have found far more "functional" proteins in his experiment. Also, recall that Axe substituted several amino acids at a time in his tests. There simply wouldn't be time to try every possible single mutation, double mutation, triple mutation, and so on. Many of those small mutations would not be expected to remove the residual function of the engineered protein as well. Evolution, as we have seen, typically works via single mutations, not numerous simultaneous ones. Axe's experiment needed to use multiple, simultaneous mutations in order to reduce the number of samples, but this means his setup is less relevant to the question of how evolution might build new protein structures over time. In fact, biologists expect that simultaneous mutation of multiple amino acids will diminish function—especially for a protein that is already mutated to the point of barely functioning in the first place.

A second issue is that Axe's experiment is designed to find proteins that can function as one specific enzyme—a beta-lactamase. Even if Axe's estimate is correct, it is an estimate of protein folds that can function as this specific enzyme. It should be obvious that within his experiment there would be many, many proteins that have stable folds, possibly with other functions, that are nonetheless "nonfunctional" in his tests. The nature of the experiment tests for only one function.

A third concern is that Axe's experiment starts with one defined protein and modifies that. The issue here is that there are other beta-lactamases that are not similar to the one Axe chose as his test subject. These other proteins function as beta-lactamases with an amino acid sequence very different from the test enzyme. So there were surely sequences in the experiment that could function as a beta-lactamase, but not as part of the beta-lactamase structure Axe chose. In other words, his experiment would miss sequences even for the function under consideration.

Now, these issues are not a problem for Axe's paper, since scientists understand these sorts of limitations and caveats. The average layperson who reads Meyer's works, however, may simply take him at his word that scientists have concluded that functional, folded proteins *in general* are exceedingly rare and thus agree with his assessment that they cannot be produced by natural mechanisms.

Of course, caveats aside, what would truly settle the issue is a concrete example of a "truly new" gene coming into being—one that is not a duplicate of a preexisting protein sequence—that nonetheless has a new function and new protein folds. If scientists could observe such an event, then it would indicate that Axe's math (and Meyer's use of it) is not a reliable estimate for the prevalence of functional protein folds. Interestingly, there are many known cases of exactly this, though Meyer does not seem to be aware of them, or of the implications they hold for his line of argument. Let's examine a few in detail.

Nylonase, de Novo

In the mid 1970s, scientists in Japan made a startling discovery when examining bacteria collected from chemical waste ponds: a bacterium that could use nylon as its sole source of carbon and nitrogen.[25] Since nylon is a synthetic chemical invented in the 1930s, this indicated that these bacteria had adapted to use it as a food source in a mere forty years—in less than the blink of an eye, in evolutionary timescales. The underlying cause of this ability was naturally of great interest, and further research showed that the bacteria harbored a set of three enzymes that performed the tasks of clipping nylon chains into smaller fragments and metabolizing them. These three enzymes and the genes that encode them are collectively known as "nylonases."

Where these nylonases had come from was naturally the next question. The answer for one of them was a surprise—it was a de novo enzyme. Rather than being a modified version of another enzyme, this functional sequence of amino acids had popped into existence in a moment, through a single mutation.[26]

Recall from our prior discussion on protein translation that the DNA code is read off in codons—groups of three DNA letters. In this case, an insertion mutation that added one DNA letter occurred in a previously existing gene sequence. Interestingly, this addition of one letter did two things at once: it introduced a "stop" codon very early in the amino acid sequence of a gene and at the same time created a new "start" codon. This new start codon, however, is not lined up with the codons of the previous gene sequence; it shifts every codon over by one DNA letter, resulting in an entirely new sequence of amino acids. This new sequence, however, was a weakly functional nylonase. Later, this sequence would be duplicated, and the sequences of the two copies would diverge from each other due to mutations. The duplicated copy would go on to become a highly active nylonase, with 200 times the activity of the original.[27]

Now, the very fact that the initial de novo protein sequence could function as an enzyme strongly supported the hypothesis that it was stably folded. Recent work has actually determined the precise structure of these enzymes, and they indeed have a number of stable folds within them, as expected. Ironically, their three-dimensional structures most closely match the shape of the lactamase group of proteins, including beta-lactamases.[28] Though their amino acid sequences are nothing like known lactamases, they nonetheless have the same overall shape. Thus, not only do they demonstrate that properly folded, functional proteins can indeed arise de novo (replete with protein folds), but they are also an example of how very dissimilar sequences can fold to similar shapes and perform similar functions—both of which we noted as caveats in Axe's work.

So what Meyer claims should be absolutely impossible—finding a functional, folded protein in the vast expanse of possible protein sequences—appears to be trivial for evolution to achieve.[29] Moreover, this is an example of evolution finding a structure that is far from optimal, and then refining its function through duplication and further mutations. Not forty years after the introduction of nylon into the environment, we observe complex, specified biological information devoted to utilizing it. Moreover, we can observe from the features of this information that it was easily produced through a well-known and probable series of mutation events.

De Novo, Over and Over Again

Now, if this was a one-off example, it might be possible to discount it as an incredibly rare, freak event. Also, one might argue that this sort of thing is only possible in bacteria, with their rapid generation times and vast numbers. Interestingly, this appears not to be the case. There is now strong evidence for brand-new, de novo genes in organisms as disparate as *Drosophila*, yeast, primates, and even humans. Though Meyer claims that "evolutionary biologists typically use the term '*de novo* origination' to describe *unexplained* increases in genetic information" and that the term "does not refer to any known mutational process," this is simply not the case.[30] De novo genes come from DNA sequences that are only a few mutational steps away from becoming a transcribed and translated gene. For example, the original, weakly functional nylonase was created by the insertion of only one DNA letter. While this new enzyme had a completely new amino acid sequence, it was generated from an existing gene. Many de novo genes, however, appear to have arisen from nongene sequences. Let's examine the evidence for this.

Researchers looking for de novo genes start by looking for protein-coding genes that are found in only one organism, and not its close relatives. To use human de novo genes as an example, researchers look for genes that are unique to humans but missing from our closest living relatives: chimpanzees and gorillas (fig. 4.6). Now, this pattern could be generated if a gene that was present in the last common ancestral population of all three species was independently deleted in the gorilla and chimpanzee lineages. Since such genes would not be de novo genes, researchers look at the sequences surrounding

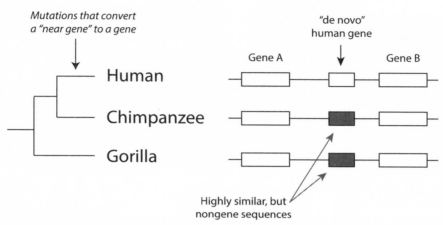

FIGURE 4.6. De novo genes in the human genome can be found by identifying genes unique to humans that nonetheless have highly similar nongene sequences in other apes.

a proposed candidate. For example, if a proposed de novo gene in humans sits between "gene A" and "gene B," researchers look for those same genes in chimps and gorillas. Since our genomes are nearly identical to those of these two apes, most often "gene A" and "gene B" also sit side by side in these other species. Geneticists can then look at the sequence between these genes in these apes. De novo genes in humans are those genes that have highly similar sequences in the corresponding chromosomal location in apes that are nonetheless not genes in those species. Typically, such sequences are only a few mutations away from becoming a new gene. With this evidence then, we can identify genes that have been newly formed from nongene sequences. In humans, three such genes have been identified thus far.[31] In *Drosophila* species, it appears that about 12 percent of new genes may be due to this process, in contrast to gene duplication.[32] There is also evidence that many de novo genes are lost shortly after they are gained. This is not surprising, since they cannot be necessary genes when they are first formed. A proportion of them are retained, however, and some of those go on to become essential genes, just as we saw for p24-2 (though, as you will recall, p24-2 arose not as a de novo gene but rather was the result of a gene duplication event). Thus genomes are in constant, slow turnover: gaining genes, losing genes, and shifting their biochemical relationships to one another over time. Once again, the evidence simply does not support Meyer's claim that the new genes, new functions, and new folds required for genetic innovation are beyond the reach of known evolutionary mechanisms. If this turnover can be observed over short timescales in present-day organisms, we have good evidence that similar innovation occurred in the past, even for events like the "Cambrian explosion" that took place over tens of millions of years, and were likely also bolstered through WGD events, as we have seen.[33] Though de novo genes can add new protein folds and functions to a genome, other more "usual" processes like gene duplication, cobbling new genes together out of parts of other genes, and other mutations also add to the mix. Moreover, these processes provide the fodder for new components to be added to existing complex biochemical systems, shifting their states and functions over time—further suggesting that Behe's claims are unfounded.

Back to the Beginning

So if there is good evidence that "complex, specified information" can arise in sufficient quantity to account for the diversity of life, and that "irreducibly complex" biochemical systems can indeed be built up over time, is there anything left to argue for within ID? Indeed there is, as Meyer has already made plain: even if the origin of new genes, functions, and folds can be demonstrated, these processes beg the question since they assume the prior existence of large amounts of biological information.[34] What is needed is an account of how that information system came into being, and this is another point in the history of life where Meyer claims ID is needed, because natural mechanisms are inadequate.

Meyer's main argument in this area is that the origin of the biochemical machinery needed to translate the DNA code into proteins cannot be explained in terms of chemical interactions. As we have seen, each DNA codon is translated when a complementary RNA molecule, called a "transfer RNA" (tRNA), brings the appropriate amino acid to the ribosome and binds to the codon through its anticodon sequence. Meyer's point is that in the present system, there is no physical reason why any particular codon should be paired up with any specific amino acid. In principle, he argues, any codon could have been assigned to any amino acid, since there are no direct physical interactions between them:

> Thus, chemical affinities between nucleotide codons and amino acids do not determine the correspondences between codons and amino acids that define the genetic code. From the standpoint of the properties of the constituents that comprise the code, the code is physically and chemically arbitrary. All possible codes are equally likely; none is favored chemically. . . . To claim that deterministic chemical affinities made the origin of this system inevitable lacks empirical foundation.[35]

Meyer even uses a diagram emphatically labeled "No direct chemical interaction!" and pointing to an amino acid, the codon coding for it, and the intervening tRNA molecule bridging the two to underscore his point.[36] This is a key argument for Meyer: if chemical interactions do not explain how the code is translated today, then there is no evidence that chemical interactions could have built the current code from a simpler system. Rather, he argues, it means that the "genetic code" is in fact a *genuine, arbitrary code*, such as a designer would create from scratch.

The problem with this line of argumentation is that there is evidence that the genetic code has a chemical basis. Some amino acids do, in fact, bind directly to their codons in the absence of tRNA molecules.[37] Now, they do not do so in current organisms because of the tRNA system, but the chemical affinities are there nonetheless. This suggests that at least part of the genetic code passed through a stage where amino acids lined up directly on their codons rather than with the help of tRNA molecules. Now obviously this observation does not give a complete picture of how the code originated, but such an observation is difficult to explain from an ID perspective. Why is it in an arbitrary, designed code that such affinities are found? Why might a designer place these affinities within the code when it would be trivial to design a code without them, since they do not contribute to the function of the current code? Like Behe's, Meyer's designer seems to choose designs that have the appearance of having evolved.[38]

Evolution ~~versus~~ *Is* Design

Though many Christians view *evolution* and *design* as opposites, there is another way to think about these issues. Simply put, they need not be mutually exclusive categories. Evolution, rather, may be God's chosen design to bring about biodiversity on earth. My friend and colleague Ard Louis puts it well, using an analogy drawn from his work as a biophysicist:

> If I took Lego blocks, and put them together and made you a train, it would be pretty cool. But if I made Lego blocks that, when I put them into a box and shake the box for a little while . . . and I open it, and they've spontaneously assembled into a train—even if the train has a few little scratches on it—that might be potentially even cooler.[39]

Indeed, making an object that can self-assemble would require a design far superior to that of an object that requires manual assembly. Rather than suggesting that a self-assembling object was evidence that a designer was not needed, we would be convinced that a powerful intellect was behind it. Evolution, as a mechanism, works wonderfully to adapt populations to their environments—to allow them to "self-assemble," as it were. Many scientists have agreed with Darwin's famous assessment that evolution produces "endless forms most beautiful."[40] Could it be that God, in his wisdom, chose to use what we would call a "natural" mechanism to fill his creation with biodiversity adapted to its environment? And to use evolution to allow his creation to continue to adapt as that environment's conditions shifted over time? If he did, would he be any less a creator than if he had done so miraculously? I think not. Though it is not something that science can speak to—since it goes beyond what science can establish—I view evolution as God's grand design for creating life.

Taking Stock

Over the course of my personal journey away from ID, I came to an uncomfortable conclusion: ID seemed strong only where there was a lack of relevant evidence. Though ID proponents strenuously deny the charge, I came to view ID as a God-of-the-gaps argument. The less one knows about the fossil record, the more compelling ID appears. The less one knows about the details of biochemical systems and how they change over time, the more compelling ID appears. The less one knows about the genetic code, the more compelling ID appears. The less one knows about the organization of genomes, the more compelling ID appears. The origin of life, the Cambrian explosion, and the origin of most complex biochemical structures are deep in the past, making them challenging, though not impossible, to study. Yet despite the challenges scientists face in these areas of inquiry, evidence continues to trickle in that undermines the ID view and supports evolution. Have chemists solved how life arose on earth? Not remotely, nor will they in the foreseeable future, if ever. Have biologists determined the detailed mechanism by which every complex biochemical structure arose through an evolutionary process? Not at all, nor will they. Is this good reason to claim that evolution has failed, that God must have created genetic information or complex biochemical structures directly? Or are such arguments merely the present-day equivalent of asserting that we know the earth does not move because we would feel it if it did? The track record of these sorts of arguments is poor, even for the ID movement over the last twenty years.[41]

Moreover, as I reflected on what Scripture says about creation, I came to view ID as counter to its witness. In Romans 1 Paul declares that observing creation bespeaks a creator. This was something that any first-century individual could observe and deduce, though they be Jew or gentile, slave or free. Importantly, Paul was not speaking to unexplained features of the created order, but rather to its functional integrity and glory. The idea that one would need a DNA sequencer or an electron microscope to discover unexplained phenomena and thereby declare the cosmos as the work of the Creator is far removed from what Paul is saying. Creation reveals the Creator, and we are without excuse. Learning more about how that creation works only deepens our wonder. To paraphrase Bonhoeffer, Paul calls us to see God *in what we know*, not in what we don't know—and as science reveals ever more about creation, we know more and more about how God chose to bring his creation into being.

Adam, Eve, and the Genome:
Four Principles for Reading the Bible
after the Human Genome Project

What happens when the church or, in my case, a Bible professor, encounters the kind of science found in the first part of this book? What happens, not to put too fine a point on it, when evolutionary theory and the Human Genome Project encounter the Bible's creation narratives? What happens then when we are told that the best of science today teaches that the DNA characteristic of modern humans could not have come from less than approximately 10,000 hominins? What happens when we are told there were pre-Adamite humans?[1] What about those two humans in Genesis 1–3? And what about the eight that survived Noah's flood? Which are we to believe, some ask: the Bible or science?

That last question leads some of us to dig in our heels while others shift with the latest conclusions of science. Some relish the countercultural stance

I am grateful to my colleague and friend Dr. Claude Mariottini for a careful reading of this chapter and the next. His wisdom eliminated some infelicities and made me rethink and revise a few points. Also, John Walton, Tremper Longman, and Jason Gile were kind enough to offer many helpful suggestions. In addition, I offer my deepest thanks to my coblogger Roseanne Sension, who made comments on my chapters in this book. I've caught more science from her than she has taught me, and she's been a brilliant help for many of us in the science-faith dialogue. Finally, I express deep thanks to the new president at Northern Seminary, William Shiell—a leader, pastor, and New Testament scholar—for his thoughtful suggestions on my chapters.

of digging in their heels, and, to switch imagery, the second group at times refers to their counterparts as hiding their heads in the sand of the past or even of religious superstition. What the first thinks is faithfulness to the Bible, the second thinks is intellectual compromise. The accusations go both ways. You've probably heard them as often as I have. To illustrate I pose the great Protestant Reformer Martin Luther, who dug in against scientists, with Galileo from the generation following Luther, who permitted science to reshape his thinking. Luther said this of the facts in the Bible that seem to conflict with the external realities: "The more it seems to conflict with all experience and reason, the more carefully it must be noted and the more surely believed." When Luther turns to Eve being formed from a rib, he says, "This is extravagant fiction and the silliest kind of nonsense if you set aside the authority of Scripture and follow the judgment of reason." But perhaps this illustrates his heel digging the most: "Although it sounds like a fairy tale to reason, it is the most certain truth."[2] Here Luther contrasts "reason" (or scientific thinking) and faith or Scripture. One might call Luther's approach the dominating approach to science and faith because he chooses—against reason, he admits—for the Bible to dominate the evidence. Galileo mirrors Luther with another kind of domination: "A natural phenomenon which is placed before our eyes by sense experience or proved by necessary demonstration should not be called into question, let alone condemned, on account of scriptural passages whose words appear to have a different meaning."[3]

The choice to let either the Bible or science dominate the other is common enough, but there is a better way, one that permits each of the disciplines to speak its own language but also requires each of the voices to speak to one another. Science, after all, can help the interpreter of the Bible just as the Bible can provide horizons and vistas for the scientist. Three Old Testament scholars are modeling how this dialogue between the Bible and science can be fruitful—John Walton, Tremper Longman, and Peter Enns. They don't agree with one another always, nor do I always agree with them in the pages that follow, but they have opened up new pathways for this kind of dialogue to occur.[4]

My Witness

But first let me speak for myself and for myself alone.[5] I grew up being told that evolution was for atheists and that those who embraced evolution could not embrace the Bible. But over time I encountered Christian scientists who informed me, sometimes off the record, that evolution was more or less how it all happened and that they believed God guided that evolutionary process. Their testimony gave me more courage to listen to how science works and to wait on the evidence. I found these Christian scientists to be faithful in their discipleship and humble in their knowledge of science, but clearheaded in believing that, while science didn't offer all the answers, there was very good evidence to trust much of what was being claimed. Their trustworthiness at the personal level made their science more credible as an option, and I'll say a bit more about that later in this chapter.

I have to admit that the encounter with science made me wonder at times about what I had been taught, about what the Bible said, about whether or not the Bible was wrong, and—this was for me a defining intellectual moment— *about whether traditional interpretations of Genesis 1–2 were perhaps well intended but misguided and in need of rethinking.* In other words, my encounters with trustworthy scientists and their works taught me to go back to the Bible with other questions and other possible interpretations and to ask what Genesis meant in its world. In this I believe I was motivated by a quest to know the truth. I went back to the Bible to read Genesis in context and to ask if what many *thought* the Bible was saying (that is, its interpreted meaning) was not in fact what the Bible *was actually* saying (its original meaning). But there's more: my encounter with science that prompted renewed study of Genesis also led me to challenge science about some of its assumptions. Modernity, expressed in extreme form in the "New Atheists" such as Richard Dawkins and Sam Harris, presses into our minds that the only reality is the empirical. If only what studies the empirical world (science) ascertains reality, then only science tells us the truth about reality. However, this common assumption in modernity is a case of concluding what one already assumes. How so? This approach restricts discoveries to empirically testable realities. Nothing else is real. But what if there is more? What if some kind of non-empirical reality exists? This is the sort of question the Bible presses on the scientist. I am convinced that there is more than the empirical, or perhaps I should say the more is hyperreality or suprareality. If so, there is a reality not knowable exclusively by the empirical methods of science. Theology, which is designed to investigate that nonempirical reality in some ways, can provide a map onto which we can locate science and which can challenge science.

In my own witness there were three defining moments, three moments when I lurched forward in utter gratitude to God for the relief of my own intellectual questions about science and the Bible, especially Genesis 1–11.[6] The first was when I read a book nearly forty years ago on the Bible and evolution that discussed "macro" versus "micro" evolution. That book, combined with reading a biography of Darwin, pried open my mind gently but firmly.[7] The second moment in my journey involved the last few years of blogging with the scientist Roseanne Sension (who goes on my blog by her initials "RJS") along with reading Dennis Venema's article "Genesis and the Genome," with Daniel Harlow's exposition following it,[8] and then finally John Walton's book *The Lost World of Genesis One*. Sension's blog posts and those writings combined to open my mind to a new way of reading the Bible. My third moment was the day a college student in tears told me that, had I not taught about reading Genesis 1 in the context of the ancient Near East, he would have abandoned the Christian faith. He wanted to be a scientist but knew there were some nonnegotiables about science that were totally convincing to him. One of which was some kind of evolution. That Genesis could be read in ways other than what he had been taught—young-earth creationism—was a defining moment for him and for me. I am convinced that a kind of evolution—theistic, evolutionary creationism, or planned evolution—fits the evidence best and does not threaten the Christian faith or a fair reading of Genesis.[9]

Genesis itself awakens us to fresh readings of itself because the text itself has some mighty unusual features that make an honest reader wonder whether they are meant to be strictly historical. For example, the earth has a dome over it, the man is formed out of dust while the woman is formed by removing a rib (or more) from the man, their names are fraught with meaning (the Earthling and the Mother of All Living), a snake talks and fools two nonsinners into sinning, there is this majestic garden of Eden (or "park") with angels twirling swords at the entrance, Cain finds a wife when there was every reason to believe there weren't any women other than sisters available, Cain is given a mark to distinguish him and protect him, the names of Cain ("spear") and Abel ("fleeting breath") seem allegorical,[10] people live to incredible ages, a flood covers the whole earth leading to nothing less than a cosmic do-over starting with eight human beings who immediately do stupid things, and then we get a group of humans intent on building a tower into the skies, and so God sorts them out into different languages. If these features don't at least make you wonder about what kind of literature this is, then nothing will.[11] Only someone trained to think otherwise will think otherwise.

What made me think otherwise were personal encounters with science and scientists, including the Human Genome Project. Thinking otherwise, in other words, asks us each to reconsider our interpretations as possible misinterpretations. In his elegant history of the interpretation of the book of Genesis, Ronald Hendel offers us this ironic reminder: "One theme within the interpretation of Genesis has been the falsity of many of its interpretations. . . . Modern biblical scholarship also argues that much of the history of interpretation of Genesis is a history of error."[12] And that reminder is from an expert on Genesis, who on the very next page refers to these mistaken views as "creative illusions"! A few pages later he says with force: "People do things with Genesis in order to influence and change reality."[13] Why? Because Genesis is a sacred book with profound power and authority. This means it deserves to be interpreted with the utmost care and respect, which means that the most important approach to reading the Bible and to understanding every form of communication—something I have learned over and over and over again—is contextual.

A Text out of Context Is a Pretext

Every statement about Adam and Eve in the Old Testament, in Jewish literature, and in the New Testament is made from a context and into a context. Furthermore, some of the statements about Adam and Eve in all this literature are designed to speak against that context. That is, those statements are polemics and apologetics. Learning about those contexts and polemics often brings fresh understanding of the intention of the Bible and hence of what God wants his people to hear. In addition, this contextual approach to Adam and Eve provides a model for how Christians today can think about Adam and Eve in the context of the faith-and-science debate. If the Human Genome Project provides brilliant discoveries about the origin of life and the development of humans into who we are today, we will all gain clarity if Christians learn how to speak about Adam and Eve in a context that both affirms conclusions about the genome and challenges some conclusions drawn from the Human Genome Project. Contexts, both ancient and modern, shape what we see, what we hear, and how we respond.

Hence, in what follows we will look at Adam and Eve in context. This means we need to interpret Genesis 1–3 in the context of some ancient Near Eastern texts like *Enuma Elish*, the *Gilgamesh Epic*, and *Atrahasis*.[14] In a later chapter we will discover that the ancient Hebrew texts continued to interact with specific cultures—apocalyptic, wisdom, Greek philosophy like Plato's *Symposium*—and that by the time Paul wrote what he said about Adam (and Eve) in Romans 5 and 1 Corinthians 15, he was taking that *interactive relationship of what Jews thought about Adam and Eve in their contexts to the next level*. In what follows we will see that God speaks to the church through a process of his people interacting with their cultures, absorbing and appreciating their cultures, differing from their cultures, and battling their cultures. Such an interactive relationship between Israel and its surrounding cultures provides a template for our own interactive relationship with our culture. We will, in fact, show that the Bible's template of presenting Adam and Eve to various cultural contexts provides fresh ways of interacting with science today. The Bible's Adam and Eve, in fact, may be what our culture most needs to hear from Christians about how to think about humans.[15]

To back up now to reading the Bible in context, my own interaction with scientists and the Bible has made clear some fundamental principles that the best readers of the Bible constantly bring into play. I want to focus on four of these principles for reading the Bible: respect, honesty, sensitivity to science students, and the primacy of Scripture.

The First Principle: Respect

To understand what someone is telling us, we must respect that person as a person, we must respect that person's speech, and we must do our best to understand that person's speech from that person's context.[16] We perhaps learned this the first time we met someone from a different culture—perhaps as a child meeting someone from Africa or South America or Europe. As they attempted to speak English, we at times heard not only an accent but also some odd combinations of words and phrases, and we learned that to comprehend them we had to listen especially well—and at times ask some questions. The same principle of respect is needed for reading the Bible, especially a section of the Bible like Genesis 1–11, a text that, no matter how embattled it is, resounds with some of life's deepest themes. Terence Fretheim, a noted Old Testament scholar, asks these big questions about the opening chapters of Genesis: "Did Israel inherit theological perspectives from the larger ancient Near Eastern culture? How old is the earth? What about evolution? Does the dominion passage commend the exploitation of the earth? Are these texts inimical to the proper role of women in church and society?"[17]

We can add more questions that pop into our minds in careful readings of this wonderful text: What about gender and identity? What about marriage and family? Is the agrarian life the divine design? How are vocation and work understood here? Is this a foundation for ecological activism? How about society and culture—are they present too? What is the primal sin? Is a sinful nature inherited or is only the inclination to sin inherited? Are humans condemned from birth because of Adam's sin? Why the persistence of evil?[18] Why do humans think they can reach God? What of the pride of empire building? And the granddaddy of them all: How, to quote a line in the opening to John Milton's *Paradise Lost*, do we "justify the ways of God to men"? Does

Genesis 1–3 explain why it is that our world blankets itself with injustice, evil, and sin as it also covers us at times with the grandeurs of goodness, love, justice, and peace? At the end of our own questions, questions about death rise to the surface in our text: What does death mean? And was there death before Adam and Eve?[19]

This text came on the scene in the ancient Near East, and Genesis 1–11 sounds like that world, uses categories and terms and ideas from that world, and, not least, has the "pre-"scientific assumptions of that world. We must respect that text as *designed for the ancient Near Eastern culture*.[20] What we have learned from specialists in the ancient Near Eastern creation stories is that these stories did double duty: they not only explored the (largely mythic) "past" but also were designed to speak into the present. They were, in other words, some kind of history and some kind of theology mixed with each other. Old Testament specialist Joseph Blenkinsopp takes us to the heart of what these ancient Near Eastern texts were designed to do:

> These ancient stories were not written to entertain. Those who first set them down in writing may have been curious about the remote past, but historical curiosity was not their main purpose in writing. Rather, the creation of narratives, active genealogies of gods and mortals, and dramas featuring characters and situations set in the remote past provided their authors with a vehicle for thinking through basic issues, for expressing convictions and ideas about life in the present, the life of their societies and, no doubt, their own individual lives as well. We should expect to find something comparable in the biblical history of cosmic and human origins.[21]

The most respectful reading knows this double-duty feature of the ancient Near Eastern creation narratives, and it gives the same respect to the Bible's own account, which is also doing double duty.

Just as it is culturally disrespectful for an American shopping in Costa Rica to think Costa Ricans should understand English, so it is disrespectful to Genesis 1–11 to think it somehow should understand modern science, DNA, and the Human Genome Project, or for that matter the science of any generation after the writing down of Genesis 1–11! An example of this is the kind of "science" assumed by Severian of Gabala in his famous sermons on the creation narrative from the beginning of the fifth century AD, in which he rants about a flat earth over against the more scientific-minded of his time, who thought it was more globular.[22] Severian, we need to say clearly, was flat-out wrong because he imposed his reading of the Bible on his time, and, we need also to say clearly, there are plenty of "Severians" today who impose their readings of the Bible on our time. Each era of the church mirrors each era of science, and each era sadly often reveals a profound disrespect for the text itself.[23] Genuine respect begins when we let Genesis 1–11 be Genesis 1–11, which means letting Genesis 1–11 be ancient Near Eastern and not modern Western science.

To provide examples of letting Genesis be Genesis, think of this: Genesis 1–11 records stories that sound like other cultures' Top First Lists. That is, Genesis 1–11 is an account of not only creation but also the first sin, the first murder, firsts in various technologies, the first (and we hope last) mating of the Nephilim with women, the first empire builder, the first act of divine discipline against the world, and the first attempt by humans to build a city that reached into the heavens with God.[24] It is not disrespectful to Genesis to perceive it as Israel's Top First List over against other Top First Lists in the ancient Near East. When I was in college I learned a line from the German poet Johann von Goethe that I have repeated in lecture after lecture. In German he said, "Willst ein Dichter du versteh'n, mußt in Dichter's Lande geh'n," which in English translation says, "If you want to understand a poet [or an author], you must go to that poet's land." Respect, then, means we learn to listen to Genesis 1–11 in its own world (and not our own).

The Second Principle: Honesty

In keeping with the topic of this book, we need to be honest about two things: the Bible and science. As a professor I teach my students this method: *face the facts* and *do not fear the facts*. I believe this means we have to face *both* what the Bible teaches *and* what science teaches. So we are right back with our two facts: science's view that human DNA goes back to more than two people and the Bible's apparent teaching that it all goes back to two people, Adam and Eve. So we face the facts. The Bible really does make it look like Adam and Eve are humans from whom we descend. But scientists are going to tell us straightaway that Adam and Eve themselves had ancestors, reminding me of an old cave I walked into just outside Johannesburg, South Africa, in what is called "the Cradle of Humankind." Here I encountered a place and pictures where they discovered hominin fossils 2–4 million years old. Others are going to tell us that the DNA makeup of humans today goes back to thousands of hominins, and on and on . . . So we come to this point, and it is for me the most significant pastoral question pastors need to ask in tandem with scientists: *Are you willing to face the facts—the facts of the Bible and the facts of science?*

Many well-meaning people get irritated over probings and understandings like this. I am convinced with Ron Osborn that at times the vitriol flowing from the more fundamentalist side of this debate, sometimes from so-called scientific creationists and other times from intelligent-design folks, indicates something deeper at work—namely, fear. They fear that they might be wrong about how to read Genesis, and some of them fear that the Bible might be wrong and their entire faith might collapse. This fear often enough is expressed as defending the Bible. I know this fear and the faithful defense posture because I've experienced them, and I've had more than one (now embarrassing to remember) heated discussion with Christian evolutionists because I was afraid of the implications of facts, facts I knew could be "real-er" than my reality. I will look at this below in our fourth principle, but before we get there, I want to quote what Osborn has said so well, and I'd like you to know that what he says could well have been spoken of me at one time in my life:

> One of the reasons I became convinced that there is something deeply unhealthy gnawing at the heart of biblical literalism on Genesis and "scientific" creationism is because of the toxic speech habits, blatant power maneuvers (wrapped in exalted religious rhetoric) and tactics of misrepresentation and incrimination I have witnessed in some of the movement's most vocal defenders within my own tradition. Those who manifest such uncharitable spirits, I concluded early on in my wrestling with questions of faith and science, are probably not the divinely anointed guardians of truth.[25]

One might be tempted to say his deck is loaded against the fundamentalists of my own ilk, but Osborn points as well to analogous problems with the other side:

> At the same time, I have often been equally dismayed by the attitudes evinced by some individuals on the other side of the debate over creation and evolution—by how quickly some are prepared to write off people of sincere faith who are at different places in their intellectual and spiritual journeys, by how little pastoral sensitivity they show in introducing unsettling ideas to others, and by how often their sense of scientific certainty and mastery of technical knowledge assumes the character of its own ersatz religion. Some of these individuals, I have concluded, have indeed broken faith with their Christian communities, though not for reasons as facile as whether or not they affirm literalistic dogmas.[26]

What is needed by both sides is honesty—fearless honesty about what the texts and empirical studies actually say, honesty about what they don't say, and perhaps most of all, honesty about what each permits the thinker to conclude. Conclusions that reach too far are as dishonest as ignoring or distorting the evidence. I've been on both sides of that fear, but I think I've found a more honest way.

Pondering honesty leads me to being honest about Genesis. One way to read Genesis 1–2 is to see two separable creation stories (1:1–2:4a; 2:4b–25). Some think Genesis 2 fills in what is not found in Genesis 1, while others think they are two originally separate creation stories in Israel that have been brought together to complement each other. The first is cosmic history, while the second is about how God's created humans are to live in God's world. The first has what seems like a sudden creation of both the man and the woman, while the second has first the man and then from man the woman. In the second the man is given a clearer role over other creatures. The first seems, well, somewhat idyllic, while the second creates that rather sad scene of the man needing a companion. The first is the bare fact of man and woman, while the second turns them into a married couple ready for procreation. In the first, God creates the man and woman out of thin air by a word, while in the second, God creates the man from the earth and the woman from the rib of the man.

Most scholars today, even if they want to read the narrative from Genesis 1 to Genesis 3 seamlessly, acknowledge that there are two separable creation accounts in Genesis 1–2. An honest and wise reader listens to this interpretation. A good example of how they are different is that in Genesis 1 the creation of animals precedes that of humans, while in Genesis 2 the man appears to be created first. Some translations, like the NIV, attempt to smooth over the differences. For instance, in Genesis 2:19 the NRSV has "the LORD God formed . . . ," while the NIV reads, "Now the LORD God *had formed* out of the ground all the wild animals . . ." (emphasis added). The NIV suggests that the formation of the animals was prior to that of the humans, as we read in Genesis 1, but Genesis 2 does not say this. In fact, the Hebrew verb *yatsar*, which describes God as a potter, is not a pluperfect ("had formed") but simple perfect/past ("formed"). The NIV wants us to think Genesis 2:19 assumes the original creation of Genesis 1. This oddity in translation illustrates the tension between Genesis 1 and Genesis 2, and that tension deserves to be kept—for that is the most honest reading of the text.[27]

Honesty leads us to say that Genesis 1–2 sounds like other creation narratives in the ancient Near East. If it does, it does. Where there are similarities, we admit them; where there are dissimilarities, we admit them. We don't need Genesis 1–2 to be totally unlike other ancient Near Eastern texts in order for it to be true, just as we don't need Jesus to be totally different from the rabbinic teaching of his day for his teaching to be truth. What we need most in studying the ancient Near East and Genesis 1–2 is an openness to truth wherever it might be found. Openness to truth is the most Christian principle I know of.

Two principles—respect and honesty—and now a third.

The Third Principle: Sensitivity to the Student of Science

Everything we teach about Genesis 1–11 needs to be examined, pondered, and thought through with respect to contemporary students of science. By "students" I mean students nurtured in Christians homes and churches and under the tutelage of public school teachers.[28] This means they hear the Bible in one context and science and evolution in another (and sometimes hostile) context, and it is they who are put in the hot box Monday through Friday in front of their peers and before teachers who will grade their papers and assess their intelligence. While pulling students out of the public school system may suspend the tension, eventually the student will experience the raw capacity of evolutionary theory to explain scientific realities.

Here is a story about one of the Western world's truly great thinkers, Alexis de Toqueville, encountering the same tension some two hundred years ago:

> Doubt had seeped into his soul through his readings in the prefect's library, where he had encountered the writings of Voltaire, Buffon, and other philosophes. He was devastated by what he encountered in their books. Here is this well-brought-up boy, certain in his belief in the church and respectful toward the monarchy, everything in his world in perfect place, and suddenly he discovers that nothing of what he believes is anywhere near so solid as he thinks—that institutions are not divine or even hallowed by tradition and man-made and thus easily unmade by man; that religion is merely another human invention and a blockade to reason; that science holds all the significant secrets of the universe.[29]

The impact can be devastating, which Tocqueville also describes in a colorful metaphor:

> "All of a sudden," the fifty-one-year-old Tocqueville writes to Madame Swetchine, "I experience the sensation people talk about who have been through an earthquake, when the ground shakes under their feet, as do the walls around them, the ceilings over their heads, the furniture beneath their hands, all of nature before their eyes. I was seized by the blackest melancholy, then by an extreme disgust with life."[30]

More than three decades later he called his doubt "a sad and frightening illness." In a beautiful book on Tocqueville, the Jewish essayist Joseph Epstein describes Tocqueville's problem that goes back to that early encounter with science:

> What was this illness? To believe in God, to feel even that one has glimmerings of understanding of God's complex reasoning, and yet not to be able to give oneself over to God—this would seem to be at the heart of Tocqueville's crisis, a crisis of faith. His inability to resolve this crisis left him in spiritual shambles.[31]

The identical experience of two centuries ago happens today. At the end of a class on Genesis 1 at North Park University, where I used to teach, and after I had finished a freshly brushed-up lecture I gave at least once a school year, a student whose name I had just learned approached me with the kind of seriousness in his eyes a professor recognizes. He looked me in the eye and said, "Thank you. This lecture saved my faith." He hadn't said a word in class, and he hadn't given off the signals one sometimes sees in student behavior that indicate mountains are moving in a student's head. I simply looked at him with the invitation to go on. So he did. "My pastor told me that I couldn't be a Christian if I didn't believe in six-day creationism. He told me if God didn't create the universe some 10,000 years ago, then the whole Bible fell apart." He paused and then said this: "I love science and I want to be a biologist, and the earth is more than 10,000 years old. So I was wondering if I could believe in the Bible and the Christian faith any longer."

Let's be honest again. Here's the common theology at work in the mind of the kind of student about whom we are concerned: God made Adam and Eve directly, out of the dust. That primal couple sinned, and death first entered into the world through their sin. Adam is almost entirely absent from the rest of the Old Testament, and so the next really important text (for our purposes) is either Romans 5:12–21 or 1 Corinthians 15:21–22. Nuances aside, Paul contends that as sin and death entered into the world through one man, Adam, so righteousness and life enter back into the world through one man, Christ. Salvation then is wrapped in one interpretation of Adam. We can ramp this up one notch: Luke has a genealogy that runs from Jesus all the way back to Adam. This means Adam is "historical," and this means the Bible tells the true story about history and origins. Those are assumed to be the Bible's scientific and theological facts. This becomes the template for understanding the Bible and reality, and any threat to that template receives serious blowback, which works itself out logically like this: if Christ is real, then Adam is real, and also if Adam isn't real, then the whole thing falls apart. This is what was at work in my student's worldview as he struggled with what he was learning in biology.

Whether in the teeth of the Enlightenment with Tocqueville or in the early decades of the twenty-first century, the same experience is had by many: the Bible, with Genesis 1–2 leading the way, encounters science, and for many the Bible loses. So the Bible folks fight back and accuse science of being wrong, dangerously wrong. Those most in need of guidance in the midst of and through such encounters are students, and the better the student, the more their need of guidance.

The number one reason young Christians leave the faith is the conflict between science and faith, and that conflict can be narrowed to the conflict between evolutionary theory and human origins as traditionally read in Genesis 1–2.[32] It works like this: many Christians grow up with a view of Scripture as inerrant, and that means for them—and I speak here of the popular impression—that it is not only true but also more or less magically true, true beyond its time, true when everything else says something else. Connected to this view of inerrancy is a view of Bible reading that takes a sound Christian idea (the perspicuity of Scripture, that the Bible's message is clear to any able-minded Bible reader) and ratchets it up one notch so that the Bible reader thinks *whatever I see in the Bible is what the Bible is saying*—although there is no promise in the Bible that everything will be clear to every reader.[33] One's interpretations of Scripture become as infallible as the Bible itself, and since everything interlocks, giving in one inch is the first step toward apostasy. One of those interpretations is that the Bible teaches science in Genesis 1–2. When the evangelical student marches off to university, takes a biology class from an able-minded, rhetorically skilled, and atheistic/agnostic professor who makes it more than clear that the earth is not 6,000–10,000 years old but is in fact closer to 4.5 billion years old, tosses in some *Gilgamesh Epic* or some *Atrahasis*, and then loads into that the thoroughly vain notion that intelligent people don't believe such things any longer, a student's faith can be more than shaken. Many walk away or, more significant today, embrace an ironic faith.

This is why my third principle is unlike any principle you will find in any textbook: the student is in my rearview mirror in all I have to say in my section of this book. Attentiveness to students is a principle that must guide us as we read Genesis. I have committed myself never to utter a word in public or in print that might discourage the budding scientist from trusting the Bible for what it is, which leads to our fourth principle.

The Fourth Principle: The Primacy of Scripture

Christians affirm the Bible as God's revelation to God's people. This is sometimes called the Scripture Principle, while others use the Latin words of the Reformation, *sola scriptura*. A slight but important modification is to turn *sola* into *prima* so that we affirm *first of all* what the Bible says.

To go to the Bible first means respecting the Bible as it is—a developing narrative. God doesn't give us a systematic theology textbook, nor does God give us a question-and-answer resource book. Rather, the Bible is an ongoing and constantly updating narrative, what we often call a "story." When it comes to Genesis 1–3, which is the focus of this section in the book, we read Genesis 1–3 in light of Genesis 1–11, and Genesis 1–11 in light of Genesis

12–50, and then we baptize Genesis into the Pentateuch (Genesis through Deuteronomy) and into the rest of the Bible as it develops. As a Christian, I interpret everything in Genesis 1–3 in light of how the New Testament will reveal the gospel and how it frames answers to the same kinds of issues in Genesis 1–3.

In affirming this Scripture Principle, however, I hasten to add that we don't go *only* to the Bible. The affirmation of *prima scriptura* means we look to the Bible in its context first, as we have already stated above. Reading the Bible in context leads us to the Bible's dialogue with its context. We will discover already at work in the Bible an interaction between the Bible and its culture—both challenging culture and affirming culture. At the most basic of levels, the Bible comes from a Semitic and Hebraic culture, Jesus came out of a Galilean Jewish culture, and the apostle Paul was reared in a Roman world as a deeply observant Jewish man and so became a man of two worlds in a profound way as he evangelized gentiles. To read any of these without respect to their contexts is to misread them.

Four principles, then, for reading the Bible in context: respect, honesty, sensitivity to students, and *prima scriptura*.

A Final Observation: Which Adam and Eve Are We Talking About?

Sometimes we have to play a game of adjectives, as when *conservative* Christians are compared with *progressive* Christians, or *evangelical* is compared with *liberal*, and we know that game. We can try to live in a world without adjectives or labels, but eventually we realize that our minds categorize by default. Adjectives are here to stay, and we are challenged to use them as accurately and as respectfully as need be. The same issue about adjectives applies to Adam and, as I will say more than once and never with a wink and nod, his oft-neglected partner, Eve. When I say "Adam" I mean almost every time "Adam and Eve."

The adjective most popular in the Adam (and Eve) discussion is "historical." I'm frequently asked when this science-faith discussion arises, "Do you believe in the *historical* Adam?" For some that adjective will give the questioner the right word, and the answer will determine if the answerer is safe, faithful, orthodox, evangelical, and all sorts of other adjectives. We cannot dodge that adjective. One can pretend that "historical" before Adam doesn't matter, just as one can pretend that it is all that matters, and both views will end up dodging something. Here's how important this is: Zondervan recently published a book edited by Matthew Barrett and Ardel Caneday called *Four Views of the Historical Adam*. Here are the titles of the chapters:

No Historical Adam: Evolutionary Creation View
Historical Adam: Archetypal Creation View
Historical Adam: Old-Earth Creation View
Historical Adam: Young-Earth Creation View

Notice the importance of the adjective! (Notice, too, that there is evidently no need for Eve in this one.) The entire debate is sorted out by whether or not one believes in the *historical* Adam. Adjectives evidently matter when it comes to Adam and Eve.

The term "historical" is stubborn and resilient and has become the line in the sand for many; however, the adjective "historical" with Adam and Eve is a prejudice. By "prejudice" I mean exactly what Russell Kirk said it meant. When describing the great English politician and political theorist Edmund Burke, who was known for his approval of the importance of "prejudice," Kirk defined it this way: "Prejudice is pre-judgment, the answer with which intuition and ancestral consensus of opinion supply a man when he lacks either time or knowledge to arrive at a decision predicated upon pure reason."[34]

Yes, "historical" as our ruling adjective is undeniably the intuition of many as well as the ancestral consensus. Such prejudice enters into our minds whenever we confront decisions, but at times it is nothing but unthinking prejudice. It operates, Kirk knows, when we lack time and knowledge to decide on the basis of the evidence. In what follows I want to contend that a new kind of prejudice needs to be developed, a new kind of intuition, one based not on the ruling consensus alone but on the basis of the evidence itself.

So I want to contest the appropriateness of this adjective as the controlling issue, but let's first clarify who this *historical* Adam and Eve are. The adjective "historical" when attached to Adam and Eve means that

1. two *actual* (and sometimes only two) persons named Adam and Eve existed suddenly as a result of God's creation;
2. those two persons have a *biological* relationship to all human beings that are alive today (biological Adam and Eve);
3. their *DNA* is our DNA (genetic Adam and Eve); and that often means
4. those two *sinned*, *died*, and *brought death into the world* (fallen Adam and Eve); and

5. those two *passed on their sin natures* (according to many) to all human beings (sin-nature Adam and Eve), which means

6. without their sinning and passing on that sin nature to all human beings, *not all human beings would be in need of salvation*;

7. therefore, if one denies the *historical* Adam, one denies the gospel of salvation.[35]

That much, and probably more, is inherent to the adjective "historical" when pressed into singing alongside Adam and Eve. The so-called historical Adam then includes the biological, genetic, and sin-nature Adam and Eve. The stakes are high, then, for some uses of *historical* Adam—way too high.

I have major doubts that when Genesis 1–2 was written, *any* of that or at least *most of that* was what was meant by "Adam and Eve." I'll put it in terms of my principles: I'm not sure we are being respectful or honest with the Bible (and therefore the Scripture Principle comes into play too) when we make Genesis 1–2 speak about something it was not speaking about—biology, transmission of sin, genetics, and the like. I don't dispute that the adjective has an important role to play in our theology, but I do dispute that what most mean by "*historical* Adam" is what Genesis meant in its world. When we use the adjective "historical" with Adam or Eve, we must know that the author of Genesis *intended all or most, or at least #1 and #2*, of the seven points above, if we want to use "historical" accurately.

The alternative to using an adjective like "historical" when it transcends what the text says is to find more organic terms that are more natural to the world of these texts, and in what follows—especially in chapters 7 and 8—I will use other adjectives and labels. Some of these lead or at least point us to someone on the order of a historical Adam and Eve, but these other adjectives are more organic and restricted to what the Bible or the extrabiblical Jewish texts were actually saying. So I will use terms such as "archetypal,"[36] "genealogical," and "literary."[37] "Archetypal Adam and Eve" refers to their representation of all humanity—Adam as Everyman and Eve as Everywoman. "Genealogical Adam" refers to Adam (and Eve) in genealogical lists, giving off (at least) the hint that the composer of the genealogy saw them as real persons (#1 above). "Literary Adam (and Eve)" refers to the Adam and Eve of Genesis taking on a life of their own because they are found in a text within Israel's Scriptures. In each text we examine, we will have to ask which Adam and Eve are in view in this context rather than assume that it is the historical, actual, or real Adam and Eve.

Hence, when Paul speaks about "Adam" in a text like Romans 5:12–21, he could be interpreted (see chap. 8) as saying "the Adam in Genesis" and not necessarily the "historical" Adam. Or, as John Walton has argued regarding the use of the "first" and "last" Adam in 1 Corinthians 15:45, the Adam of Paul is the archetypal (and not biological) Adam:

> Here Adam is called the "first" man, but in the context of the contrast with Christ as the "last" Adam, it cannot be seen as a claim that Adam was the first biological specimen. Since Christ was not the last biological specimen, we must instead conclude that this text is talking about the first archetype and the last archetype. We might say that Adam was an initial archetype replaced by the ultimate archetype in Christ. It is insufficient to bring in biology simply because Christ was biologically descended from Adam.[38]

Again, we need to be sensitive to context to discover which Adam is in view. Only when there is some kind of organic biological idea at work will I use "historical Adam"; and as we will see, many have read Romans 5:12–21 this way, and much theological weight has been laid on that reading of Romans.

Adam and Eve of Genesis in Their Context: Twelve Theses

This is not the place to settle all the skirmishes in the old battle between science and faith, but it is worth knowing that part of the interactive dynamic today between the Bible and our culture's science has a dynamic parallel in the interaction of Israel's faith with its culture's science. The Bible, and especially Genesis 1–11, came from a premodern-science culture, but it would be blinkered to think the Bible itself wasn't already forming some scientific principles—and it was! People in the ancient Near East were already observing, testing, thinking, and drawing conclusions about reality.[1] Their conclusions weren't ours, and some of their theories amuse us, but we need to respect who they were and where they were and when they were, and that they were offering an early form of science. What they say about various elements in the cosmos and how it works are their perceptions and were as much "facts" to them as DNA reveals "facts" to us. What is also characteristic of all science is that it grows and shifts and accumulates over time. This much, then, needs to be on the table from the outset: the Bible's opening chapter is an ancient Near Eastern form of science.[2]

Like some actor suddenly appearing out of the darkness on a stage before the curtain rises, the Bible opens—without introduction and without definition and without a character list—with this: "In the beginning God created the heavens and the earth" (NIV) or "In the beginning when God created the heavens and the earth" (Gen. 1:1 NRSV). There is no context, no introduction to Genesis for those who need one; there is just that opening line. Because every text comes to expression in a context, we have to do our best to find that context. If we don't, we will unknowingly disrespect the text. Indeed, the absence of context has led many to impose their own worldview on the Bible's, as Bill Arnold has observed:

> For many today, the lack of immediately preceding literary context is taken as permission to read contemporary sensibilities into Genesis 1, and since our context is so technological and scientific, this has produced a regrettable and unnecessary dichotomy between science and religion. Keeping the ancient Near Eastern backdrop for Genesis 1 in mind helps avoid this pitfall.[3]

I confess, as stated in the previous chapter, to a *prima scriptura* approach to truth, but I also confess that Scripture has a context and that part of Scripture reading is to discern the dialogue at work in the Bible between revelation and culture. We are challenged to listen once again to the Bible, to let the Bible be the Bible, and *to let the Bible be the Bible in its interactive relationship with the ancient Near East*. That is the most respectful, the most honest, and the most *prima scriptura* approach I can think of.

The following words about the dialogue of faith and culture by Walter Brueggemann will keep us on track as we look at Adam and Eve from Genesis to the New Testament:

> On the one hand, they [the theologians who he thinks wrote Genesis 1–11] break with the "mythological" perception of reality which assumes that all the real action is with the gods and creation in and of itself has no significant value. On the other hand, they resist a "scientific" view of creation which assumes that the world contains its own mysteries and can be understood in terms of itself without any transcendent referent. The theologians who work in a distinctively Israelite way in Genesis 1–11 want to affirm at the same time (a) that the ultimate meaning of creation is to be found in the heart and purpose of the creator (cf. 6:5–7; 8:21) and (b) that the world has been positively valued by God for itself. It must be valued by the creatures to whom it has been provisionally entrusted (1:31).[4]

Reading Genesis in context, Brueggemann reminds us, means knowing that context well enough to see the Bible speaking in a contextually sensitive way and breaking from that context and offering instead a powerful message about God as creator and creation as good. That's a glimpse of what lies before us.

We begin by sketching four ancient Near Eastern creation stories, three of which touch directly upon Adam and Eve (or the origin and purpose of humans). In what follows I do not assume the author of Genesis 1–3 knew these texts, knew about them, had read them, or was consciously interacting with them. I assume only the generally recognized conclusion that *these texts express the kinds of ideas "in the air" when Genesis 1 and 2 were drafted.*[5]

An Ancient Near Eastern Creation Story: *Enuma Elish*[6]

The first story hails from Mesopotamia, which refers to the eastern area of the Fertile Crescent and includes, over centuries, peoples who lived in ancient Akkad, Babylon, and Sumer. This region, along with Egypt, produced some fascinating creation stories, legends, myths, and sagas. The texts are not easy to date since the stories have been passed on and on from one generation to another. They were not produced or passed on at the same time, though in gathering information about ancient Near Eastern creation stories it is reasonable to take a look at each of them to see what we might glean from that world. Most importantly, these ancient stories express the "science" or "cosmology" of the time; they were the world into which the ancient Hebrews entered, and that means the Bible's records of creation (e.g., Gen. 1–2; Job 38–41; Pss. 19; 74:13–16; 136; Prov. 8; Isa. 40–45; Jer. 10:12–16; 27:5) reflect similar ideas and categories from these sorts of creation traditions.

Babylon had become the most powerful city in Mesopotamia at the mighty hand and sword of Hammurabi, and he installed Marduk as god. What we call today *Enuma Elish* (its opening words, "When on high") remains one of the most important creation narratives from the ancient world. It makes for fascinating reading, but we will need to get to the creation of humans as quickly as possible since that's our concern.

A noisy collection of gods was created out of a watery chaos when the god of fresh water (Apsu) mixed with the god of salt water (Tiamat),[7] and so noisy were they that Apsu wanted to kill them. But Ea, his son, killed Apsu first. Then more gods came into existence, including the impressive Marduk, son of Ea and Damkina—Hammurabi's favorite. Apsu is dead, you will recall, and Tiamat marries Qingu, who has had enough with the gods and wants them destroyed. Tiamat creates some monsters to defeat the gods. The serpents and dragons join forces with Tiamat and Qingu and put the fear of the one set of gods into the gods associated with Marduk. Marduk rises to the challenge with an obligation: if Marduk wins, Marduk rules all and his commands will be permanent. The story is clear: Marduk defeats Tiamat and stands over her body as the conqueror and then builds a temple where Tiamat's monsters become statues reminding all who enter what resistance to Marduk will mean. From Tiamat's body Marduk creates the sky and the earth, and he places her gods into the sky (as planets). This is when Ea and Marduk decide to create humans.

Here is an excerpt from tablet 6 of *Enuma Elish*, describing the creation of humans:[8]

> I will bring together blood and form bone,
> I will bring into being Lullu, whose name shall be "man,"
> I will create Lullu-man
> On whom the toil of the gods will be laid that they may rest. (6.5–8)

You might ask, whose blood? Here is the answer:

> They bound him [Qingu], holding him before Ea,
> They inflicted the penalty on him and severed his blood-vessels.
> From his blood he (Ea) created mankind,
> On whom he imposed the service of the gods, and set the gods free.
> After the wise Ea had created mankind
> And had imposed the service of the gods upon them—
> That task is beyond comprehension
> For Nudimmud performed the creation with the skills of Marduk—
> King Marduk divided the gods,
> All the Annunaki into upper and lower groups. (6.31–40)

All of this leads to the building of Etemenanki, a ziggurat, where Marduk was annually worshiped and the *Enuma Elish* was retold.

Connections to the Bible? Some. Differences? Plenty. Before we discuss how the Bible speaks to the culture of the *Enuma Elish*, however, we need to look at another account that has an even more sweeping theory of history, the famous *Gilgamesh Epic*, though this story is not as important for Adam and Eve as it is for revealing themes similar to those found in Genesis.

Gilgamesh: Another Ancient Near Eastern Story

In the mythic narrative of the *Gilgamesh Epic* one finds the themes of the gods and humans in relation, a great flood, sexual intercourse, the search for immortality, and the inevitability of death. Notably, one-third of the king of Uruk, Gilgamesh, is human while two-thirds is divine.[9] As a tyrant over Uruk he has no equal, so the divine assembly creates Enkidu to be his companion, but Enkidu dwells in the wild with the animals. He is tamed, as it were, by prolonged sexual intercourse with the prostitute Shamhat. When Enkidu returns to the wild, three things have happened: the animals are now uncomfortable with him, he has been physically weakened, and he has acquired "reason." The woman then says, "You are handsome, Enkidu, you are just like a god!" She teaches him how to become a human being by teaching him to eat bread and drink beer. He becomes a friend to Gilgamesh. To shorten an adventurous story: Enkidu is put to death by the divine assembly. So the grieving Gilgamesh sets out to find immortality with some special advice from Siduri, a female beer maker, and she tells him to go home and drink and be merry, for he will die. Only the gods of the divine assembly possess immortality. His persistence pays off when she tells him how to cross the Sea of Death, and when he gets there he is told a story of how the gods sought to destroy humans by sending a massive flood to drown them all.

Once again we are breathing an ancient Near Eastern air of ideas and motifs that are both similar to those in Genesis—including the release of a dove to determine if there was sufficient land after the flood—and profoundly dissimilar, not least in terms of the groundbreaking ideas in Genesis that there is but one God and this God is not in competition with others (called "theomachy," "war of the gods").

A Third Story: *Atrahasis*[10]

My favorite extrabiblical account about creation and humans, originally from Sumer but which spread around to other cultures, is called *Atrahasis* (after its main character).[11] The connections of Genesis to *Atrahasis* are far more numerous, leading some (with caution) to suggest that Genesis 2–8 is Israel's *Atrahasis*. I want to begin by quoting the opening of this text to give an impression of its worldview. The world is populated only by the gods, divine warriors, and divine elders, and the warriors find the chores too much.

> When the gods like men
> Bore the work and suffered the toil—
> The toil of the gods was great,
> The work was heavy, the distress was much—
> The Seven great Anunaki
> Were making the Igigi suffer the work. . . .

Excessive [. . .] for 40 years
[. . .] they suffered the work night and day.
They [were complaining], backbiting,
Grumbling in the excavation . . .
"[Enlil], counsellor of the gods, the hero,
Come, let us unnerve him in his dwelling!" (I.i.1–6, 37–40, 45–56)

Their pain causes Enlil to weep, so the solution is a new order of beings. Ea-Enki settles with them by creating workers (humans) who will do the work the divine warriors no longer want to do. As with similar stories in the ancient Near East, the gods are bothered by the noisy humans, so they send a flood to destroy them. Again, all of this sounds like themes in Genesis 1–11, with both fascinating similarities and yet profoundly different theological ideas. What matters to us most especially is what is said about humans as they are created.

They summoned and asked the goddess,
The midwife of the gods, wise Mami . . .
Create *Lullu* [worker] that he may bear the yoke,
Let him bear the yoke assigned by Enlil,
Let them carry the toil of the gods. (I.ii.192–93, 195–97)

Humans, then, are created because the divine assembly is lazy, so the gods can enjoy their leisure. The task of humans in this text is to work for the gods. One has to think that the Genesis 3 account of males working the land would have been heard by some in the ancient Near East as an echo of other creation narratives.

The creation of humans is told in three different ways in *Atrahasis*, but notice the presence of clay in the following passage:[12]

Nintu opened her mouth
And addressed the great gods,
"It is not possible for me to make things,
Skill lies with Enki.
Since he can cleanse everything
Let him give me the clay so that I can make it."
Enki opened his mouth
And addressed the great gods,
"On the first, seventh, and fifteenth day of the month
I will make a purifying bath." . . .
From his flesh and blood
Nintu mixed clay. . . .
It proclaimed living (man) as its sign. (I.198–207, 225–26, 229)

A second account mixes the clay with the divine warriors' and divine elders' saliva, while a third account comes closer to the human norm—sexual intercourse produces seven males and seven females. These "workers" then free the gods from their labor. But the workers—humans—are so noisy that the god Enlil wants them destroyed. First, he sends plagues upon the land. Atrahasis, through Ea-Enki, learns how to stop the plague, which leads Enlil to try other measures (like famine), but the workers figure out how to beat Enlil's destructive designs. Finally, he sends a flood to discipline the workers. Ea-Enki informs Atrahasis how to build a "barge" (ark), which he fills with animals and his own family. For seven days and seven nights the flood fills the earth with destruction as the divine assembly weeps over what it has done. Their final resolution is to create infertile women to keep the population in line!

A Fourth Story: The Assur Bilingual Creation Story

This Sumerian creation account slightly varies from *Atrahasis* and opens with a wonderful setting of the scene—with terms and beliefs that sound like Genesis 1 but at the same time are different:[13]

> When Heaven had been separated from Earth
> —hitherto they were joined firmly together—
> After the earth-mothers had appeared;
> When the earth had been founded and set in place;
> After the gods had established the plan of the universe,
> And, to prepare the irrigation system,
> Had determined the course of the Tigris and Euphrates,
> Then An, Enlil, Ninmah (correction) and Enki, the chief gods,
> With the other great gods, the Anunna,
> Took their place on the high dais,
> And held an assembly. . . .
>
> \<Enlil asked them,\> "And now what are we going to do?
> What are we going to make now?
> O Anunna, great gods, what are we going to do now?
> What are we going to create?"

The gods answer with the recommendation to create humans:

> And the great gods who were present there,
> With the Anunna who assign destinies,

Responded in chorus to Enlil:
"In the 'Flesh-Growing Place' of Duranki (Nippur),
We are going to slay two divine *Alla* . . .
And from their blood give birth to human beings!"

With these sorts of gods ever concerned with the purpose of life and the importance of land and the profitability of unpaid labor, humans are made. Their assignment is not unlike the assignment given to Adam and Eve to govern the earth and to work the land so that it produces:

They will fix the boundaries of the fields once and for all,
And take in their hands hoes and baskets,
To benefit the House of the great gods,
Worthy seat of their high Dais! . . .
They will install the irrigation system . . .
And thus make all kinds of plants grow.

They are named, as in Genesis 1–2:

They will be named Ullegarra and Annegarra,
And they will multiply, for the prosperity of the land,
Cattle, sheep, (other) animals, fish, and birds.

Reading Genesis 1–3 in Context

Returning to our opening category of interpretation—a text without a context is a pretext—we now want to read Genesis in its context. We will see that this reading taps into both similarities and dissimilarities with respect to these ancient Near Eastern texts while it forms a theology and an anthropology that contest that context. I propose twelve theses about Genesis 1–3 that clarify a theology of Adam and Eve in that world—in other words, a theology of Adam and Eve in the ancient Near East as a template of interaction between faith and culture.[14]

A contextual approach to reading Genesis 1–3 immediately establishes that the Adam and Eve of the Bible are *a literary Adam and Eve.* That is, Adam and Eve are part of a narrative designed to speak into a world that had similar and dissimilar narratives. Making use of this context does not mean Adam and Eve are "fictional," and neither does it mean they are "historical." To be as honest as we can with the text in its context, we need to begin with the undeniable: Adam and Eve are literary—are part of a narrative that is designed to reveal how God wants his people to understand who humans are and what humans are called to do in God's creation.

Thesis 1

God is one, and this one God is outside the cosmos, not inside the cosmos as the gods of the ancient Near East are. The God of Adam and Eve is unique as the superior one. Genesis 1–2 is more about God than Adam and Eve or the creation of the world. This one true God of Israel, as the New Testament will state explicitly, creates the universe through the Son of God, who is the Wisdom of God.

Most notable perhaps about the Bible's presentation is that the God of Genesis is not like the gods of the Mesopotamian accounts. In fact, the God of the Bible is the one and only God, as stated in Deuteronomy 6:4–9, which will become the Jewish creed, the Shema. There are many gods in the Mesopotamian stories: Marduk, Tiamat, Enlil, and others. The Bible's own most important parallel to Genesis 1 is Isaiah 40–48, because what is implicit in Genesis is explicit in Isaiah: the God of Israel is all-powerful, while the gods of the pagans, especially the Babylonians, are powerless and, not to put too fine a point on it, nonexistent.[15] Genesis 1, then, is a claim that "our God is the one and only true God."

There is a notable difference not only regarding God but also regarding creation itself. The gods go back and forth and get in tangles with one another while working the earth. Those deities are irritable, worn down by working, in need of help—and not entirely able to resolve their own problem without permission from the higher-up gods, who seem at the same time to be at odds with themselves. No one seems to be totally in control. The God of Genesis 1–2 is different: this God, like Michelangelo's creator God with the all-powerful, creative finger, controls the whole lot. God creates by a word deriving from God's own sovereign choice. The fundamental event of Genesis 1 is God saying, "Let there be," and there is. The waters may be primal chaos, but the waters are easily and simply subdued by God's own command. The swirl of the *tohu va-bohu*, translated "formless and empty," is untangled into orchestrated order, function, and purpose. This God is transcendent and exceedingly powerful, exalted above creation and responsible for all of creation; this God, then, is not part of the created order but outside and over the created order. All of the gods of the ancient Near East are eliminated in the theology of Genesis 1, and one supreme God, YHWH, is left standing.

The "lilting and graceful rhythm" of Genesis 1 is designed to give such an impression of God's all-powerful and graceful ordering of creation.[16] Hence, the summary of Bill Arnold sets the tone for reading Genesis 1–3 in context: "In a word, ancient religion was polytheistic, mythological, and anthropomorphic, describing the gods in human forms and functions, while Genesis 1 is monotheistic, scornful of mythology, and engages in anthropomorphism only as figures of speech."[17]

This fundamental set of contrasts between the God of Genesis and the gods of the ancient Near East doesn't mean there isn't borrowing of ideas and terms. For example, there appears to be a trace of the divine council of the ancient Near East—the belief that God was surrounded by "advisors" in the form of supernatural beings—in Genesis 1:26 where it reads, "Let *us* make mankind in our image." The "us" of this verse has generated no end of speculations—who else was there? Is this the Trinity?[18] Is this simply a magisterial or a deliberative plural where a supreme being speaks of himself alone in plural terms?[19] Or is this a residue from other ancient Near Eastern theologies and texts, a hint of the divine council, a possible connection with the neighboring peoples and what they believed? Or, which seems more likely, is this a reference not to other "gods" in a divine council but to the Bible's cosmology of a heaven indwelt by myriads of worshiping and serving angels?[20]

But there is more to consider about this one and only one God the Creator, and it involves looking at the Bible from its beginning as a story moving toward a clearer ending. Proverbs has a most interesting reflection about Wisdom, who is personified and who reveals her beginning before creation itself. One must read all of Proverbs 8:22–31 to see what is meant:

> The Lord brought me forth as the first of his works,
>   before his deeds of old;
> I was formed long ages ago,
>   at the very beginning, when the world came to be.
> When there were no watery depths, I was given birth,
>   when there were no springs overflowing with water;
> before the mountains were settled in place,
>   before the hills, I was given birth,
> before he made the world or its fields
>   or any of the dust of the earth.
> I was there when he set the heavens in place,
>   when he marked out the horizon on the face of the deep,
> when he established the clouds above
>   and fixed securely the fountains of the deep,
> when he gave the sea its boundary
>   so the waters would not overstep his command,
> and when he marked out the foundations of the earth.
>   Then I was constantly at his side.
> I was filled with delight day after day,
>   rejoicing always in his presence,
> rejoicing in his whole world
>   and delighting in mankind.

Wisdom personified is a separate creation, but this Wisdom reflection gives rise to a kind of New Testament thinking that sees Jesus as that personified Wisdom so that Jesus the Sage becomes Jesus the Creator. Reading the Bible as a canonical narrative prompts us to see the ordering of Genesis 1 as something the Son of God has accomplished. Here are the New Testament texts that absorb Wisdom into Christology:

> . . . but to those whom God has called, both Jews and Greeks, Christ the power of God and the wisdom of God. (1 Cor. 1:24)

> The Son is the image of the invisible God, the firstborn over all creation. For in him all things were created: things in heaven and on earth, visible and invisible, whether thrones or powers or rulers or authorities; all things have been created through him and for him. He is before all things, and in him all things hold together. And he is the head of the body, the church; he is the beginning and the firstborn from among the dead, so that in everything he might have the supremacy. For God was pleased to have all his fullness dwell in him, and through him to reconcile to himself all things, whether things on earth or things in heaven, by making peace through his blood, shed on the cross. (Col. 1:15–20)

> In the past God spoke to our ancestors through the prophets at many times and in various ways, but in these last days he has spoken to us by his Son, whom he appointed heir of all things, and through whom also he made the universe. The Son is the radiance of God's glory and the exact representation of his being, sustaining all things by his powerful word. After he had provided purification for sins, he sat down at the right hand of the Majesty in heaven. So he became as much superior to the angels as the name he has inherited is superior to theirs. (Heb. 1:1–4)

> In the beginning was the Word, and the Word was with God, and the Word was God. He was with God in the beginning. Through him all things were made; without him nothing was made that has been made. In him was life, and that life was the light of all mankind. (John 1:1–4)

The God of creation, then, the one true God of Israel, creates through the Son of God.

Thesis 2

There are occasional elements of theomachy in the Bible, even if the Bible routinely minimizes and perhaps even deconstructs the ideas of theomachy. Adam and Eve are not the result of a cosmic battle but the product of God's good design for the cosmos.

Historians use the term "theomachy" to describe "conflict among the gods," and it is a common feature of the Mesopotamian creation stories. John Walton defines it for us:

> In the cognitive environment of the ancient Near East, the gods become involved in conflict under a variety of circumstances and at various levels: (1) they fight among themselves on an individual or corporate level, (2) they battle with entities or nonentities that represent a threat of some kind, and (3) they enter into conflict with humans.[21]

I cited a text from *Enuma Elish* above that deserves to be cited again to make clear this battle among the gods:

> They bound him [Qingu], holding him before Ea,
> They inflicted the penalty on him and severed his blood-vessels.
> From his blood he (Ea) created mankind,
> On whom he imposed the service of the gods, and set the gods free.
> After the wise Ea had created mankind
> And had imposed the service of the gods upon them—
> That task is beyond comprehension
> For Nudimmud performed the creation with the skills of Marduk—
> King Marduk divided the gods,
> All the Annunaki into upper and lower groups. (6.31–40)

A second instance comes from *Atrahasis*, also cited above, indicating the same kind of strife among the gods that leads to a resolution of a labor conflict by the creation of humans to do the work of the gods:

> The Seven great Anunaki
> Were making the Igigi suffer the work. . . .
> Excessive [. . .] for 40 years
> [. . .] they suffered the work night and day.
> They [were complaining], backbiting,
> Grumbling in the excavation . . .
> "[Enlil], counsellor of the gods, the hero,
> Come, let us unnerve him in his dwelling!" (I.i.5–6, 37–40, 45–46)

There are hints of this in the Bible. It is hard not to see the battle with a kind of Tiamat, here called Leviathan, in Psalm 74:13–16:[22]

> It was you who split open the sea by your power;
>   you broke the heads of the monster in the waters.

> It was you who crushed the heads of Leviathan
> and gave it as food to the creatures of the desert.
> It was you who opened up springs and streams;
> you dried up the ever-flowing rivers.
> The day is yours, and yours also the night;
> you established the sun and moon.

This is where the principles of respect and honesty come into play: one can suspect that the psalmist is using ancient language to express something he knows better, or one can suspect that the author shared those ideas. Either way, the Bible forms a marvelous parallel with the ancient Near Eastern literature, while it offers a significantly different theology of creation: *Israel's God conquered the forces of evil in creation because those "gods" were not capable of resisting the one true God.* One is allowed to ask *how* God conquered, which we will do below, but *that* God conquers evil is not up for question.

Another element of theomachy in the ancient Near East was the cosmos itself, what John Walton calls "macrocosmic disorder."[23] The belief of the ancient Near East was that the gods had established order but that rebellious elements in creation occasionally emerged and needed to be battled and defeated. In the *Enuma Elish* above we saw that Tiamat, the god of the sea (or salt water), is defeated by Marduk in order to bring order to the universe. Some have detected that very theme—subduing the god of the sea, the sea monster, Leviathan—in Genesis 1:1's "formless and empty" and "the Spirit of God hovering over the waters." That is, the waters were under the control of rebellious forces and needed to be tamed and ordered into goodness in God's design for creation. One need not assume that the ancient Hebrews embraced the fullness of anything like the Tiamat myth when they referred to Leviathan, but one should at least admit that mythical themes and language have some role in the Bible's creation accounts.

There is, then, an occasional hint of this theomachy theme of the combat myth, but it is, comparatively speaking, underserved. Neither creation nor the ordering of creation is seen as a battle among the gods or as God subduing the restless, rebellious sea monster. Instead, God rather serenely utters a command, and order ensues. Put more boldly, God doesn't win a battle, because there never has been a battle for God to wage! God has always been the sovereign God. But at times God's sovereignty or serenity is highlighted by appeal to themes emerging from ancient Near Eastern theomachy.

In fact, there is more than one way to explain the Bible's use of the so-called combat myth. Richard Middleton has offered an important suggestion that it need not carry overtones of violence but instead needs to be seen through a theology of God, not as warrior, but as artisan.[24] A close reading of Genesis 1 prompts us to ask how it is that God subdued these primordial elements. Did YHWH pull out a sword, Zeus-like, and charge into battle, whipping his sword this way and that? Middleton pushes us to consider another form of conquest. God conquers *not by counterviolence but by ordering creation through his artful work and through the word*. The suggestion of Middleton is brilliant and explains better than any other I've seen both the slight presence of the combat myth and even more how it is contextualized in Genesis: the creating order of the Divine Artisan is the way of God.

Thesis 3

God orders creation into a temple. Adam and Eve are designed by God to worship and to lead all creation to see its God.

Recent scholarship has proposed an important reorientation of how we are to read Genesis 1.[25] It is not necessary here to enter into a deep discussion since we only want to put the big idea on the table: Genesis 1 is to be read as God forming the universe into a cosmic temple. Now to some details.

Walton has concluded that Genesis 1, like other ancient cosmologies, is concerned far more with *function* than *materiality*, with what he calls a "functional ontology" as opposed to a "material ontology."[26] This means that the Bible's creation narrative in Genesis 1 concerns the *purpose* of what is created and not the *physical origins* of what is created. Another way of expressing this has been offered by the Jewish scholar Jon Levenson, who concludes his sketch of creation in the Bible with this:

What emerges in those stories is not the physical universe, but an environment ordered for peaceful human habitation and secure against the onslaughts of chaos and anarchy. The concern of the creation theology is not *creatio ex nihilo*, but the establishment of a benevolent and life-sustaining order, founded upon the demonstrated authority of the God who is triumphant over all rivals.[27]

That is, Genesis attempts to show not so much that God created the world out of nothing but *that God ordered all creation for a purpose*.[28]

Thus when God creates light, the issue is not the *material origin* of light but the *function* of light: time, or ordering life into day and night. Day 2's concern is not with the creation of the material substance of the vault above (the dome) and the waters below but with space to live and to experience weather, the need for rain for plants to grow and for humans to have drink. Day 3 is about food—vegetables and plants. Day 4, to continue with the functions theme (versus the material origins theme), fills in the time with seasons, and day 5 fills in the theme of cosmic space. Finally, day 6 places humans in God's good world. What is the point here? To establish the material origins of humans? Walton says yes to the material origins of humans through God's creation, but the *function* of animals and humans is the focus of Genesis 1: the function of the animals is to fill the earth and reproduce, while the humans are to order creation and to rule creation under God, taking their nourishment from the plants and animals.

Functions:

Day 1: Time
Day 2: Space for weather
Day 3: Food

Functionaries:

Day 4: Day and night and seasons
Day 5: Beautification and filling of the space for weather
Day 6: Animals to reproduce, humans to reproduce and rule

The creation narrative of Genesis 1, then, as is seen in the complementary motifs of functions and functionaries, is a beautifully ordered cosmos. What may lie unnoticed in this text, perhaps because we are so modern in our perceptions, is that God seized control of these elements *by forming them into an order*. It seems then that God creates by providing an order to it all, by containing it all, by giving direction to it all. God subdues by being the Cosmic Artisan.

This way of looking at creation as divine ordering is, to remind us of our topic, "ancient science." Whether we think it is science or not, Genesis 1 is shaped by how science has always been done: by observation. The author of Genesis 1, by observation and theorizing, comes to the conclusion that the sky is a dome or a "vault" (NIV) in day 2, but that kind of observation is focused on its purpose, its ordering. That is, the "vault" is designed to express the glory of God's creative work in terms of the ancient Near East's understanding of the universe. What matters here is that God designed it all, then God put Adam and Eve in charge of it all, and . . .

. . . then God clarifies what creation is all about. Our next observation is one of the most important discoveries I have happened upon: God places humans on the earth in order to worship God and to lead the rest of creation to

God. The world is designed by God to be God's cosmic temple. Again, John Walton has most recently established this case. We may be inclined to think that the climax of creation was the creation of Adam and Eve—humans—but this would be just one more instance of humans creating an anthropocentric world. Rather, the climax of creation is not day 6 but day 7, the day God rests in the created world as if it were a temple designed for God. The purpose of creation is *rest*, which doesn't mean vacation or leisure, but instead describes freedom, peace, and rightful living in God's good world. *All of creation is ordered so we can live an ordered life under God in God's ordered cosmos.* Here is how Walton sums it up:

> When God rests on the seventh day, he is taking up his residence in the ordered system that he has brought about in the previous six days. It is not something that he does only on the seventh day; it is what he does every day thereafter. Furthermore, his rest is not just a matter of having a place of residence—he is exercising his control over this ordered system where he intends to relate to people whom he has placed there and for whom he has made the system function. It is his place of residence, it is a place for relationship, but, beyond those, it is also a place of his rule. Note Psalm 132:7–8, where the temple is identified both as God's dwelling place and as his resting place. Psalm 132:14 goes on to identify this resting place as the place where he sits "enthroned." The temple account in Ezekiel 40–48 also identifies this element clearly: "Son of man, this is the place of my throne and the place for the soles of my feet. This is where I will live among the Israelites forever" (Ezek. 43:7).[29]

To put this in the ancient Near Eastern context, we need to know simply that the ancient gods "rested" in their temples. To "rest" in that world is to enter into a temple, to enter into the temple is to rest. Bill Arnold summarizes that context well:

> Comparisons with creation accounts from the ancient Near East are again instructive. Both the *Enuma Elish* and the Ugaritic *Baal Cycle* close their creation accounts in cultic dramas, in the building of great temples, and in the case of *Enuma Elish*, specifically as a place of "rest." Likewise in the Memphite theology of ancient Egypt, the god Ptah rested after creating everything. At the conclusion of each of these, the cultic drama gives reason for the preeminence of a deity, of a temple, or of a specific cultic feature of life or worship.[30]

Like other ancient Near Eastern texts, Genesis 1 has a liturgical event at the end of creation; unlike those texts, it is the Sabbath that forms the completion (Gen. 2:1–3). The similarities and dissimilarities, however, lead to the conclusion that creation is depicted in Genesis 1 in very ancient Near Eastern terms as God's cosmic temple. As Solomon took seven years to build a temple *and only then did God enter into his rest in that temple*, so God took seven days to create the cosmos *before he took up residence among humans*.

The earth, then, is not designed as a scene of conflict but a scene of worship. The gods are not fighting for control, because God is in control. All of creation is designed not for humans but for God, and all things on earth are called to worship this one true God. In worship of the one true God, all creation is subdued. Creation is God's space, so that the radical scientific theory called "materialism" or "naturalism"—in which what we see, taste, feel, and can test is all there is—is challenged by our creation account with this message: Look and see! God created this space; and in worship and service of God, others, and the rest of creation, we enter into God's purpose for all of creation.

Thesis 4

All humans—male and female—are made in God's image. Adam and Eve are unique and special and carry both great freedom and great responsibility for the earth.

The Bible's breathtaking presentation of God making two humans—the man and the woman—"in his own image" (Gen. 1:26–27) has influenced the world's perception of human beings.[31] To be sure, the importance of humans as made in the "image of God" has been taken to extremes because it has led many humans to think the world revolves around themselves or that they can exploit animals or the environment.

What does "image of God" mean? Better yet, *what did "image of God" mean in the ancient Near East*? Before we answer that question, I want to present how John Walton has summarized the purpose of humans in the Mesopotamian creation narratives:

> The foundation of religion in Mesopotamia is that humanity has been created to serve the gods by meeting their needs for food (sacrifices), housing (temples), clothing, and in general giving them worship and privacy so that these gods can do the work of running the cosmos. The other side of the symbiosis is that the gods will protect their investment by protecting their worshipers and providing for them. Humans thus find dignity in the role that they have in this symbiosis to aid the gods (through their rituals) in running the cosmos.[32]

While humans are not overly despised by the gods—though at times they can be depicted in the ancient Near East as piddly little puddles of nonsense—the general drift is that humans are created to do the work of the gods and to make the life of the gods easier. Humans are put up with, though kings and queens are given far more respect. This falls short of the glory of humans in the Bible. Here is what the Bible says in Genesis 1:26–28:

> Then God said, "Let us make mankind *in our image, in our likeness*, so that they may *rule* over the fish in the sea and the birds in the sky, over the livestock and all the wild animals, and over all the creatures that move along the ground."
>
> So God created mankind *in his own image,*
> *in the image of God* he created them;
> *male and female* he created them.
>
> God blessed them and said to them, "*Be fruitful* and *increase* in number; *fill* the earth and *subdue* it. *Rule* over the fish in the sea and the birds in the sky and over every living creature that moves on the ground."

I have highlighted (in italics) important words that both provide connections with the ancient Near East and interpret the meaning of "image of God." In what follows I will make use (with some additions and subtractions) of the outstanding study of J. Richard Middleton entitled *The Liberating Image*, a study whose conclusions have now become widely accepted among Bible scholars and theologians. The term "image of God" in Hebrew is *tselem elohim*, while "likeness" translates *demut*. *Tselem* and *demut* are found with "of God" only in three places in the Old Testament, all in the opening section of Genesis (chaps. 1–11): 1:26–28; 5:1; and 9:6. Here are those other two references:

> When God created mankind, he made them in the *likeness* of God. (5:1)
>
> Whoever sheds human blood,
> by humans shall their blood be shed;
> for in the *image* of God
> has God made mankind. (9:6)

So we ask again, what does "image of God" mean? The principle of respect has gone unheeded by too many in the Christian theological tradition because far too many have theorized what "image of God" means without paying one bit of attention to the ancient Near East, the very context out of which and into which the author of Genesis 1 was writing. In a recent study of the meaning of "image of God," Ryan Peterson sketches the various meanings of this expression in the history of the church, and few of these are sensitive to the ancient Near East:

> There is agreement among scholars that Genesis 1 indicates that human existence is somehow modeled after God. However, there are many ways this modeling has been construed. The image has been taken to refer to *the human soul* (since God is spiritual), *the human mind* (since God is rational), *the human body* (since ancient Near Eastern people thought that the gods had physical forms), *human dominion* (since God rules all things), *human relations* (since God, being triune, is eternally relational), *human virtue* (since God is good), and *human existence* (since God is). The general strategy has been to look for some particular human attribute that matches analogously a divine attribute.[33]

In the middle of this welter of competing views, most today, represented especially by Middleton, propose that we cut through the options by examining the text in its context. Hence, we might call this view the *contextual* view— that is, humans are made in God's image in the sense that they are called by God to mediate God's power and authority in this world.[34] The word *tselem* (image) often is used to refer to a man-made idol of a god; that is, in the ancient Near East "image" was a "localized, visible, corporeal representation of the divine."[35] Thus, *Adam and Eve are placed on the earth to rule over creation and to represent God to creation.* Here is Middleton's definition: "On this reading, the *imago Dei* designates the royal office or calling of human beings as God's representatives and agents in the world, granted authorized power to share in God's rule or administration of the earth's resources and creatures."[36]

We can get even more specific now. In the ancient world kings often placed an image of themselves in a temple in a city in order to represent their rule and their presence. Many examples of this from the ancient Near East have been found, so I will limit myself to three, again found in Middleton's *The Liberating Image*:

> Amenhotep II (1427–1400 B.C.E.) is described variously as "image of Re," "image of Horus," "image of Atum," "holy image of the lord of the gods," "foremost image of Re," "holy image of Re," "holy image of Amon, image of Amon like Re," and so on. Amenhotep III (1390–1352 B.C.E.) is addressed by Amon as "my living image, creation of my members, whom Mut bare to me." Amenhotep III is also addressed by Amon-Re: "You are my beloved son, who came forth from my members, my image, whom I have put on earth. I have given to you to rule the earth in peace."[37]

In the claim that Adam and Eve are made in the "image of God," Genesis 1 not only *borrows* the language about Mesopotamian royals but also *challenges* that royalty with another royalty (God) and another idea: all humans, male and female, are images of God, not just kings! In the Mesopotamian royal ideology, humans are vassals of the king; in Genesis's divine royal ideology, God rules and humans share in divine rule by subduing creation to its divinely intended designs. What the Mesopotamians devalued—humans in general—the Bible values: all humans, male and female.

Middleton's approach is remarkable on a number of fronts. I mention four:

1. Adam and Eve, or humans in general, are physical, embodied images of the invisible God;
2. the royal rule of humans is challenged by divine rule;
3. all humans are assigned to a royal and priestly status; and
4. all humans are called to rule creation but are not made to rule over other humans.

This set of conclusions does not establish anarchy but the summons for all human beings to submit to God's rule instead of human rule. These themes are bubbling in Psalm 8 when the psalmist describes humans (the "son of man"): humans are made "a little lower than the angels," and God has "crowned them with glory" and most especially "made them rulers over the works of [God's] hands" (8:5–6a). The psalmist has Genesis 1 in mind:

> You put everything under their feet:
> all flocks and herds,
> > and the animals of the wild,
> > the birds in the sky,
> > and the fish in the sea,
> > all that swim the paths of the seas. (Ps. 8:6b–8)

This is the *context* from which and into which Adam and Eve are set when they are called "image of God."

So to be made in God's image is to be a physical, embodied representative of God with the mission of governing and prospering God's creation. This completely forms and reshapes *identity*, as Peterson has observed:

> My claim is that every human person's identity is determined by the reality described in Genesis 1:26–28: a human knows who she is and how she is oriented within creation when she recognizes that she is made in God's image. Of course, each person has many secondary and tertiary aspects to her identity that give shape to the particularities of her life and its distinction from another person's

life. But everyone's "fundamental orientation" is established in the fact that they are made by God to represent God in the world.[38]

This understanding of "image of God" thus forms our identity and our mission to represent God in ruling creation.

Two more observations make explicit what has been only suggested so far. The first is that *because humans are divine images, humans/Israelites are prohibited from making idols.*[39]

> You shall not make for yourself an image in the form of anything in heaven above or on the earth beneath or in the waters below. (Exod. 20:4; cf. Deut. 5:8)

There is contained in this prohibition of making idols something that powerfully highlights the significance of humans: in all of creation, *only humans image God.* This is not to say one can't comprehend something about God through creation (Ps. 19; Rom. 1), but it is to say that *only humans* are designed to image God. This is why Jesus, God incarnate, is the true image of God (2 Cor. 4:4; Col. 1:15).

What I don't see as often in this discussion is a second consideration, something that mattered then and matters perhaps even more now: *humans are not given the responsibility to rule other humans but to rule creation.* They are images *of God*, which means they are not to make images of themselves as kings and gods in the world. Genesis 3's temptation reveals that humans wanted to be gods and goddesses and not undergods and undergoddesses. The temptation of Israel, made most famous in the wonderful dialogue between Samuel and God in 1 Samuel 8, was to find a king who would be like the kings of the other nations. God made humans as *his images* to rule *on behalf of God*, but this rule was to be *over creation* and not over other humans. We have a sad story to tell about human history from this angle: instead of accepting our role as subrulers, time and time again we have attempted to become gods and goddesses to the degree that we have enslaved other humans in our rule of others. *The strongest form of idolatry, then, is tyranny.* The tyrant thinks he or she has become a god; the emperor over the empire does the same.

Thesis 5

Humans are distinct from the rest of creation. Adam and Eve are unlike other creatures and therefore have a responsibility for them.

All of life is by God's design, and all of life—from the tiniest microbe to the largest mammal and to humans—comes into being as a result of God's own display of creative power. The history of evolutionary theory, from the angle of creative evolution (a God-planned process, whether as a result of intrusion or, more likely, by the way God constructed the DNA of the smallest organic matter to unfold in our direction), is a history that shows humans at the "end" of a spectrum or a process. From this angle, we are led to see ourselves as utterly created matter and utterly like all other created matter. This can't be denied, and need not be for those who trust the Bible and the Christian tradition.

But, but, but. Genesis 1 says that humans not only are designed by God to rule on his behalf but are also profoundly unique and distinct in comparison with the rest of creation. Three observations. First, read Genesis 1 briskly, and here's what happens: day 1, day 2, day 3, and God sees that it is "good"; then day 4, day 5, day 6, and God sees that it is "good." After God makes humans, God sees that everything he has made is *very* good" (Gen. 1:31). Not until God has all the elements in place, made just right for Adam and Eve, and just after placing them in his newly fashioned world, does God see that it is all good. In God's mind, a world run by Adam and Eve is very good. This narrative flow in Genesis 1 makes humans distinct from all creation. Second, God makes humans after making all the rest of creation, and it is only humans who have the task of ruling and subduing and nurturing. This makes humans distinct. Third, we have already seen that humans are "images of God," and that the application of that expression to Adam and Eve was an application of what was reserved for kings and queens to all human beings. This makes humans different from all creation, too.

In some sense this makes humans superior to nonhuman creation, but in another sense it is a reminder of their responsible station in life: humans remain created beings like all other created beings even if they have a special task among all of God's creatures. Their task is not to exploit or kill and distort creation but to extend the work of the Creator—namely, to subdue creation into divine order so that it functions as God designed it.[40] *The task of humans over creation is to participate in creation's flourishing.* Humans are most human in God's economy when they are, like God, artisans causing all creation to flourish: when they plant and water seeds, care for the sprouts, nurture the plants, and eat the produce in deep respect for the earth and how it works; when they care for the environment, not by the reckless production of nonbiodegradables but by sustaining creation in respect for what it can consume;[41] and when they beautify their homes and their gardens and find the proper color and the right pattern for the houses they transform into a space called "home."

The diminishment of the glory of humans—whom God made "just a little lower than angels"—in writers like Peter Singer or Samuel Harris or Stephen

Pinker (who do so in differing ways) must be challenged by this powerful expression of two terms in Genesis 1: we are "images" and "likenesses" of God; the Artisan Creator of all creation summoned us to share in that creative task. This dignifies each and every person in the world for all time, but it carries with it an awe-inspiring responsibility to respect one another.

Thesis 6

Humans are gendered for procreation (one flesh) and mutuality. Adam and Eve are to multiply in order to populate the earth with more and more "images of God" to rule and govern and nurture the earth.

A dramatic moment in Genesis 1–2 occurs with respect to humans, an aspect of the Genesis story that seems unparalleled in the ancient Near East. This in itself summons us to think about something distinct that may well challenge other cultures. I begin with Genesis 1:26–27:

Then God said, "Let us make mankind in our image, in our likeness, so that they may rule over the fish in the sea and the birds in the sky, over the livestock and all the wild animals, and over all the creatures that move along the ground."

So God created mankind in his own image,
in the image of God he created them;
male and female he created them.

We know what "image of God" means, so we can narrow our discussion to a singular element: "male and female he created them." Adam and Eve, each separately and both together, are the image of God. Though some in the early church mistakenly and tragically thought only males were in the image of God, all theologians today know the image of God applies to both Adam and Eve. Further, each of them images God: Adam images God, and Eve images God, not just when they are together but also when they are apart. But this means also that they image God when they are together in a unique manner. How so? *They image God whenever each separately or whenever both together rule, subdue, or cause any element of creation to flourish in God's design for it.* Herein is established both the individuality of God's creation of humans and the teamwork (on which see below) expected of humans. The diminishment of individuality in some collective political environments and the exaggeration of individuality in other liberal democracies—think Mao Tse-Tung and Joseph Stalin or Jean-Jacques Rousseau and Thomas Paine—are challenged by the dual expectation of the Genesis account: each person images God and we together image God *whenever we participate in the flourishing of creation.*

Another passage in Genesis 2—namely, 2:18, 20–25—brings our gendered relations with an emphasis on mutuality to the surface:

> The LORD God said, "It is not good for the man to be alone. I will make a helper suitable for him." . . .
>
> So the man gave names to all the livestock, the birds in the sky and all the wild animals. But for Adam no suitable helper was found. So the LORD God caused the man to fall into a deep sleep; and while he was sleeping, he took one of the man's ribs and then closed up the place with flesh. Then the LORD God made a woman from the rib he had taken out of the man, and he brought her to the man. (Gen. 2:18, 20–22)

In one of the great understatements by a biblical scholar, Joseph Blenkinsopp observes that "the operation [on Adam] was a spectacular success to judge by the man's joyful reaction":[42]

> The man said,
>
> "This is now bone of my bones
>   and flesh of my flesh;
> she shall be called 'woman,'
>   for she was taken out of man."

> That is why a man leaves his father and mother and is united to his wife, and they become one flesh. Adam and his wife were both naked, and they felt no shame. (Gen. 2:23–25)

The story is told in such a way that the act of naming gives Adam an opportunity to observe that he is alone and in need of someone to love and to help him image God to the world. Thus, the first paragraph (Gen. 2:18, 20–22) highlights Adam's aloneness and God's design for a "helper suitable for him," *ezer kenegdo* in Hebrew. Adam goes through animals one by one, giving them names, which is a vital element in imaging God to this world: observing, defining, naming, and learning the way of life of each animal. (As a bird-watcher I do wonder if Adam caught on to the variety of warblers. Perhaps he never got beyond seeing all of them as "bird.") But he finds no *ezer kenegdo*. The man is now utterly alone because he has not found one like himself. So God puts him to sleep or sends him into a deep vision—surely we are here dealing with a great story that speaks not only to human origins but also to the deep and enduring connection of males to females and females to males.[43]

Adam finds in Eve "bone of my bones," and he knows that they will be-come "one flesh," which is an ancient Hebrew, subtle way of talking not just about sexual relations but also about the unity discovered when a man and a woman form a loving relationship called "marriage." There is a commentary on innocence when the author of Genesis 2 says they were "both naked, and they felt no shame." (It's also a hint of what is to happen in Gen. 3.) Their nakedness and sexual congress now in view, the Bible indicates yet one more feature of human flourishing as images of God: they are called to reproduce and populate God's good creation. *Procreation stands tall in the divine plan of being images of God.*

God genders humans into male and female so they can relate to one another in mutuality and reproduce. Mutuality flows out of being images of God and expresses what being an image of God means at its deepest core. This is not to say that only married persons image God. Rather, persons who mutually relate to one another are imaging God.[44] The mutuality of Genesis 1–2 is about a man and a woman bringing two personalities, two sets of gifts, and two dis-tinct genders into relationship. This relationship in the Bible is called "love," and love begs for some definition in our world. It is not possible to discuss at length, but love in the Bible has four elements: it is (1) a rugged commitment, or covenant, (2) to be with one another as physical and personal presences, (3) to be for one another as advocates for what God designs for each of us and for us together, and (4) all of this with the design to grow into becoming Christlike.[45]

Thesis 7

Humans are called to work the earth for its flourishing. Adam and Eve are not like the ancient Near Eastern gods desiring leisure, nor are Adam and Eve like the humans whom the ancient Near Eastern gods want as slaves, but instead are called to cocreate and conurture as part of God's design for this earth.

We image God when we, like God, generate new life through procreation, and we also image God when we work as artisans in making the land flour-ish. This is indicated in two verses in Genesis 2, but it dominates like a silent background the rest of the Bible—and of human history.[46]

Now no shrub had yet appeared on the earth and no plant had yet sprung up, for the LORD God had not sent rain on the earth and there was *no one to work the ground.* (2:5)

The LORD God took the man and put him in the Garden of Eden *to work it and take care of it.* (2:15)

We may think of work and labor as post-fall activities, and so we diminish their significance in life—not to mention for the new heavens and the new earth. You may not have caught that hint, so let me say it: not unlike the Mesopotamian creation stories, in Genesis humans are created to work. So once again the Bible speaks the language of the ancient Near East, but there are a few distinctions worthy of note. Humans aren't workers replacing some worn-out deities who'd rather have leisure. Instead they are cocreators, colaborers, and corulers in the work of God to subdue and make the world flourish. Instead of slaves of God they are colaborers with God. In so working with God they become like God: an artisan designing as a way of entering into the Divine Artisan's designs.

The word used for "work" (*'bad*) in "work the ground" (Gen. 2:5) is used for a number of kinds of labor in the Old Testament: vineyard working, working in flax, working in a city, and doing military service. While the context in Genesis 2 is farming, that term grows into all kinds of work in the Bible and in history, and would therefore include our own work. I'm a teacher, a writer, a deacon, a (sometimes) preacher and speaker; Kris, my wife, is a psychologist and works out the details of my speaking engagements with admirable efficiency and attention to detail, and she tends to our garden and our home and our grandchildren and a multitude of other things that she neatly balances in her mind (and that I far too often forget). We both "garden" and beautify our home and yard as part of our work, and we both cook. We've done our procreating task, and now we get to grandparent Aksel and Finley. I add that *humans* are called to procreate *as humans*, but this does not mean that each one of us is called to marriage and having children—some are called to be single, some parents are unable to have children, and others choose not to have children.

Another term is used for our work: "to take care" (*shamar*, Gen. 2:15). This refers to the task of guarding, watching, inspecting, evaluating, and protecting God's good creation. Ours is the task to keep our eyes on God's creation to make sure it is not being exploited, ruined, or distorted. I grieve over the plastics swirling by the tons in our God-made oceans. Genesis 1–2 summons us to care for God's creation as a reflection of God's own creation and our calling.

Back to an important theme in this section of the book. So far we've seen no sign of a historical or biological or genetic Adam and Eve; rather, those adjectives are categories from an important but later interpretive history that will prove themselves useful for understanding humans. Genesis gives us a *literary* Adam and Eve, a genealogical Adam and Eve, but most importantly an *imaging* Adam and Eve. Genesis 1–2 is focused entirely on that literary, imaging feature of Adam and Eve.

Thesis 8

Humans are called to name creatures in order to understand fit and function so that creatures might flourish. Adam and Eve, following in the way of God, are to name creatures as a result of observing and knowing them in order to nurture them into their divinely ordained functions.

We can begin by citing Genesis 2:10–14 as the focus of this unit.

> A river watering the garden flowed from Eden; from there it was separated into four headwaters. The name of the first is the Pishon; it winds through the entire land of Havilah, where there is gold. (The gold of that land is good; aromatic resin and onyx are also there.) The name of the second river is the Gihon; it winds through the entire land of Cush. The name of the third river is the Tigris; it runs along the east side of Ashur. And the fourth river is the Euphrates.

Both Genesis 1 and 2 show that God creates, and it is implied (so I think) that God names what is created. Naming is found as well in other ancient Near Eastern creation narratives, like *Enuma Elish*, so it makes sense to see Israel's God naming.[47] To name is to know and understand by observation, and then to assign oneself a relationship to and a responsibility for that which is named. In fact, the absence of a name is virtual nonexistence in the ancient Near East, and hence naming in a sense gives something an existence in the knowable and known world. Others also contend that naming is an act of authority over that which is named, but that cannot always be the case since Hagar "names" God (Gen. 16:13). On each day of creation, elements come into view that now have names at some level—light, darkness, sun, animals, and "male and female."

In Genesis 2 we see that God creates the man (or earthling)[48] and places him in Eden[49] and in the middle of the garden places a tree of the knowledge of good and evil.[50] Then there are four *named* rivers and their locations. The Hebrew word for "name" (*shem*) stands out ("the name of . . .") particularly in Genesis 2:10–14. Then God brings before the earthling all the animals in Eden and presents them to him to name them. In this, so it appears to me, the man is called to do what God does. Naming them will give the creatures a known existence, and the man will, by naming the creatures, be given a role as the governor (or subgovernor under God) of those creatures. Naming involves observation, discernment, labeling, and therefore relating.

We need to observe two more elements of Genesis 2. To begin with, notice in 2:19 that God brings before the man what "God had formed out of the ground"; that is, just as God had formed the man out of the ground, so he had formed the animals too. This means that the wild animals, the livestock and the birds, are created beings like the man. Furthermore, God brings before the man all these animals in such a way that the reader perceives that God is revealing to the man that these creatures are good but not like the man. Hence, the man learns he is alone by evaluating, knowing, and naming the creatures. The narrative works—rather briskly—to leave us wondering if the man didn't say to God, "Is this all there is? Is there yet one more, one like me?"

So the narrator tells us the reason for the naming: "But for Adam [or the man, the earthling] no suitable helper [*ezer kenegdo*] was found" (2:20). Naming, then, is about observing and evaluating in order to determine fit and function. This "no suitable helper" is the consequence of the man naming all the animals, and as the consequence it makes sense that naming was intended to find someone to fit with the man. God creates the woman out of the man's rib or side—that is, one half of the man or one half of his entire rib cage.[51] Then the man explodes in joy and relief and then in some way names her by saying, "She shall be called 'woman' [*ishah*], for she was taken out of man [*ish*]" (2:23). The man thus joyously names her relationship to him, a relationship that speaks of both sameness and distinction.

What God calls her is even more important, for God speaks of an *ezer kenegdo*, with *ezer* meaning "helper" and *kenegdo* meaning "corresponding to." The man needs someone to be with him, someone to work alongside him, and someone with whom he can form mutuality.[52] Noticeably, the term *ezer* is used in the Old Testament for God and evokes divine help, strength, and accomplishment.[53] The term is used often for a stronger person helping a weaker person, so while it is an indicator of mutuality, it also evokes the sense of a "strong helper."[54] The idea is that the man needed an "ally."[55] If we read Genesis 1–2 in context with Genesis 3 and beyond, the *ezer* is clarified: she cogardens, corules, cogoverns, conurtures, and cocreates with the man to form new children[56] who will expand the number of images of God on earth. This means she and the man will coparent their children and coteach them how to govern the world God has designed.

This "fit and function" theme is developed into marriage (2:24), into sexual relations, and into the theme of gendered embodiment or sexuality: "Adam [or, the man] and his wife were both naked, and they felt no shame" (2:25). But it cannot be narrowed to sexual relations, for the term is a comprehensive description of the benefits of the woman to the relationship in their joint task of imaging God. Once again, what we get in Genesis 1–3 is a *literary and imaging-God Adam and Eve.*

Thesis 9

Humans want to be more than they are and to extend their reach. Adam and Eve, designed by God to subgovern and subnurture creation in leading it to God, have the freedom to choose to defy God and the arrogance to think they can be "like" God.

Over and over we have observed that God creates Adam and Eve and shares with them divine responsibility for creation. The profundity of this ought to stir us repeatedly. This sharing of responsibility implies *freedom*. Like God, humans have the power of choice. Here is the text that reveals the power of our freedom: "And the LORD God commanded the man, 'You are free to eat from any tree in the garden; but you must not eat from the tree of the knowledge of good and evil, for when you eat from it you will certainly die'" (Gen. 2:16–17).

What is at work here is both permission and prohibition. As Bible readers, and perhaps far too familiar with the text itself, we know where this story will end up in Genesis 3. What we call the "fall" story of Genesis 3 borrows a later Christian term and, more importantly, in borrowing a later category, reads the text in ways that miss what the text meant in the ancient Near East. That is, our much later and far more theological use of the category "the fall" to understand Genesis 3 violates the principle of respect and perhaps even the principle of honesty in reading this text. In fact, the whole of Genesis 1–3 barely—if ever—makes another appearance in the entire Old Testament; so while many would say Genesis 1–11 is the foundation for reading the whole Bible, that is certainly at least an exaggeration if not a serious error.[57] Neither the Old Testament nor Romans 5 blames Adam for the sin of others or blames Adam for our own death. We sin by choice; we die because we sin.[58] Our text speaks of sin in terms of pride, arrogance, and a failure to trust the loving word of God. We need to respect Genesis 1–3 for what it says and also for its silences; what it does make clear is that Adam and Eve's sin was disastrous for them—and for their children.

The serpent—a common image of chaos, mystery, and deceit in the ancient Near East—questions God's instructions to Adam and Eve and, in so doing, puts questions in the mind of Eve (Gen. 3:1). Then the serpent denies what God has threatened Adam and Eve with if they touched or ate from the tree: death (3:4).[59] Or, as some have suggested, did the serpent know the ways of God and know that God would be compassionate and gracious?[60] The serpent then tempts Eve (and her silent partner) to eat by promising Eve that she will be "like" God (3:5). And here is the fundamental tension of the first three chapters of Genesis when read together: Adam and Eve are images of God, but that means they are to follow through on the divine assignment of governing the earth on God's behalf. They can be god*ly* by doing so, but they are not designed to become god*like*. The temptation for Eve is to be a goddess; the temptation for Adam is to be a god. They both succumb to their mistaken drive to become gods. As Terence Fretheim describes the tragic moment,

> the woman takes some of the fruit and gives it to her husband [3:6]. As a silent partner "with her" throughout this exchange, the man puts up no resistance, raises no questions, and considers no theological issues; he simply and silently takes his turn. The woman does not act as a temptress in this scene; they both have succumbed to the same source of temptation. They stand together as "one flesh" at this point as well.[61]

They choose not to be god*ly* but god*like*, and they fail on both counts. Consequently, the world shifts for them. One thinks here of *Pleasantville* in reverse: instead of the world suddenly shifting from black-and-white to color, their world loses its sparkle and shifts into a foggy gray. The fullness in which they were dwelling is diminished. They realize their nakedness; their embodied sexuality now becomes a source of shame (Gen. 3:7).

More important is how Adam responds to God when God finds him hiding out in Eden, a place designed by God for delight in one another, for nourishment, and for worshiping God. First, Adam hides from God; second, Adam expresses his fear of God (not the good kind of "fear of God" in the Bible); third, he blames Eve for succumbing to the serpent's temptation to become a god (Gen. 3:8–12). Or, as the Venerable Bede said so poetically: Adam "had the burden of embarrassment but not the humility for confession."[62] Fourth, Eve blames the serpent (3:13). Every conceivable relationship is affected by their choice, and this infection begins to spread until in 8:21 God can say this of humans: "Every inclination of the human heart is evil from childhood."

The consequences, though often stretched and pulled and misinterpreted, follow (Gen. 3:14–15): the serpent will be despised as a creeping creature of the dust; the serpent will be at war with Adam and Eve, and here we see that the serpent's influence on Adam and Eve becomes a metaphor of the devil's power among humans in the Bible;[63] and there will be a battle that the humans will eventually win (and Paul says the victor will be the Second Adam). Surely this battle is part of the divine assignment to image God by coruling; the ruling will entail the struggle. The woman will experience pain in childbearing (3:16a) and, perhaps most noticeably, will now at times be at odds with her husband (3:16b). The language of 3:16b can be either a *description* of what may and will happen or a *prescription* of what is ordered by God to happen. I prefer the former reading, but here is the text:

> Your desire[64] will be for your husband,
> and he will rule over you.

This text has been a battlefield between the hierarchicalists (complementarians) and the mutualists (egalitarians), with at least some of the former thinking the text is divine prescription (women will now submit to husbands because they sinned)[65] while the latter think this is description (there will be at times a war of wills in male-female relations).[66] I agree that this text is about description, and no one has put this more poetically than Walter Brueggemann, who compares the original garden with the garden after their sin: "In God's garden, as God wills it, there is *mutuality and equity*. In God's garden now, permeated by distrust, there is *control and distortion*. But that distortion is not for one moment accepted as the will of the Gardener."[67]

Some think that to protect Adam and Eve from eternal lockdown to sinfulness and this war of wills, God clothes them and then ushers them from the garden of Eden so they won't eat of the tree of life and become immortally sinful (see Gen. 3:21–24). This could be an example of disrespecting the text and reading the fall into what is said there. So perhaps all the text says is that God doesn't want Adam and Eve to be immortal. The text reads: "He must not be allowed to reach out his hand and take also from the tree of life and eat, and live forever" (3:22). This perhaps only says that now Adam and Eve will die; it may have nothing to do with an immortal sinful existence. I'm inclined to think that this act of God is an act of grace that protects Adam and Eve on a journey that leads them to redemption. Adam and Eve are depicted as the literary characters in a story that goes wrong. We see them as *imaging-but-failing* Adam and Eve.

Thesis 10

Humans are called by God to relieve suffering, to undo the curse, and to labor in a creation now tempted to return to chaos. Adam and Eve are called by God to continue in their role as God's images in this world: cocreating, cogoverning, and conurturing one another and the created order.

In powerful contrast to the ancient Near Eastern texts that depict the gods creating humans—sometimes from muddy clay—so they can do the slave labor the undergods are tired of doing, in Genesis God *exalts* humans from a status of slaves to a status of cocreators, coartisans, cogovernors, and conurturers. They are under God, to be sure, but not slaves. One of the most stunning elements of Genesis is to be found in the seamless but suspenseful move from God making the man and woman in the divine image (Gen. 1:26–28) to the act of rebellion in chapter 3 and the question prompted by Genesis 5:1–2: "When God created mankind [or Adam],[68] he made them in the likeness of God. He created them male and female and blessed them. And he named them 'Mankind' [or "Adam"] when they were created."

The question left hanging here is: But after they sinned, did they remain images of God? The answer to that question, which an attentive reader asks (and therefore wonders about an answer), is found four chapters later in a few lines drawn out of Genesis 9:1–7, and here the reader may well notice in some versions that the language is poetic, as in 1:26–28:

> Whoever sheds human blood,
>   by humans shall their blood be shed;
> for in the image of God
>   has God made mankind.

As for you, be fruitful and increase in number; multiply on the earth and increase upon it. (9:6–7)

Yes, the suspense is over: *all humans, male and female, remain images of God*, and the same directions given to Adam and Eve in Genesis 1 are given to Noah and his descendants in Genesis 9. The mission remains: humans are summoned by God, not to be slaves working irrigation ditches as in the Mesopotamian texts, but cocreators, cogovernors, and conurturers of God's creation. They still are summoned by God to see the earth as God's cosmic temple and to mediate that knowledge to all creation. They are summoned to procreate in order to form more images of God in this cosmic temple. Once again, what kind of Adam and Eve do we find? The *literary Adam and Eve who will always be the image-of-God Adam and Eve.*

Thesis 11

To read the Bible in context means to know where the Adam and Eve story will go in the pages ahead. What will become evident to the one who reads the whole Bible is that Adam and Eve are not just two individuals but representatives of both Israel and Everyone. Hence, Adam and Eve's sin is Israel's prototypical sin, their "exile" is Israel's exile, and they therefore represent the sin and discipline of Everyone.

An adventure is suggested in Genesis 1–3 to any reader of the Bible with an ear for the themes that are yet to come in the Old Testament as it tells the story of Israel.[69] Peter Enns explains how Adam (and Eve) corresponds to what will be said of Israel as a nation in the rest of the Bible:

> The Adam story mirrors Israel's story from exodus to exile. God creates a special person, Adam; places him in a special land, the garden; and gives him law as a stipulation of continued communion with God (not to eat of the tree of the knowledge of good and evil). Adam and Eve disobey the command and as a result are cursed with various curses, but primarily their punishment is death and exile from paradise. So too Israel was "created" at the exodus . . . and brought to the good and spacious land of Canaan, a land "flowing with milk and honey" (e.g., Exod. 3:8, 17; 13:5)—a description of superabundance with rich ancient Near Eastern overtones that evoke images of paradise. Israel also has law to keep, in this case the law given to Moses on Mt. Sinai. But Israel continually disobeys the law, which eventually results in an exile from the land God gave them.[70]

The details to establish each of these observations could consume us, but notice these:

Genesis 1:1 speaks of the creation of the "heavens and the *earth*" where "earth" is the Hebrew word used usually for the "land" of Israel (*ha-arets*).

Genesis 1:2 speaks of "formless and empty," terms used in Jeremiah for the condition of the land of Israel after exile (Jer. 4:23).

Genesis 1:28 speaks of *subduing* the earth, and this is the same term (*ka-bash*) used in Numbers 32:22, 29 for conquering the land.

Genesis 2:17 announces a death sentence for the one who eats of the tree, and in Ezekiel 37 exile is described as a valley of dead bones.

It is the accumulation of details like this that leads to the theory that Genesis 1–3 foreshadows Israel's entry into the land. One must admit that not all agree with each of these observations. Enough has been said to establish that Adam and Eve are at least paradigms or archetypes of Israel's own experience, just as the creation of the earth/land is a paradigm of God's gift of the land to Israel. Adam and Eve *are* Israel just as Israel *is depicted* in Adam and Eve. Our point is not to argue that this view of Genesis 1–3 is the one and only reading, for that would claim too much. Rather, it is to show that this account of Adam and Eve has suggestive theological overtones that must not be ignored when reading the text. To read the text respectfully, honestly, and in the context of Scripture itself means we are to learn to hear what the text was saying to its audience. To put this more bluntly in the context of our own book, this text is far more about *Adam and Eve as Israel* than about the historical, biological, and genetic Adam and Eve.

Inherent to Israel's calling, as is made clear in Genesis 12:3, is that Israel is to be a blessing to "all peoples on earth." Israel's calling, if we tie together Genesis 1 and Genesis 12, is to image God in the world before the nations in order to mediate God's presence, God's redemption, and God's will for the sake of the world's redemption (not just Israel's).[71] Adam and Eve represent Israel in its mission and its failure to fulfill that mission by not living faithfully under God's covenant.

The implication of this understanding of Adam and Eve forms the basis for the primary focus of the Jewish presentation of Adam (and only sometimes Eve) outside the Old Testament. We will develop this in the next chapter, but this must be said at this point: the notion of Adam and Eve as representative of unfaithful and exiled Israelites forms a, if not the, fundamental theme about Adam in the Jewish literature. Adam becomes the archetypal Israelite and archetypal sinner and archetypal exile. Hence, the Jewish literature will focus on Adam as the one challenged to obey the Torah but who failed and therefore as the archetypal sinner. (Eve will play for the most part the silent wife in that same literature, as she will for the apostle Paul.) Another interpretation, to which attention is rarely called, is the fruitful comparison of the garden of Eden scene with themes of wisdom in Proverbs, and this too will be developed in the Jewish traditions examined in the next chapter.[72]

What happens then to Adam and Eve in Genesis 1–3 is that they become *archetypal Adam and Eve*, not only for Israel but also for universal humanity. They become by extension—somewhat indirectly in Genesis 1–3 but explicitly in the Jewish literature and explicitly as well in Romans 5—"Adam and Eve as Everyone." Nothing is more true about humans than what is said about Adam and Eve in Genesis 3: offered the world, humans somehow find a way to want more. Given great standing, but filled with pride and the desire for honor, the primal pair want more. That is to say, the Adam and Eve narrative of Genesis 1–3 depicts them as free and capable of choice, but that freedom and choice can become the power that takes over and grows as if fed by steroids to become more than freedom and more than choice. This freedom becomes a self-intoxication.

Thesis 12

No matter how much emphasis is given to a literary, archetypal, and image-of-God reading of Adam and Eve, the fact remains that Genesis 1–2 presents Adam and Eve as what might be called the *genealogical* Adam and Eve.

I have said little about the much-debated *historical* Adam in Genesis 1–3 for a simple reason. The category of "historical Adam" is an anachronism with respect to our text because (1) it comes from the modern world of science, history, anthropology, biology, and genetics, and it also is accompanied by the quest to see if what the Bible says about the past can be proved true (and therefore believed as true); (2) any talk of the "historical Adam" is steeped in the theological conversation about original sin, which is not present in Genesis 3; and (3) the historical, biological, and genetic Adam and Eve are not, strictly speaking, what the writers of Genesis 1–3 were focused on. The writers of Genesis were focused on the above themes about imaging God in this world. Adam and Eve were, to use John Walton's preferred adjective, "archetypal" humans.[73] That is, the primal couple is created to reveal what humans in general are assigned to do in God's cosmic temple. The singular focus of Genesis 1–3 is that Adam and Eve are images of God and all that that entails. Hence, they are presented as the imaging Adam and Eve, not (as I defined it in the previous chapter) as the historical Adam and Eve.

However, some elements in the idea of a historical Adam that developed in Judaism prior to the apostle Paul will be shown in our next chapter (on Adam and Eve in Judaism) and then will be given a fair hearing in our study of how the apostle Paul talked about Adam (and his silenced wife, Eve). It needs to be pointed out early on, however, that if the Human Genome Project has any weight in our worldview, to insist that our DNA comes from two humans, Adam and Eve, is intentionally to run contrary to what science now teaches with considerable evidence. Perhaps one can, with someone like N. T. Wright,[74] suggest that Adam and Eve were elected out of the other 10,000 hominins, were endowed with representative power as images of God, and failed in that imaging responsibility. One might suggest that, but it is rather obvious to all readers of Genesis 1–2 that *there are no other humans present from whom Adam and Eve could have been chosen.* Yes, to be sure, that odd wife of Cain who seems to come from nowhere might just be the speck of evidence such an interpretation is seeking, but even that interpretation eventually crashes into the lone eight survivors of Noah's flood, and we are back to the same problem: the Human Genome Project concluding that our DNA comes from no less than around 10,000 hominins and the Bible's restriction of the origin to two or eight.[75] Instead of fighting that concordist approach to the "historical Adam (and Eve),"[76] I prefer to read Genesis in context to see what light it sheds on humans and human history. What we discover here, so it seems to this Bible reader, is not the historical or biological or genetic Adam and Eve but the literary, image-of-God Adam and Eve.

Having observed that all talk about a "historical" Adam emerges more from modern sciences and history than from the world of the ancient Near East and early Judaism, I must add that an honest reading of the Bible also leads at least to what might be called "the genealogical Adam." I would contend first, though, that the genealogical Adam is rooted in the literary portrait of Adam and Eve over against their ancient Near Eastern contexts. That is, the *literary Adam and Eve are the "front porch" to the genealogical Adam and Eve.* From this literary presentation of Adam and Eve in Genesis on into early Judaism, the first man will be Adam and the first woman will be Eve. *All Jewish genealogies*—when they do appear (and they are not frequent)—that take us back to the origins will take us back to Adam and Eve. Thus, Genesis 5:3–5:

> When Adam had lived 130 years, he had a son in his own likeness, in his own image; and he named him Seth. After Seth was born, Adam lived 800 years and had other sons and daughters. Altogether, Adam lived a total of 930 years, and then he died.

And 1 Chronicles 1:1–3 followed by Luke 3:38:

> Adam, Seth, Enosh, Kenan, Mahalalel, Jared, Enoch, Methuselah, Lamech, Noah. (1 Chron. 1:1–3)

> . . . the son of Seth, the son of Adam, the son of God. (Luke 3:38)

This needs to be seen for what it is: the *literary* Adam and Eve of Genesis 1–2 gave rise to a *genealogical* Adam and Eve of Genesis 5:1–5. All reflections about the first human being derive from Genesis 1–2 and 5:1–5, and Genesis 1–2 is not an example of ancient or modern historiography. Thus, a literary text—Genesis in its ancient Near Eastern context—with these two humans entering the scene first gives rise to a genealogy that runs from Adam onward. The *literary Adam of Genesis became the genealogical Adam in the biblical story.* Our text was designed for a specific context with a message for that context. The next two chapters will attempt to show that we need to be careful not to confuse the genealogical Adam with the historical Adam, for what we will see is that the literary-genealogical Adam is a man with a wax body who can be molded and formed into a variety of Adams (and Eves).

The Variety of Adams and Eves in the Jewish World

The old adage that all roads lead to Rome has a biblical and theological parallel: all theology eventually leads to Adam (and Eve, his neglected partner). Not to whittle the pen to a fine point, but one can reasonably say that theology from the Cappadocians or Augustine, to the intricacies of Thomism, to the foundational themes of the Reformers Luther and Calvin, and then on into the Wesleyan movement as well as the synthesis in the United States established through the famous American theologian Jonathan Edwards, and perhaps most noticeably in the evangelical form of gospel preaching, is rooted in a theology of Adam as the first human, the first sinner, and the one from whom sin was passed on to all humans. Human solidarity and human sinfulness are the foundations of Christian theologies of salvation. The human needs to be saved, one can say, because the human is Adamic, and to be Adamic is to be fallen, sinful, and (in some articulations, therefore) damned.[1] To think like this is also to believe in what I have already described as the "historical" Adam. Without that historical Adam, many think there is no need for the gospel, for Christ, or for salvation history. To question the historical Adam suggests to some that one is flirting with serious theological error.

Questioning a Common Assumption

For much of evangelical theology, then, all roads lead to Adam. But what if, on the basis of evidence and careful thinking, one concludes with the scientists

147

that the earth is some 4.5 billion years old and that the DNA of humans on
earth today could not have derived from two solitary hominins, Adam and
Eve in the garden of Eden?[2] No sooner does one affirm such a conclusion than
someone with Bible in hand opens it to Romans 5:12–21 and begins rattling
off Bible verses that say something else. Thus,

> Therefore, just as sin entered the world through one man [Adam—and Eve,
> don't forget], and death through sin, and in this way death came to all people,
> because all sinned . . . (5:12)

> For if the many died by the trespass of the one man, how much more did God's
> grace and the gift that came by the grace of the one man, Jesus Christ, overflow
> to the many! (5:15)

There you have it. One man was created (with his partner Eve) and brought
death, and one man brought life—Adam and Jesus. The thought of course
is that Adam's sin (and Eve's sin) corrupted his nature, and that nature—
sometimes called the "sin nature" and often discussed as "original sin"—was
passed on from one human (Eve too) to all others. For this to have happened,
it is also assumed that *it had to happen physically or soul-fully* in some manner. Therefore, if you disturb that physical reality, whether by suggesting there
was actually, by the way, more than one man (or hominin) or that creation
was actually evolution and therefore "image of God" is not as simple as one
might think, you disturb the sinful reality, or the sinfulness of each human,
and that means the entire message of salvation is out the window. This is a
rather tiring and fast-paced presentation of a view that, while hoary and assumed, has as much against it as for it.

What it has against it is a common assumption: *that the literary image-
of-God Adam and Eve of Genesis were a historical, biological, and genetic
Adam and Eve* and, furthermore, *that Judaism at the time of Jesus and Paul
believed in that same historical, biological, and genetic Adam and Eve.* But
the questions become these: What did Jews between the Old Testament and
the New Testament believe about Adam and Eve? How did they bring into
play that literary, genealogical, image-of-God Adam and Eve of Genesis?
Did they follow the example of Genesis and create their own literary understanding of Adam and Eve and do so in a way that both made them a part of
the writer's context and simultaneously challenged that context? The answer
to this last question is a resounding yes, and in what follows I want to sketch
the wide variety of Adams and Eves we encounter in Judaism. This will then
lead to a final chapter on Paul, where to be honest and respectful of Paul will

mean recognizing that the Adam (and Eve) of Paul *was the result of both an engagement with these other literary Adams and Eves and the articulation of Paul's own literary Adam and Eve.*

The Many Adams (and Not as Many Eves) in the Jewish Traditions[3]

There is, then, a history of interpretation of Adam from Genesis to the first century AD, a history revealing a bold and astonishing diversity in which one might say accurately that authors made of Adam what they needed of Adam. Or, if you prefer, one might say that the literary Adam was a wax Adam and that Jesus's and Paul's views do not stand over against but instead are instances of this diversity of interpretations. In his thorough study of Adam in Jewish literature, Felipe de Jesús Legarreta-Castillo sketches three reconfigurations of Adam (and Eve) in the Jewish interpretive tradition: (1) Hellenistic interpretations,[4] (2) the "rewritten" Bible interpretations,[5] and (3) apocalyptic interpretations.[6] Each spells out a particular understanding of Adam and Eve, and I italicize the important summary expressions.

> The *Hellenistic* authors "interpret the story of the creation of Adam and the fall incorporating Hellenistic traditions and thoughts to preserve Judaism or accommodate it to their larger historical and cultural milieu. They portray Adam as *paradigm of humankind and the ancestor of Israel who faces the dilemma of freedom and its implications.*"[7]
>
> The *"rewritten" Bible* texts "freely follow the biblical narrative in order to find the place and function of Israel in the world. These interpretations include apocalyptic and wisdom features that express hope in a future reward on the condition that one keep God's commandments contained in the Law. In these interpretations Adam's sin is characterized as disobedience to God's commandment and functions as *the prototype of the historical transgressions of Israel and the nations that brought into the world all sorts of misfortunes for humankind*, especially untimely death. The story of the fall also explains the misfortunes of Israel, typically the destruction of the temple and Jerusalem. In this context, the righteous are exhorted to adhere to the Law in order to attain the promised restoration in the eschaton."[8]
>
> The *apocalyptic* texts "emphasize the story of the fall over the story of the creation of humankind to explain the hardships and the destruction of Jerusalem and its temple. It is interpreted as *an example and an effect of the protoplasts' disobedience to God's commandment on*

their descendants as well as their own unfaithfulness to the covenant.
In these interpretations, heavenly beings typically reveal the destruction
of the wicked—Israel's enemies or sinners—and the salvation of the
righteous in the eschaton. The destruction of this world anticipates the
coming of a new creation."[9]

This is but a quick sketch of major themes in these three blocks of Jewish
literature, but already the respectful and honest reader of the New Testament
will have to be asking, which Adam are we talking about in the various New
Testament texts we might need to consider? To find our bearings for probing
what the apostle Paul will say, I now want to sketch seven kinds of Adam and
Eve that can be discovered in the Jewish literature prior to the New Testament. In what follows I will use a basic label for each text—simplifying for
the sake of clarity—though one must read each text carefully to observe the
nuances of each label.

Sirach: Archetypal, Moral Adam (and Eve)

The name of the author of this book of wisdom is "Jesus son of Eleazar son
of Sirach of Jerusalem" (Sir. 50:27)[10]—in Hebrew, Yeshua ben Elazar ben
Sira; and the book he wrote around 200 BC is often called Sirach or, more
traditionally, Ecclesiasticus ("Church Book") or the Wisdom of Jesus Son of
Sirach. (I will refer to the author as "Ben Sira" and to the book as "Sirach.")
The book is found between the Old Testament and the New Testament in
Bibles that include the Old Testament Apocrypha. Sirach lands in what is
called the "wisdom tradition," a tradition in which Jews expressed—on the
basis of observations about life, worshiping God, and reading Torah in the
context of Israel as God's people—how best to live in God's world in God's
ways. In Sirach the Torah is itself wisdom, and, therefore, wisdom is to live by
the Torah (e.g., Sir. 1:26; 6:32–37; 15:1; 19:20; 23:27; 24:23–29). The book has
some noteworthy observations and uses of Adam (and not Eve), and it serves
as the opening to our discussion of the diversity of Adams in Jewish literature.

What Sirach says about Adam can be sorted into four themes: (1) Adam is
the glorious ancestor of Israel (49:16), (2) Adam lacked wisdom as a mortal
human being (24:28), and (3) Genesis 1–3's account of Adam and Eve becomes
a text that can be universalized to describe all humans. For the mess of sin
that the world is, Ben Sira blames Adam, who is both Israel and all humans.
(4) Humans are given the faculty to choose, and therein lies the significance of
Adam for Ben Sira. Adam is the one who has the power to do God's will or not.

The Adam of Sirach is the *volitional* Adam. God made "humankind" (Sir. 15:14), and because God is good, humans are not to blame God for their sins (15:11–13). Instead, God "left them in the power of their own free choice" (15:14). This power of choice makes Adam a volitional Adam, and it explains the sin of Adam and Eve in Genesis 3.[11] Adam is archetypal: Ben Sira turns to his audience to say, "If you choose, you can keep the commandments, and to act faithfully is a matter of your own choice" (15:15). God gave to each person in the world the choice, and each can do with it whatever one wishes, but it remains that person's choice. This notion is at the heart of Deuteronomy (30:15–20), and Sirach has broadened it from Adam to Israel and to Everyone.[12] Because Sirach ties wisdom to Torah, wisdom as Torah becomes a gift to all humans. Ben Sira can therefore say that God "has not commanded anyone to be wicked, and he has not given anyone permission to sin" (Sir. 15:20). Why? Because each knows at some level what God wants and each is responsible for his or her choice. For Ben Sira, God's final judgment, because God can see each person in the entire world (16:17–23), correlates with how one has chosen: "Everyone receives in accordance with his or her deeds" (16:14).[13]

Ben Sira's theology of free choice is embodied in all of the created order (16:26–17:14). The celestial bodies have a place in the cosmos, and they, unlike humans, do what God orders (16:26–28). Here is where Ben Sira once again "renders" an interpretation of Adam (and Eve):

> The Lord created human beings out of earth,
>   and makes them return to it again.
> He gave them a fixed number of days,
>   but granted them authority over everything on the earth.
> He endowed them with strength like his own,
>   and made them in his own image.
> He put the fear of them in all living beings,
>   and gave them dominion over beasts and birds.
> Discretion and tongue and eyes,
>   ears and a mind for thinking he gave them.
> He filled them with knowledge and understanding,
>   and showed them good and evil.
> He put the fear of him into their hearts
>   to show them the majesty of his works.
> And they will praise his holy name,
>   to proclaim the grandeur of his works.[14]
> He bestowed knowledge upon them,
>   and allotted to them the law of life.

> He established with them an eternal covenant,
>   and revealed to them his decrees.
> Their eyes saw his glorious majesty,
>   and their ears heard the glory of his voice.
> He said to them, "Beware of all evil."
> And he gave commandment to each of them concerning the neighbor.
>   (17:1–14)

Notice the following: "man" or "human beings" are from the earth and return to that same earth (v. 1; cf. 33:10); their days are ordered temporally (17:2a). More importantly, the author interprets the *literary* Adam and Eve in accordance with Genesis 1 as having a mission from God: he "granted them authority over everything on the earth" (v. 2b). The image-bearing Adam and Eve are designed to rule over other created beings under God. The "image" of God, so famous from Genesis 1:26–27, is understood as God-created "strength" (Sir. 17:3), so much so that the rest of creation fears humans or, which is perhaps more likely, fears God because of humans (17:4). But the literary depiction in Genesis 1 of Adam and Eve as made in God's "image" is further unfolded in these terms: "discretion and tongue and eyes, ears and a mind for thinking" (17:6). All this is granted to human beings—once again his focus—for the purpose of moral, free choice: God "showed them good and evil" (17:7). As the image of God, humans are to praise God and "proclaim the grandeur of his works" (17:9). So God granted them knowledge and moral discernment and revealed to humans his covenant and decrees (17:11–12), and they saw God's "glorious majesty" (17:13). And here's the focus yet again: "He said to them, 'Beware of all evil.' And he gave commandment to each of them concerning the neighbor" (17:14).[15] Put into a tight circle: God created humans, revealed his will, and put the matter of obedience into their hands. What strikes the reader here is the generalization of Adam (and Eve): somewhere along the line Adam ceases being simply a literary Adam and has become the *archetypal* Adam. Adam is not responsible for the sins of others; everyone is Adam, everyone experiences what Adam experienced, and therefore everyone is accountable to God for the choices he or she makes. Adam then is used by Ben Sira for ethical purposes. That is to say, the literary and archetypal Adam in this book of wisdom has become more narrowly focused into the *moral or ethical Adam (and Eve)*.

Furthermore, as we observed in thesis 11 in the previous chapter, the Adam of Sirach is the *archetypal* Israel, or Israel is Adam (17:15–32). How so? Ben Sira recounts the story of Israel as the recitation of the life of Adam: created, chosen by God, educated by God's revelation, and put on the path of life to choose life or death. If Israel sins, Israel can repent and find restoration (17:24–26, 29). Again, Sirach shifts the lens slightly so that Israel expands to include all. Humans have limitations: "For not everything is within human capability" (17:30a). Why? Because "human beings are not immortal" and are in need of grace (17:30b, 32; more at 18:1–10). God is more merciful, compassionate, and kind than humans—so God can forgive Israel of its sins. A note of grace frames much of Ben Sira's theology, not least in 18:1–14, where the fallibility of humans is swallowed by the forgiving grace of God (vv. 11–14).

Thus, free choice is constrained in Sirach by some kind of limitation of the human ability to choose what is good. However, there is in this text not a trace of the idea that Adam (or Eve) passed on their original sin to other humans. Later in Sirach this limitation of humans may be connected to the way God made humans (33:13), but the scope of Sirach is far more focused on the choice of humans (32:14–24), as one reads in 32:24 ("The one who keeps the law preserves himself, and the one who trusts the Lord will not suffer loss") or 33:1 ("No evil will befall the one who fears the Lord, but in trials such a one will be rescued again and again"). Obedience, then, is a matter of being "wise" (33:2) and "sensible" (33:3). For Ben Sira, God's creation has some who are good and some who are bad (33:7–15), or as he puts it to finish off that section: "They come in pairs, one the opposite of the other" (33:15). This does not appear to me to be a rigid doctrine of election or predestination, but instead a covenantal election that is shaped by free choice. Ben Sira looks out into the world and sees binary opposites, and the good humans are the wise, sensible people of God who choose obedience.[16]

Ben Sira brings up that most demanding of texts, the so-called curse text of Genesis 3:14–19, in Sirach 40:1–11, and his reflections here deserve our consideration, for they reveal how he uses the *literary* Adam. Adam's sin, as God promised, led to hard work for humans, but Ben Sira expands God's curse of the land and labor in a number of directions, each of which could be inferred from the text—but most are not explicitly mentioned in the text of Genesis 3. Here is Sirach 40:1–11, with the appropriate curse words italicized:

> *Hard work* was created for everyone,
>   and a *heavy yoke* is laid on the children of Adam,
> from the day they come forth from their mother's womb
>   until the day they return to the mother of all the living.
> *Perplexities* and *fear of heart* are theirs,
>   and *anxious thought of the day of their death*.
> From the one who sits on a splendid throne
>   to the one who *grovels* in dust and ashes,

from the one who wears purple and a crown
  to the one who is *clothed in burlap*,
there is *anger* and *envy* and *trouble* and *unrest*,
  and *fear of death*, and *fury* and *strife*.
And when one rests upon his bed,
  his sleep at night confuses his mind.
He gets little or no rest;
  he struggles in his sleep as he did by day.
He is troubled by the visions of his mind
  like one who has escaped from the battlefield.
At the moment he reaches safety he wakes up,
  astonished that his fears were groundless.
To all creatures, human and animal,
  but to sinners seven times more,
come death and bloodshed and strife and sword,
  calamities and famine and ruin and plague.
All these were created for the wicked,
  and on their account the flood came.
All that is of earth returns to earth,
  and what is from above returns above.

Our observations must be limited. First, Eve is skipped over to focus on Adam's curse, which is actually not a curse of Adam but of the land. Because the land is cursed, Adam's life is full of "painful toil" and "sweat of [the] brow" until Adam dies (Gen. 3:17–19). Second, Ben Sira explores "painful toil" and "sweat of [the] brow" in psychological directions, not least in fear of death. Third, all humans, not just the poor, will experience this manifold pain; and it will result, fourth, in social strife and tension. Finally, and in bold in the text above, this expansion of pain from Adam is especially ("seven times more") severe for "sinners," who must stand over against Israel, or at least obedient Israelites.

Here one must conclude that the implications of Adam's sin (again, Eve is ignored) continue to ramify among humans and spread in all directions. *Adam, however, is not blamed; humans are blamed for their choices.* Adam for Ben Sira is the *archetypal, moral human being standing before God on the basis of choice.* In fact, in Sirach 49:16 Adam is sketched as more than a little superior to all human beings: "Shem and Seth and Enosh were honored, but above every other created living being was Adam." Here Ben Sira assumes his readers know that Shem, one of Noah's sons, was the father of the Semites and therefore Abraham (Gen. 6:10; 11:10–26); Seth was considered a prototypical righteous man for his obedience; and Enoch was taken up to be with God (Gen. 5:24; Sir. 49:14). They were honored, "but above every other created living being[17] was Adam" (Sir. 49:16). How so? As Alexander Di Lella observes in his commentary on this verse, Adam "was created directly by God (Gen. 2:7) and made in God's image and likeness (Gen. 1:26–27), [and thus] could be considered 'the son of God,' as Luke 3:38 puts it."[18] Yet in connecting Adam to others in Israel's story, it is clear that Ben Sira glorifies Adam as the *primal ancestor of Israel*; his glory, in effect, is derived from his relationship to God's elected people.[19] Adam is hereby idealized, but Ben Sira's "wisdom" will not let Adam get beyond his capacities and limitations: "The first man did not know wisdom fully, nor will the last one fathom her" (Sir. 24:28).

Eve, however, is not ignored in Sirach 25, where the author begins with a construct of the evil woman but ends up expressing his belief that it was a woman—namely, Eve—who permitted entry of sin into the world (25:24, italicized below):

> There is no venom worse than a snake's venom,
>   and no anger worse than a woman's wrath.
> I would rather live with a lion and a dragon
>   than live with an evil woman.
> A woman's wickedness changes her appearance,
>   and darkens her face like that of a bear.
> Her husband sits among the neighbors,
>   and he cannot help sighing bitterly.
> Any iniquity is small compared to a woman's iniquity;
>   may a sinner's lot befall her!
> A sandy ascent for the feet of the aged—
>   such is a garrulous wife to a quiet husband.
> Do not be ensnared by a woman's beauty,
>   and do not desire a woman for her possessions.
> There is wrath and impudence and great disgrace
>   when a wife supports her husband.
> Dejected mind, gloomy face,
>   and wounded heart come from an evil wife.
> Drooping hands and weak knees
>   come from the wife who does not make her husband happy.
> *From a woman [Eve] sin had its beginning,*
>   *and because of her we all die.*
> Allow no outlet to water,
>   and no boldness of speech to an evil wife.
> If she does not go as you direct,
>   separate her from yourself. (25:15–26)

Eve here is the *archetypal sinner* whose sinfulness has passed on to all humans, creating evidently the prototypical evil woman with whom Ben Sira's kind of man seems forced to dwell.[20]

Adam (and Eve) in Sirach, then, can be called archetypal figures for the human summons and responsibility to live well before God. The Adam of Sirach is the *archetypal, moral* Adam, who is summoned before God on the basis of obedience or disobedience. While there are traces of a genealogical Adam, the Adam of Sirach is not the historical Adam who plays such an important role in Christian theology.

Wisdom of Solomon: Immortal and Just Adam of Wisdom

In his attempt to win back Jews who had shifted toward Hellenism, the author of the Wisdom of Solomon, another Old Testament apocryphal book and written in Egypt in the first three or four decades of the first century AD, uses wisdom as his strategy—but the irony is that the author expresses his thoughts in eloquent Greek and in Greek rhetorical forms. An eschatology more Greek than what one could hear in the classical texts of Israel shapes Wisdom of Solomon's image of Adam. We observe these themes: (1) Adam was shaped by wisdom, (2) which means by the Torah-observant practice of justice or righteousness, and this observance indicates (3) that the soul is alive and at work in Adam and (4) will produce immortality. Now to the text itself.

In Wisdom of Solomon's opening statement about the destinies of the wicked and righteous we find Adam (not Eve) dressed in Greek, Platonic clothing while debating contemporary Epicureans who devalue humans and distance God:

> For God created us for incorruption,
> and made us in the image of his own eternity,
> but through the devil's envy death entered the world,
> and those who belong to his company experience it. (2:23–24)[21]

The author is interested in "incorruption"[22] and "eternity," each tucked away in a dualistic framework of body versus soul (1:4; 8:19–20; 9:15; 15:8, 11), all concerned with avoiding "death." In other words, God created Adam with an immortal soul, with what he calls in 15:11 "active souls" and a "living spirit,"[23] but humans are by nature mortal (7:1; 15:8). The "image" of God is God's "own eternity" (2:23)—that is, immortality—over against Genesis's sense of the relationship between the image and dominion as God's vice-regents.[24] These themes of immortality, eternal life, and their cousin, heaven, find expression only in the later traditions of the Old Testament, and most today would argue that the impact of Persia and Greece was necessary for their development.[25] They clearly are not present in Genesis 1–2, another indicator of how the literary Adam is supple and useful in other contexts.

Yet "image" for Wisdom of Solomon entails an ethical dimension as well: the love of wisdom means following the Torah, which leads to "assurance of immortality" and being "near to God" (6:17–19). Immortality for the soul, then, requires wisdom and Torah observance, or righteousness (1:15), which is the supreme characteristic of Adam and Solomon (7:1–6), who are made in God's image. It is wisdom that can protect Adam and Eve and all humans (see 15:8–13) from corruption unto death and preserve them to immortality.

> Wisdom protected the first-formed father of the world, when he alone
>   had been created;
> she delivered him from his transgression,
> and gave him strength to rule all things. (10:1–2)

Jack Levison concludes that "the image [of God] is not a metaphysical trait possessed by all; it is the capacity to live a holy life which issues in immortality."[26] Those who choose disobedience, in the form of either Adam and Eve's disobedience or Cain's murder (10:3), will experience eternal death.

In addition, "image" connotes dominion to the author of Wisdom of Solomon (as in Gen. 1):

> [O God, who] by your wisdom have formed humankind
> to have dominion over the creatures you have made,
> and rule the world in holiness and righteousness,
> and pronounce judgment in uprightness of soul . . . (9:2–3)

Hence, the ethical dimension of "image" includes this ruling/judging vocation. We begin to hear again the emphasis of Genesis on the vocation of Adam and Eve that they failed to fulfill, as the author also points to kings and rulers of his day and their vocation to be Torah observant in pursuing righteousness and holiness and judging in "uprightness of soul." As Levison observes, the "sage presents human rule in Greek categories as the imitation of divine rule."[27]

Since we believe that all Jewish thought about Adam begins with the *literary* Adam and Eve, we need to observe here that Wisdom of Solomon 7:1 states that each human is "a descendant of the first-formed child[28] of earth," and this appears to indicate that the author believed in what we have labeled the *genealogical* and (perhaps at some level of science) a *biological* Adam. This falls well short of the list of markers for believing in a *historical* Adam, but, like Genesis 5:1's indication of a genealogical Adam, it is one step toward that historical Adam. The same may be present in Wisdom of Solomon 10:1, where it is said, "Wisdom protected the first-formed father of the world, when he alone had been created." How, we might ask, did the author know this? He knew this from the Bible as understood in his Jewish tradition; that is, the author of the Wisdom of Solomon affirms the *literary* Adam as a *genealogical* Adam and so knows from that literary tradition that there was one common ancestor for all humans. He is not thinking scientifically, biologically, genetically, or even historically but instead is affirming his tradition and theologizing in light of it.

Philo of Alexandria: Logos Adam

Philo of Alexandria (ca. 30 BC–AD 50) is the paradigmatic example of our thesis that each Jewish author saw in Adam what one believed and used Adam to prop up a theology or philosophy. Adam for Philo is the paradigm of the Greek theory of the human made of body and soul. Writing in Alexandria, Egypt, and fully conversant with Greek philosophical categories of his day (Platonism and Stoicism), Philo combined exegesis of Scripture, philosophy, and apologetics into a strategy for articulating Judaism in a way that made it palatable to non-Jews. One might be accurate in saying that Philo sought to argue that God's revelation is mediated through Wisdom, the Logos, and when interpreted aright, the Torah of Moses and the entire Jewish tradition is a manifestation of that cosmic Logos-Wisdom.[29] Philo opens one of his studies of Moses's Torah with this:

> [The Torah] consists of an account of the creation of the world, implying [because the Torah includes the laws in Exodus–Deuteronomy] that the world is in harmony with the Law, and the Law with the world, and that the man who observes the Law is constituted thereby a loyal citizen of the world, regulating his doings by the purpose and will of Nature, in accordance with which the entire world itself also is administered. (*Creation* 3)[30]

Notice how "Nature," "Law," and "world" are connected in Philo's thought with the Torah; notice, too, that Philo uses Adam ("the man") for an ethical agenda.

With Philo we have hit a stroke of luck: not only is he from the first century AD, but he also discusses Genesis in a number of settings, and, while each reveals Philo's own theology, his treatments make clear that Adam was capable of being interpreted in a number of ways. We are, however, out of luck when it comes to substantive similarities with the apostle Paul, for the two are rarely writing on the same kind of papyrus.[31] The texts of significance in Philo are, with their English titles, *On the Account of the World's Creation Given by Moses* (here *Creation*), *On the Virtues*, *On the Life of Moses*, *Allegorical Interpretation of Genesis 2 and 3*, and, finally, *Questions and Answers on Genesis*. I will make brief comments on them in that order, relying on and interacting once again with the path-shaping work of Levison along with the important recent study of Legarreta-Castillo.[32]

First, in Platonic fashion the entire cosmos is a copy or replica of Logos-Wisdom since creation is a "copy of the Divine image" (*Creation* 25).[33] It must be emphasized that creation is an image of the Logos, an "image of His nature, the visible of the Invisible, the created of the Eternal" (*Life of Moses* 2.65). The Logos-Wisdom-Mind theme of the created order is deepened in *Creation* 64–88, where humankind (Philo uses *anthrōpos* throughout in reference to humankind, not just to Adam as a male) is the climax of creation as the one with Mind. Thus, God "bestowed on him mind [*nous*] *par excellence*, life-principle [*psychē*] of the life-principle itself" (66). "Image of God" thus means Mind, which is made even clearer when Philo aggressively distances the "body" of the human from God and "image" (69). In a later section, Philo distances the Adam of Genesis 1 from the Adam of Genesis 2, the former being "an idea or type or seal, an object of thought (only), incorporeal, neither male nor female, by nature incorruptible" (134). The Adam of Genesis 2, however, made as he is from clay, is marked by body and "sense-perception" (134). Again, man is therefore both immortal and mortal, and what is immortal is Mind (135). This notion of two types of humans is expressed yet again in his *Allegorical Interpretation* (1.31–42; 2.4):

> There are two types of men; the one a heavenly man, the other an earthly. The heavenly man, being made after the image of God, is altogether without part or lot in corruptible and terrestrial substance; but the earthly one was compacted out of the matter scattered here and there, which Moses calls "clay." (1.31)

In distinguishing the Adam of Genesis 1 from the Adam of Genesis 2, the author is concerned with ethics: one kind of man does what is reasonable, wise, Logos-based, and of the mind, while the other does what comes from the passions; the former is immortal, the latter mortal.[34]

Mind forms the core of the "image of God," and, in a move sounding like Stoicism, this makes humans superior to all creation. The Mind, sent from God to be stored in the body as a "sacred dwelling place or shrine"

(*Creation* 137), is designed by God to rule the human with its body. All of this is played out on a cosmic map: God creates a spectrum from virtue and vice and reason; plants and animals are devoid of reason; heavenly beings have mind but no virtue. Humans, however, are of a "mixed nature" and "liable to contraries, wisdom and folly" (73–74). There is also a kind of dualism at work in Philo that reveals just how much he is influenced by Platonism,[35] and is something that will be developed intensively in later gnosticism. For example, according to Philo, the "us" of "let us make" in Genesis 1:26 refers to God's subordinates who are capable of creating "thoughts and deeds of a contrary [to God] sort" (76).

Philo blames Adam's partner, Eve, for the fall of Adam, who had been a man who was altogether happy and virtuous prior to her arrival.[36] She, he says, "becomes for him the beginning of a blameworthy life" (151). Her bodily beauty becomes for both of them a source of pursuing "that pleasure [*hēdonē*] for the sake of which men bring on themselves the life of mortality and wretchedness in lieu of that of immortality and bliss" (152). Sex is at the root of all evil. Seemingly repeating a traditional interpretation that he knows, Philo says this of Eve: "She, without looking into the suggestion, prompted by a mind devoid of steadfastness and firm foundation, gave her consent and ate of the fruit, and gave some of it to her husband" (156). However, no blame is accorded to Eve in *On the Virtues* 203–5, where Adam—the "first and earth-born man" who "stands beyond comparison" with other humans because he was created "by the hand of God" and received his soul from the same God directly—"was quick to choose the false" and so sin.

Philo also ponders the historical plausibility of the text of Genesis, preferring to read the fantastic not so much as "mythical fictions" but as allegorical symbols or "modes of making ideas visible" (*Creation* 157). Thus the garden is about the "ruling power of the soul" (154), and the tree of life symbolizes reverence toward God, and the tree of the knowledge of good and evil points toward "moral prudence" (154). By Adam and Eve's act of sin, *the soul* is driven from the garden. The serpent itself allows Philo to launch into a classic Platonic critique of bodily pleasures (157–69).

Man is the "first father of the race" (79), and this notion of Adam as "first man" and "ancestor of our whole race" (136)—in fact, the "only citizen of the world" (142)—emerges often in *Creation* 136–44. It is indeed likely that Philo believed Adam genuinely was the first human, for he believes the *literary* Adam is the *genealogical* Adam, as do other Jewish writers of his day. He also believes, according to *Questions and Answers on Genesis*, that the first man had intense sensory powers, and he speculates that he was a giant (1.32). Along the same lines, he speculates that the bodies and souls of the descendants, especially from Cain on, were quite different from Adam's (1.81). But we are entitled to ask how Philo knew these sorts of things, and we are led to only one conclusion: because he found the *literary*, *genealogical* Adam in Genesis. Thus, Adam for him is "clearly the bloom of our entire race" (*Creation* 140). He also knows, though, in true Platonic fashion, that "the copies are inferior to the originals" (141). Adam's descendants "preserve marks, though faint ones, of their kinship with their first father" (145); all humans, to be sure, carry traces of "divine Reason" (146). But what causes the difference between ancestor and descendants? Noticeably for those trained in Christian thinking, Philo does not put blame on Adam or the fall; instead, his beliefs bring to expression the Platonic theory of degeneration.[37]

Adam, then, is the image of Logos-Wisdom-Mind and as such forms the apex of creation, "a miniature of heaven" (82), the ruler of all beasts under the heavenly beings. Here Philo lands—finally, one might suggest—where the author of Genesis begins (and stays):

> So the Creator made man after all things, as a sort of driver and pilot [here he is referring to how farmers and pilots steer animals from behind, as Adam was made last in order], to drive and steer the things on earth, and charged him with the care of animals and plants, like a governor subordinate to the chief and great King. (*Creation* 88)

Adam's rule under God is why Adam names the animals, for "he was, moreover, a king, and it befits a ruler to bestow titles on his several subordinates" (148). All humans, Philo infers, carry on this ruling function of Adam, "keeping safe a torch (as it were) of sovereignty and dominion passed down from the first man" (148; see also *Life of Moses* 2.65).

To repeat, the Adam of Philo is a Logos-shaped and Wisdom-shaped Mind, an expression of the Mind of God; he is also an embodied person who chooses whether to live a life shaped by the mind or the body and so chooses immortality or mortality. Philo's Adam is a Jewish Adam who becomes a Jewish, Platonic Adam, and as in many other ancient interpretations of Genesis, Eve is largely ignored.

Jubilees: Adam of Torah Observance

The response of some Jews to the growth of Hellenistic influence and power was a stricter form of Torah observance, not least in terms of the distinguishing marks of Judaism, such as the Sabbath, reminders of the jubilee, and purity laws as observed in the temple courts. In the book of *Jubilees*, which is one example of the Bible being rewritten, we encounter another presentation of Adam, almost to the total neglect of Eve.[38] In general, the Adam of *Jubilees* is the literary Adam of Genesis, with its special emphasis on Adam and dominion, but the author of *Jubilees* uses Adam—the literary Adam no doubt—to emphasize his own concerns with Torah observance, like Sabbath practices. Adam thus becomes an *archetypal Adam of Torah observance*.[39]

The Adam narrative is expanded with detailed knowledge of the calendar. Thus, during the second week after the creation week, Adam names the animals on successive days (3:1–4); God shows Eve to Adam in the second week (3:8); forty days later he enters the garden of Eden (3:9); Eve is shown to him on the eighth day (3:9), but she does not enter the garden for eighty days in order to be pure (3:12). They tilled for seven years prior to the serpent's temptation (3:15). Their sin led to shame and covering themselves with fig leaves (3:17–25), and in so retelling this story the author takes a stand with Jewish laws about exposure and nudity—surely a concern about gentile behaviors and influence in the aftermath of the Maccabean revolt.

Some verses in Genesis are omitted (like 1:28; 2:14–17; 3:8–13, 22, 24), and those omissions seem to have been made on the basis of the author's own theology. That is, it is entirely possible that the original form of *Jubilees* recorded only the creation of Adam in the first week. Perhaps even more important are the insertions one finds in *Jubilees* 3:8–14, 27–32. In 3:8–14 we find the birth of Eve outside the garden and her need for a longer purification—incorporating the codes of Leviticus 12—to reveal Torah observance as the core human response; in 3:27–32 Adam offers incense in priestly fashion, anticipating what the later patriarchs will do. This version of the Torah, then, is not in need of historical development or subsequent revelation because it was already known from Adam on. The author of this text, as Levison observes, is responsible for "transforming him from transgressor to the first Israelite Patriarch."[40]

That does not happen in another rewriting of Scripture, one deserving here of only a brief mention: Pseudo-Philo's *Biblical Antiquities*.[41] In 13:8 Adam is framed negatively: "But that man transgressed my ways and was persuaded by his wife; and she was deceived by the serpent. And then death was ordained for the generations of men." The author of this text continues to show that humans after Adam have fallen into Adam's ways. It is up to Israel, God says, to choose to walk in his ways and save their souls or to walk in sin and find no blessings. Here we encounter again another version of the *archetypal, moral Adam*.

To return to our principal text in this section, *Jubilees*: this text is a tendentious, if conservatively so, rereading of Genesis. However, what shapes the author's rereading is the author's theology of Torah observance, a concern that emerges from Second Temple Judaism's temptation to fall into the ways of the Hellenists. Once again, Adam is turned toward an ethical purpose as the *literary* Adam of Genesis becomes even more an *archetypal, moral Adam*.

Josephus: Roman Adam

Flavius Josephus, the famous first-century AD Jewish historian and near contemporary of Jesus and Paul, rewrote the Bible's history into a pleasing narrative that made the Jewish story more palatable to Roman tastes.[42] His approach to the Genesis narrative about Adam illustrates his method and philosophy/theology, as revealed in his condensations, rearrangements, additions (like the speech of God to Adam in *Jewish Antiquities* 1.46–47), and subtle revisions. A few observations.

First, when Josephus turns to the Adam narrative, he opens with these words: "And here . . . Moses begins to interpret nature, writing on the formation of man" (*Jewish Antiquities* 1.34).[43] His Adam is more or less a Platonic portrait: "God fashioned man by taking dust from the earth and instilled [inserted] into him spirit and soul" (1.34). This created and now Platonic Adam—that is, one with both spirit and soul—is "without female partner" (1.35).[44] Eve is formed, as in the Genesis narrative, from Adam's "rib" (1.35) but in no way is understood as Adam's equal.

Second, Josephus fills in details of the Eden narrative on the basis of Jewish tradition and his own beliefs, including the following: there is a "stream" that "encircles all the earth" (1.38), the tree is the "tree of wisdom" (1.40), every created being had a "common tongue" (1.41), the serpent "grew jealous" (1.41) and tempted Eve, who tempted Adam, and they both sinned and covered themselves with "fig-leaves" (1.44). Here the ethical summons to be virtuous in order to live the good life shapes how the narrative is retold. Adam was such a virtuous man that he was able to predict the destruction of the world, once by fire and once by flood (1.70). The serpent was deprived of speech and legs, and poison was put under his tongue (1.50–51). The descendants of Adam through Cain become a depraved lot (1.66), whereas Seth's were virtuous (1.68–71; cf. 1.72).

The Adam of Josephus is the "first man" (1.67)—that is, the *genealogical* Adam of the book of Genesis, with slight modifications. There is for Josephus no "image of God" or charge by God for Adam (and Eve) to exercise subdominion on behalf of God. Inasmuch as Josephus condenses the account of Genesis dramatically, one is at a loss to know why something so important as "image" is omitted, though some have suggested it is because of Josephus's high regard for the prohibition of images (cf. *Against Apion* 2.190–92). Most notably, Josephus also makes Adam into *an archetypal virtuous figure and example*, but this is shaped to make Adam palatable to Rome. Thus, Adam is less Torah observant and more "virtuous"—a Greco-Roman category, but one that can speak to and explain the same reality as Torah observance.

4 Ezra: Fallen Adam

A late first-century AD dialogical apocalypse called *4 Ezra*,[45] perhaps originally written in Latin, presents a theology of Adam not unlike that of the apostle Paul. In the text, Ezra pleads with God for the salvation of humans, including Israel. The two voices in *4 Ezra*, the pessimistic Ezra and Uriel, differ on how to view Adam, though even their difference is at times a distinction without much difference. Ezra wants to put blame more on Adam and the fallenness of humanity, while Uriel emphasizes human will and choice.

The sketch of Adam in *4 Ezra* is summed up in these words of Uriel, and here again we find the *Torah-observant Adam*:

> This is the meaning of the contest which every man who is born on earth shall wage, that if he is defeated [in the summons to live obediently before God by following the Torah] he shall suffer what you have said [eternal torment], but if he is victorious he shall receive what I have said. (7:127–28)[46]

But there is a distinctive contribution of *4 Ezra* when we discover the emphasis on the sin of Adam having implications for all humans, not least Israelites, including their being brought to the divine dock for final judgment with very little hope for salvation. All of this is shaped by the context and setting of the book: it is a theodicy to explain Israel's suffering at the hands of Rome (and God).

Here are the emphases. First, the ordinary features of Genesis are present in *4 Ezra*: Adam is created by God from dust, and then God breathes into him immortal life (3:4–5). It is noteworthy, in distinction from the more Greco-Roman uses of Adam in other Jewish texts, that *4 Ezra* says nothing about "spirit" or "soul." Life is what God breathes into Adam. Taken directly from Genesis, Adam is the "ruler over all the works which you [God] had made" (6:54).

But, second, immediately Ezra himself turns to his theme of life as the divine test of obedience: "And you laid upon him one commandment" (3:7). He—the absence of Eve is noteworthy—failed, and God " appointed death for him." This is directly from Genesis, but it is here that something new enters: the fall. The text says that God appointed death not only for Adam but also "for his descendants" (3:7). To be sure, the later Christian belief in original sin and original guilt, with all inheriting a sinful nature, does not come to the fore. Why? Because the emphasis falls upon the will and action of all humans: "every nation walked after its own will" (3:8). The author ties Noah's sin to Adam's sin and Adam's death to Noah's flood (3:10). "The fall," Ezra says, "was not yours alone [Adam], but ours also who are your descendants" (7:118).

Third, the author of *4 Ezra* traces sin to the "evil heart" that hinders Torah observance. As Ezra puts it: "Yet you did take away from them their evil heart, so that the Law might bring forth fruit for them" (3:20). In fact, Adam evidently had an evil heart before he sinned: "For the first Adam, burdened with an evil heart, transgressed and was overcome" (3:21), and such was the case for all his descendants. Here is a noteworthy development in Adamic thinking: "Thus the disease became permanent" (3:22).[47] The contest continues: "The law was in the people's heart along with the evil root, but what was good departed, and the evil remained" (3:22). They all "had the evil heart" (3:26). Uriel will explain this as a "grain of evil seed" in 4:30. But the text of *4 Ezra* is just as quick to blame humans for their choices as it is to lay blame on Adam.

Fourth, the consequences of disobedience, a lack of Torah observance, and sin are spelled out in *4 Ezra* in a rather simplistic way: those who sin will be tormented forever; those who obey, Uriel observes, will inherit eternal life (7:11). This theme turns into a set of rhetorical questions in *4 Ezra* 7:62–74, 116–26 (Ezra), and 127–31 (Uriel): humans have chosen disobedience and will be punished. But in this conclusion Ezra places more blame on humanity, and Uriel more on individual will. The theological debate many know today is at work already in the text of *4 Ezra*, and Ezra himself eventually sides with the need for humans to choose obedience—theirs is the responsibility.

Put together into rhetorical context, the voice of Ezra blames Israel's sinfulness on its choice to permit the evil heart to have its way with them. He does not blame Adam so much as people, but he does plead with God to be merciful to Israel. Uriel's own responses say much the same thing: Israel, not Adam, is the problem; Israel chose to sin. In *4 Ezra* Adam is a *literary* Adam who has become, because he is also a *genealogical* Adam, a *moral and fallen* Adam. This portrait of Adam is not identical to the apostle Paul's, but it is much closer than the Greek- and Roman-sounding Adam.

2 Baruch: Adam as Everyone

Like the apocalypse *4 Ezra*, the apocalypse called *2 Baruch* came into existence after Jesus and Paul, probably closer to AD 130 than to AD 100.[48] Both are responses to the aftermath of Rome's sacking of Jerusalem in AD 70, and both are also attempts to come to terms theologically with what it means to be God's elect people when reality (apparently) denies it. If *4 Ezra* carries darker themes, *2 Baruch* lands squarely on the ground of the freedom of the will and the responsibility and potential of each person to be obedient. This kind of exigency then gives rise to a way of thinking about Adam, and it is not an accident that both apocalypses construe Adam from the angle of free will, choice, and the correlation between obedience and blessing.

The most memorable line about Adam in *2 Baruch* comes from 54:19:

> Adam is, therefore, not the cause, except only for himself, but each of us has become our own Adam.[49]

A fall, perhaps, but not in any way that diminishes the personal responsibility of each human, especially Jews, to choose to observe the Torah. A number of themes appear in *2 Baruch* about Adam, who is for the author a paradigmatic human being. He is, in other words, the *literary* Adam used as the *moral, archetypal* Adam.

First, since Jerusalem figures so prominently in Jewish theology, especially in the aftermath of Rome's destruction of the city, and since "as Jerusalem goes so goes Israel," it is not one bit surprising to read that God revealed the "new Jerusalem" to Adam before his choice to sin and that the same revelation was given to Abraham and Moses (4:1–7). Adam here is depicted, as he is throughout the apocalypse, as a sinner.

Second, traditional elements about Adam appear, even if little is made of them: Adam was the "guardian over [God's] works," and the world was created for him, not him for the world (14:18). Adam's many, many years (930 to be exact) did not lead him to righteousness, whereas Moses's few years (120) did just that (17:1–18:2). Adam brought death, whereas Moses brought the light of life. Here we find an alternative to the Adam-Christ typology of Christianity; for this author the typology is Adam-Moses. Death is decreed against Adam and Eve (19:8).

Third, the author broaches the fall and inherited sinfulness, but backs off before it becomes clear what he thinks: "For when Adam sinned and death was decreed against *those who were to be born* . . ." (23:4; emphasis added). He seems to back down somewhat because Adam's sin brings corruption to all: "O Adam," the author asks, "what did you do to all who were born after you?" (48:42; cf. 56:6). In fact, *2 Baruch* lists the consequences of Adam's sin (56:6–10): untimely death, mourning, affliction, illness, labor, pride, death (Sheol), conception (or better, the death) of children, passion of parents, loftiness, and goodness disappeared.[50] This takes us back to a similar list in Sirach 40:1–11 (see above).

But we come back to the original theme: Yes, Adam sinned; yes, Adam's sin impacts all; but each person is responsible for himself or herself. "And those who do not love your Law are justly perishing" (54:14). The text continues:

> For, although Adam sinned first and has brought death upon all who were not in his own time, yet each of them who has been born from him has prepared for himself the coming torment. And further, each of them has chosen for himself the coming glory. (54:15)

To sum up, for *2 Baruch*, each of us is our own Adam, meaning that our own destiny, and the destiny of this world, is in our hands—we can choose to obey God or disobey, but the matter is in our own hands. In this text we have the *literary*, *genealogical* Adam who is *archetypal* of all humanity: here we find Adam *as Everyone*.

Conclusion

We begin with something nonnegotiable but largely ignored: the Adam of each of these writings is consciously and constantly the Adam of Genesis, the *literary* Adam. Instance after instance of interpretation by these authors, from Sirach to *2 Baruch*, is an exegesis of the text of Genesis. There is no reason to repeat evidence from each author, but here are two examples—beginning with one from Sirach—that prove that the Adam of these authors is the Adam of Genesis, the literary Adam:

> The Lord created human beings out of earth,
>   and makes them return to it again.
> He gave them a fixed number of days,
>   but granted them authority over everything on the earth.
> He endowed them with strength like his own,
>   and made them in his own image.
> He put the fear of them in all living beings,
>   and gave them dominion over beasts and birds. (Sir. 17:1–4)

Ben Sira's Adam is the literary Adam, and what we read here is quite plainly what is found in Genesis, though Ben Sira doesn't mind speculating that God "put the fear" of Adam and Eve "in all living beings" and that this is inherent to their calling to "dominion." The second example is from Josephus, where we find the same pattern of recycling Genesis alongside reinterpreting Genesis. Straight out of Genesis we read, "God fashioned man by taking dust from the earth," and that Adam is "without female partner" (*Jewish Antiquities* 1.35). Genesis gave to these authors the *literary* Adam, and they embraced him, but they gave the man (and occasionally his wife) a family hug that made them part of a new family.

The second nonnegotiable is just as firm: each author used Adam to his (or her) own purposes. That is, each interpreted the Adam (and far less often Eve) of Genesis 1–3 for particular reasons and purposes in the context of debates and discussions, with the result that *Adam has an interpretive history*. No author left Adam in Genesis and read the biblical text simplistically; no author cared about giving Adam a "historical" reading; each author adapted and adopted and adjusted the Adam of Genesis. The result of this sketch of ancient interpreters, who sometimes added to and sometimes subtracted from the Adam of Genesis, is that when we talk about Adam, we are far more accurate to ask, which Adam? or, whose Adam? Is it the Adam of the Wisdom literature, where Adam is more the universal human, or the Adam of the legal or apocalyptic traditions who made his choices about Torah observance? We are then driven by the evidence to conclude that instead of a single Adam typology in Judaism, there are a variety of Adams in Judaism. It is worth pausing here to detail a few of the adaptations of Adam in this Jewish history.

The theme of Adam as capable of choosing and as paradigm of Torah observance and disobedience dominates the later apocalypses, *4 Ezra* and *2 Baruch*. Every human being is implicated in Adam's sin because every human being enters into the same contest of obedience versus disobedience. Nothing frames this better than *4 Ezra* 7:127–28, in the words of Uriel:

> This is the meaning of the contest which every man who is born on earth shall wage, that if he is defeated [in the summons to live obediently before God by following the Torah] he shall suffer what you have said [eternal torment], but if he is victorious he shall receive what I have said.

The distinctive contribution of these two pieces of literature, each one written in the world of post–AD 70 Judaism, one more pessimistic and the other less so, is the radical impact of Adam's sin on humans. They are not yet Augustine; instead they hover between, on the one hand, passing on Adam's sinfulness with an "evil heart" (*4 Ezra* 3:20) and a permanent disease (3:22) and, on the other hand, setting up a world in which sinfulness predominates. As *2 Baruch* frames it, each of us is our own Adam (54:19).

We may be wise not to synthesize all of these interpretations into a "Jewish view of Adam," but if I were to offer a synthesis of the Adam of the Jewish traditions, it would be this: Adam is the *paradigm or prototype or archetype* of the choice between the path of obedience and that of disobedience, the path of Torah observance and that of breaking the commandments, the path of Wisdom and Mind and Logos and the path of sensory perceptions and pleasure and bodily desires. The Adam of the Jewish tradition is depicted very much as the *moral* Adam. Thus, from texts not yet mentioned, in the Qumran community we discover an Adam who, though formed in the image of God (4Q504 frag. 8, line 4), is the archetype who "broke faith" (CD 10.8). Thus Israel, "like Adam, broke the covenant" (4Q167 frag. 7 9.1). Those who are faithful, however, will inherit the "glory of Adam" (1QS 4.23). Hence, the emphasis in the Dead Sea Scrolls on the two spirits derives from the interpretive history of Adam choosing disobedience and therefore becoming a prototype of the human faced with obedience or disobedience (1QS 3–4).

In some of these interpretive traditions Adam comes off more positively than in others, but in each of them Adam is not just the first human being (the *literary-genealogical* Adam) but also the first sinner, whose sin had an impact on those who followed him. Adam is never simply the first human being in a long chain of history; Adam is always the *archetype* of humans in general or Israel in particular. How did these authors learn to read Adam as an archetype and come to know these things? They did so not by historical investigation or scientific inquiry but simply by *knowing Adam as the literary Adam found in their sacred book, the Torah, in Genesis.* There are elements of the so-called *historical* Adam present—genealogical Adam, fallen Adam—in these Jewish sources, but *the historical Adam that Christians now believe in has yet to make his appearance on the pages of history.* Perhaps we will encounter him in Paul or perhaps not, but this point must be emphasized: the *construct Christians use when they speak of the historical Adam is not to be found in the Old Testament or in other Jewish sources.* This does not mean that Christian theology, even if that theology develops after the New Testament, is not true, but it does mean that it is postbiblical.

We are now ready to ask how the apostle Paul fits into this story of Jewish diversity, this story of multiple Adams, a story that has been shown to be both male centered and free-will centered. Is Paul's Adam the *literary-genealogical* Adam who becomes the *archetypal, moral* Adam? Or is Paul's Adam the *historical* Adam of Christian theology?

8

Adam, the Genome, and the Apostle Paul

At this point I want to return to the third principle of Bible study outlined in chapter 5 above: the principle of reading the Bible with sensitivity toward the student of science. I want to recall also that the number one reason Christians leave the faith and the number one reason non-Christians find the Christian faith untrustworthy is the issue of the Bible and science. At the heart of this complicated issue is the way the Bible talks about human origins—that is, about Adam and Eve. I believe that science forces us to pause long enough to question our assumptions about how to read Genesis 1–3, and I also believe the sketch I have provided so far brings to the surface another approach not only to reading Genesis 1–3 but also to understanding Adam and his oft-neglected partner, Eve.

But let us pause again to look at the issue of walking away from the faith on account of science. Theoretically speaking, all conversions are apostasies and all apostasies are therefore conversions. Everyone who converts leaves a former faith, even if that faith is ill-defined. Those who study conversions often observe that a conversion *to* something means a conversion *from* something else, but rarely does the observation work itself into the fabric of one's study of conversions themselves. One rare exception is the fine study by John Barbour, who specializes in studying autobiographies. In *Versions of Deconversion*, Barbour observes that those who tell their own stories of deconversion also reflect on their own past through four lenses:

- they doubt or deny the truth of the previous system of beliefs;
- they criticize the morality of the former life;

- they express emotional upheaval upon leaving a former faith; and
- they speak of being rejected by their former community.[1]

There is no historic profile for someone who leaves orthodoxy or, to use a clinical and historical term, for someone who commits apostasy by abandoning orthodoxy. I have sketched some of this story in a book I coauthored with Hauna Ondrey entitled *Finding Faith, Losing Faith.* Some of those we studied were nurtured into the faith in committed Christian homes (like the journalist Christine Wicker), while others experienced dramatic conversions to the faith (like the famous evangelist and rival of Billy Graham, Charles Templeton, or the strident apologist for antitheism, John Loftus). Each, for a variety of reasons, encountered issues and ideas and experiences that simply shook the faith beyond stability. In essence, those who leave the faith discover a profound, deep-seated, and existentially unnerving *intellectual incoherence* to the Christian faith. The faith that once held their life together, gave it meaning, and provided direction simply no longer makes sense. But this shift in faith does not often occur suddenly. Mary McCarthy, a luminous thinker for a generation well before mine, in her famous "My Confession" talked about her loss of faith in a way that illustrates the slow and often drawn-out process of faith slowly ebbing away: "This estrangement was not marked by any definite stages; it was a matter of tiny choices."[2]

I give one more example of someone encountering science who had a rigid view of Scripture and a theory of human origins. Kenneth Daniels is not a scientist, but his own research into questions about the origins of life and the Genesis record convinced him that the Bible was either mythical or a falsehood. "I do not want to make myself out as being more qualified to judge the matter than the typical creationist," he admits, "but I am disturbed by the flippant disregard and disdain on the part of many creationists for the patient investigation and analysis that have led most scientists in the past century to accept evolution." One fact that persuaded Daniels was the latent but inactive remains of the Vitamin C–producing gene that is not needed by humans and primates. "This can be readily accounted for within an evolutionary framework, but is simply a puzzling curiosity from a creationist standpoint." His question has been asked by many: "Why would God allow so many apparent evidences for evolution to exist in the first place?" "I see a pattern suggesting the appearance of evolution, something which an omnipotent, undeceiving God could easily have preempted in any number of ways if evolution had not happened."[3] Here is what is vital for this book: this person's faith in the Bible was challenged by his realization about evolution, and he was forced to make a choice about whether the Bible or evolution was the truest description and understanding of the world. *He chose science because the understanding of the Bible was in his view demonstrably wrong.* Dennis and I are proposing another alternative: accepting the reality of genetic evidence supporting a theory of evolution *along with* an understanding of Adam and Eve that is more in tune with the historical context of Genesis.

It would not be hard to provide additional testimonies of what happened to someone's faith when that person began to face the empirical evidence supporting evolution. I have encountered many who consider science *an excuse not to believe the Bible* rather than a reason to undertake a very serious quest to understand both science and Genesis 1–3. No one points a finger at lazy theories more than Marilynne Robinson, whose protagonist in her novel *Gilead* observes, "It seems to me some people just go around looking to get their faith unsettled."[4] We are concerned not with the simply disaffected or the one who looks for problems in the conflict between science and faith but with the truth seeker. And the truth seeker eventually wants to know what to make of Adam in what is said most especially in the apostle Paul's Letter to the Romans, and nearly everyone goes immediately to Romans 5:12–21.

All theological roads, to repeat an earlier point, lead to Adam in Romans 5:

> Therefore, just as sin entered the world through one man [Adam—and Eve, don't forget], and death through sin, and in this way death came to all people, because all sinned. . . .
> For if the many died by the trespass of the one man, how much more did God's grace and the gift that came by the grace of the one man, Jesus Christ, overflow to the many! (5:12, 15)

We must ask if the widespread belief that Adam passed on the sinful nature physically—through sexual reproduction—is found in Romans 5:12–21. (The absence of Eve in so many of these discussions is already a problem or, as will become clear, a hint that we might not be thinking right.) I will explain this more below, but we must at least raise the question early in this chapter. Notice that Paul says "because all sinned" in verse 12 and not "because all sinned in Adam." The early church father Jerome, ever fiddling with the text and not so good in Greek, translated "because [*eph' hō*] all sinned" as "in whom [*in quo*] all sinned"; then Augustine made nothing less than an extensive case for the theory of original sin and original guilt,[5] and we've been stuck with both of them and that theory ever since. Because we have dipped into the intertestamental Jewish texts about Adam (in chap. 7), we have become sensitive to the Adam of Judaism. Those texts rarely blame Adam and Eve but instead turn Adam into the *archetypal, moral* Adam who embodies the moral choice of each individual in history. The game changes, if only slightly, with this interpretation, but what does not change is the importance of Adam.

Like most texts we touched upon in chapter 7, Paul ignores Eve in his major passages about Adam that we will examine below.[6] He does mention Eve as the one deceived by the serpent in 2 Corinthians 11:3 in a way that sees her as the archetype of one who is deceived, and in 1 Timothy 2:13 we have a temporal reflection: "For Adam was formed first, then Eve." This note of primogeniture is another instance of the *literary* Adam and Eve being used for theological reasons. And Paul adds that it was Eve, not Adam, who was first deceived. In a highly provocative context where women were challenging both Roman and Jewish customs about sexuality, worship, and leadership, where some Roman women were turning everything upside down, and where Paul's concern was with young widows (see 1 Tim. 5:9–16), he returns to Genesis to find support for his position: women need instruction before they can go public with their teachings (1 Tim. 2:11–12). However one explains this difficult passage in 1 Timothy—and an appeal to specific situations at Ephesus with the worship of Artemis has become increasingly clear to historians[7]—our larger point needs to be clear: Paul's neglect of Eve in Romans and 1 Corinthians is typically Jewish. The focus of attention is on the man, Adam, rather than the woman, Eve. Thus, Paul lifts any blame from Eve and lays it all on Adam.

The important texts in Paul are 1 Corinthians 15:21–22, 45–49 and Romans 5:12–21,[8] and they deserve to be read slowly before we begin.[9] I begin with 1 Corinthians 15:21–22, 45–49:

> For since death came through a man, the resurrection of the dead comes also through a man. For as in Adam all die, so in Christ all will be made alive. . . .
>
> So it is written: "The first man Adam became a living being"; the last Adam, a life-giving spirit. The spiritual did not come first, but the natural, and after that the spiritual. The first man was of the dust of the earth; the second man is of heaven. As was the earthly man, so are those who are of the earth; and as is the heavenly man, so also are those who are of heaven. And just as we have borne the image of the earthly man, so shall we bear the image of the heavenly man.

The second passage, Romans 5:12–21, "defines the future destiny of believers just as Adam's life defined the future of his descendants."[10] Because this passage from Romans is complex, I have ordered it into an outline adapted from N. T. Wright; if one uses the outline as one reads the text, it will make the reading a bit easier to follow:[11]

The Opening Statement

[12]Therefore, just as sin entered the world through one man, and death through sin, and in this way death came to all people, because all sinned—

First Explanatory Aside

[13]To be sure, sin was in the world before the law was given, but sin is not charged against anyone's account where there is no law. [14]Nevertheless, death reigned from the time of Adam to the time of Moses, even over those who did not sin by breaking a command, as did Adam, who is a pattern of the one to come.

Second Explanatory Aside

[15]But the gift is not like the trespass. For if the many died by the trespass of the one man, how much more did God's grace and the gift that came by the grace of the one man, Jesus Christ, overflow to the many! [16]Nor can the gift of God be compared with the result of one man's sin: The judgment followed one sin and brought condemnation, but the gift followed many trespasses and brought justification. [17]For if, by the trespass of the one man, death reigned through that one man, how much more will those who receive God's abundant provision of grace and of the gift of righteousness reign in life through the one man, Jesus Christ!

Completion of Opening Statement in Verse 12

[18]Consequently, just as one trespass resulted in condemnation for all people, so also one righteous act resulted in justification and life for all people.

Filling Out of Verse 18

[19]For just as through the disobedience of the one man the many were made sinners, so also through the obedience of the one man the many will be made righteous.

The Law in This Discussion

[20]The law was brought in so that the trespass might increase. But where sin increased, grace increased all the more,

Triumphant Conclusion

[21]so that, just as sin reigned in death, so also grace might reign through righteousness to bring eternal life through Jesus Christ our Lord.

To facilitate an ease with reading, instead of a lengthy commentary and some long tangents and digressions and clarifications, I have organized this chapter as well into some theses.

Thesis 1

> The Adam of Paul is the literary, genealogical, image-of-God Adam found in Genesis.

This is nothing but an attempt to state the obvious so we can move into more detailed particulars below. By saying Paul is using the literary, genealogical Adam, I'm not assuming this is fiction or that Paul somehow got it wrong. What Paul knew about Adam was not gained by scientific examination as we now know science. Rather, like the authors of the texts we examined in chapter 7, Paul knew about Adam from the Bible, and the Adam and Eve he knew from the Bible were part of a standard Jewish genealogy (e.g., Gen. 5:1). The Adam and Eve Paul knew from Genesis were presented as made in God's image, as two who failed to do what God commanded, who were expelled from Eden, and who then occupy a part of the standard story in the history of Israel. Paul does not question this literary-genealogical tradition he inherited from his parents, teachers, and people. If these be true, then it is unfair to Paul to impose on him what many today mean by the "historical" Adam (see thesis 5 below). A reading of Josephus's account of the beginnings of life in his *Jewish Antiquities* (book 1) shows that he, too, assumed the literary-genealogical Adam as the way to begin telling the story of Israel.

Many have observed that Paul's understanding of humans—of Adam and Eve, as it were—in passages outside this important one in Romans 5 is rooted in Genesis 1–3. For instance, there are echoes of Genesis in Romans 1:18–32, that famous passage about the sinfulness of gentiles. So when Paul says in verse 22, "Although they claimed to be wise, they became fools," we hear an echo of what Adam and Eve chose to do (cf. Gen. 2:17; 3:5–6). When we read the well-known "for all have sinned and *fall short of the glory of God*" (3:23; emphasis added), we can easily make a connection with Adam and Eve's glorious state that was corrupted by sin and see that humans have in some way defaced what God made humans to be. These echoes make us walk backward until we find Genesis 1–3 and what I have called "the literary Adam." That literary Adam and Eve become the *genealogical* Adam and Eve upon whom the entire history of Israel is built. James D. G. Dunn has noted that "one of the most striking features of Romans is the fact that Paul repeatedly calls upon Genesis 1–3 to explain his understanding of the human condition."[12]

Thesis 2

> The Adam of Paul is the Adam of the Bible filtered through—both in agreement and in disagreement with—the Jewish interpretive tradition about Adam.

Again, this should be obvious.[13] Jews of Paul's day didn't pick up the book of Genesis as if it had never been read prior to them. Like you and me, when they read the Bible, they encountered the text of Genesis with terms and categories that had become familiar to them and that shaped what they saw. Furthermore, what they saw and heard was what they thought was actually in that text, intended by that text, and intended by Moses. When it comes to Genesis, I've heard this a thousand times: Christian folk read Genesis 1–2 and think they hear confirmation of their theories of science and so conclude that the Bible is wonderfully supernatural in that God revealed to them what no one understood until our times.

The same needs to be said of Paul. The literary-genealogical Adam and Eve of Genesis were filtered through the interpretive history of Adam that we read about in the last chapter. Paul's Adam was the *literary-genealogical and Jewish Adam of Jewish tradition*, but there's this to add as well: *Paul's Adam is not identical to those other Adams but has its own contours.* What is also noteworthy is that Paul shows no serious interaction with, or even awareness of, the famous scene in Plato's *Symposium* when Aristophanes proposes the following: there were originally three sexes, and humans were spheres with four hands and feet and two faces and two sets of genitals—and Zeus cut humans in two to punish them, but their primordial unity was retained, and so a man loves a woman in bonded unity as a way of returning to those origins.[14]

I will begin to illustrate how Paul's Adam shows similarities to the Jewish Adam (and Eve) of his day with an example from the Wisdom of Solomon (13:1–19). A slow reading of this text shows how often Romans 1 echoes it. I would highlight the words and phrases here that are echoed by the apostle Paul in Romans, but there are too many, so do take the time to read this passage slowly, and think too that most of what is here is *not* found in Genesis or in the rest of the Old Testament:

> For all people who were ignorant of God were foolish by nature;
> and they were unable from the good things that are seen to know the
>   one who exists,

nor did they recognize the artisan while paying heed to his works;
but they supposed that either fire or wind or swift air,
or the circle of the stars, or turbulent water,
or the luminaries of heaven were the gods that rule the world.
If through delight in the beauty of these things people assumed them
    to be gods,
let them know how much better than these is their Lord,
for the author of beauty created them.
And if people were amazed at their power and working,
let them perceive from them
how much more powerful is the one who formed them.
For from the greatness and beauty of created things
comes a corresponding perception of their Creator.
Yet these people are little to be blamed,
for perhaps they go astray
while seeking God and desiring to find him.
For while they live among his works, they keep searching,
and they trust in what they see, because the things that are seen are
    beautiful.
Yet again, not even they are to be excused;
for if they had the power to know so much
that they could investigate the world,
how did they fail to find sooner the Lord of these things?
But miserable, with their hopes set on dead things, are those
who give the name "gods" to the works of human hands,
gold and silver fashioned with skill,
and likenesses of animals,
or a useless stone, the work of an ancient hand.
A skilled woodcutter may saw down a tree easy to handle
and skillfully strip off all its bark,
and then with pleasing workmanship
make a useful vessel that serves life's needs,
and burn the cast-off pieces of his work
to prepare his food, and eat his fill.
But a cast-off piece from among them, useful for nothing,
a stick crooked and full of knots,
he takes and carves with care in his leisure,
and shapes it with skill gained in idleness;
he forms it in the likeness of a human being,
or makes it like some worthless animal,
giving it a coat of red paint and coloring its surface red
and covering every blemish in it with paint;
then he makes a suitable niche for it,

and sets it in the wall, and fastens it there with iron.
He takes thought for it, so that it may not fall,
because he knows that it cannot help itself,
for it is only an image and has need of help.
When he prays about possessions and his marriage and children,
he is not ashamed to address a lifeless thing.
For health he appeals to a thing that is weak;
for life he prays to a thing that is dead;
for aid he entreats a thing that is utterly inexperienced;
for a prosperous journey, a thing that cannot take a step;
for money-making and work and success with his hands
he asks strength of a thing whose hands have no strength.

This chapter in the Wisdom of Solomon is for New Testament readers another version of Romans 1, and it should not then surprise us that many think Paul had read the Wisdom of Solomon and was echoing it there. At a minimum it had influenced the world in which Paul learned to think about the human condition.

This idea of Adam's glory departing is found in another Jewish text called the *Apocalypse of Moses* (the Greek *Life of Adam and Eve*). A few lines from that text illustrate again that Paul's emphasis on human glory being defaced by sin is an interpretation of the Genesis narrative found in many places in Judaism.

And at that very moment my eyes were opened and I knew that I was naked of the righteousness with which I had been clothed. And I wept saying, "Why have you done this to me, that I have been estranged from my glory with which I was clothed?" (20:1–2)

And he said to me, "O evil woman! Why have you wrought destruction among us? You have estranged me from the glory of God." (21:6)[15]

That Adam lost his glory in the primal sin is found in Paul and in Jewish texts, but one cannot find it in Genesis, though it is more than easy to infer it. (The word "glory" is not even found in the entire book of Genesis.)

One more example.[16] In the Jewish world some thought that the root of all sin was *desire* (in Greek, often *epithymia*). In the text we just cited, the *Apocalypse of Moses*, we read that very idea: "For covetousness [*epithymia*] is the origin of every sin" (19:3). This is taught as well in that most Jewish of all New Testament texts, James: "Then, after desire [*epithymia*] has conceived, it gives birth to sin; and sin, when it is full-grown, gives birth to death" (James

1:15). Connecting sin to death sounds very much like Genesis 2–3. So when the apostle Paul in Romans 7:7–13 begins to explain how sin works, he sounds like this interpretive tradition about the root of all sin in desire:

> What shall we say, then? Is the law sinful? Certainly not! Nevertheless, I would not have known what sin was had it not been for the law. For I would not have known what coveting [*epithymian*] really was if the law had not said, "You shall not covet [*epithymēseis*]." But sin, seizing the opportunity afforded by the commandment, produced in me every kind of coveting [*epithymian*]. For apart from the law, sin was dead. Once I was alive apart from the law; but when the commandment came, sin sprang to life and I died. I found that the very commandment that was intended to bring life actually brought death. For sin, seizing the opportunity afforded by the commandment, deceived me, and through the commandment put me to death. So then, the law is holy, and the commandment is holy, righteous and good.
>
> Did that which is good, then, become death to me? By no means! Nevertheless, in order that sin might be recognized as sin, it used what is good to bring about my death, so that through the commandment sin might become utterly sinful.

There you have it: an echo of Adam and Eve, the reality of desire leading to sin and all leading to death—very Jewish, and most noticeably Genesis being read through the interpretive tradition in Judaism.[17]

We can now sum this up: the Adam of Paul is a Jewish Adam—that is, he is not simply the *literary-genealogical*, *image-of-God Adam* but is instead that Adam as interpreted in the Jewish tradition. The first and second theses should not be open to disagreement except in precise details of how much of the Jewish Adam Paul picked up and used. Details aside, Paul's Adam has become more than what he was in Genesis. If these two theses are not susceptible to simple denials, what follows enters us into the realm of debate.

Thesis 3

> The Adam of Paul is the archetypal, moral Adam who is the archetype for both Israel and all humanity.

This point is not so much a discussion of the *historical* Adam—or that he was a real human being—as it is a framing of how Paul *uses* Adam in Romans 5:12–21 and 1 Corinthians 15:21–22, 45–49. Very much like many uses of Adam in the Jewish literature discussed in the previous chapter, *Adam (not Eve) is presented here as the one who was summoned by God to obedience, who disobeyed, and who brought in death and destruction.* Adam is archetypal for the apostle.[18] Paul says nothing about biology and genetics (of course), but instead presents Adam as the man who made the wrong choice and whose choice ruined himself and his descendants in both Israel and all humanity.

Paul's presentation of Adam in Romans 5 and 1 Corinthians 15 sets up an antithesis between the first Adam (a tragic hero) and the second or new Adam (a redeemer hero, Christ),[19] and in this Paul's Adam is unlike anything we've seen in the Jewish traditions.[20] Paul's comparison of Adam and Christ can be schematized as follows:

Adam	Christ (the Second Adam)
Sin	Obedience
Death	Life
Condemnation	Justification
Union with others	Union with others

One could argue that Paul *began with Christ* and found opposites in Adam just as easily as one could argue that he *began with Adam* and found opposites in Christ.[21] What matters in our context is only that Paul *uses* Adam to bolster his Christology and to magnify the accomplishments in Christ. One can explain our passage as yet one more representation of reuse of the literary Adam of Genesis for theological purposes. However one explains it, the emphasis here in Paul is the comparison of Adam with Christ. For Paul, Christ is the Second Adam just as he is the true Israelite. That is, God's design all along when he created Adam and Eve was for them to reflect God's glory and rule God's creation, but they rejected that mission; so in God's right timing he created Israel to be that Adam, but Israel too did not live up to the divine calling, and so in God's right timing he sends his Son, Jesus, to be Adam and to be Israel. Jesus, then, is seen by Paul to be the true Adam and the true Israelite who, unlike Adam and Israel, accomplishes the divine mission.[22]

The comparison begins in Romans 5:14 with an explicit term that spells out Paul's point of view: "Adam, who is a type [*typos*] of the one who was to come [Christ]" (NRSV). Instead of drawing out commonalities, Paul is intent on drawing out differences. In this text, then, Adam as type is the reverse image, or the negative, of Christ. Thus, in verse 15 we read: "But the free gift [in Christ] is not like the trespass" (NRSV). Why? The trespass brought death, but in Christ the grace of God "abounded for the many." The effect of the sin of Adam, verse 16 goes on to say, is not like the gift. How so? The sin brought "judgment" and "condemnation," while the gift in Christ brings "justification." Then in verse 17 Paul enters into his penchant for the term "dominion." One man's trespass led to the "dominion" of death, while the gift of grace in

Christ means his people "exercise dominion in life through the one man, Jesus Christ" (NRSV). And Paul piles it on in verse 18: Adam's sin means death for all, but Christ's "act of righteousness," which refers to his obedient death on the cross or to his own faithfulness to God's saving plan,[23] "leads to justification and life for all."[24] He winds it all down in verse 21 with more "dominion" language: sin brings the dominion of death, but Christ ends the dominion of death in the dominion of grace that brings life. The near obsession with "rule" or "dominion" in this text echoes the mission God gave to Adam and Eve to rule creation, a mission that they forfeited and was then passed on to Israel but was not finally established until the resurrection of Jesus. As N. T. Wright has recently pointed out, when Jesus is depicted in 1 Corinthians 15:20–28 as conquering, ruling, and handing over all of creation-now-redeemed to the Father, he is doing what Adam and Eve were called to do.[25]

What kind of Adam is at work here? In his commentary on Romans, James Dunn refers to Adam and Christ as "epochal" figures, and in his later *The Theology of Paul the Apostle* he uses both "epochal" and "archetypal" with respect to Adam. Notably, Dunn turns his attention from the archetypal Adam to whether or not Paul thinks of Adam as a historical Adam:

> Whether Paul also thought of Adam as a historical individual and of a historical act of disobedience is less clear. Philo should remind us that the ancients were more alert to the diversity of literary genres than we usually give them credit for. And Paul's very next use of the Adam story (Rom. 7.7–11) is remarkably like *2 Baruch* 54.19 in using Adam as the archetype of "everyman." Be that as it may, the use Paul makes of Genesis 1–3 here is entirely of a piece with the tradition of Jewish theologizing on Adam in using the Genesis account to make sense of the human experience of sin and death.[26]

Douglas Moo, observing that Paul drops the original sinner—Eve—from the story, sees in her absence a schematic theory of salvation history at work in Paul. He writes, "The fact that Paul attributes to Adam this sin is significant since he certainly knows from Genesis that the woman, Eve, sinned first (cf. 2 Cor. 11:3; 1 Tim. 2:14). Already we see that Adam is being given a status in salvation history that is not tied only to temporal priority."[27] Moo claims more than Dunn, for Moo sees in Paul some kind of "temporal" description, which would make Adam a real, historical Adam at some level, but in any case what Moo shows is that Paul is using Adam in a salvation-historical scheme to compare and contrast Adam and Christ. Dunn is less sanguine, but both affirm that Adam is used here in some archetypal, epochal, and salvation-historical manner.

Thesis 4

> Adam and all his descendants are connected, but original sin understood as original guilt and damnation for all humans by birth is not found in Paul. In Jewish fashion, Paul points his accusing finger at humans for their sins. How there is continuity between Adam, all his descendants, and their sins and death is not stated by Paul.

We now arrive at the most significant set of observations for assessing how to understand Adam (Eve is totally ignored in Romans 5 even though she was the first to sin)[28] in light of how we have read Genesis itself (in the context of the ancient Near East) and Genesis in the history of Jewish interpretation. What is significant is that in Christian theology it has been claimed over and over that we must have a *historical* Adam to have the Christian doctrine of salvation. The issue, however, is not whether the historical Adam is important to soteriology but what kind of Adam Paul has in mind in Romans 5:12–21. Does Paul reveal an Adam who is a real person, who is biologically connected to all humans, a genetic or DNA Adam? Or does Paul have in mind the standard Jewish Adam—that is, the *literary*, *genealogical* Adam who becomes an adjustable figure who can be used in theology for a variety of presentations and ideas?

The critical words are those of Romans 5:12: "Therefore, just as sin entered the world through one man, and death through sin, and in this way death spread to all people, because all sinned . . ."[29] While it is possible to extend this discussion in a number of directions, I want to zero in quickly on the major elements for the purpose of this book. The beginning of verse 12 reads "just as sin *entered* the world," and the term in italics is a translation of *eiserchomai*. The Greek word translated as "spread" in "death spread to all people" is *dierchomai*. Thus, the two Greek verbs mean respectively "enter" and then "spread"—like a cancerous cell or a bad idea or, in this case, the cosmic power of sin that presses humans toward an inevitable death. *How* that spreading occurs is not stated by Paul. While some are attracted to the idea that Adam created the moral and social conditions where sin became inevitable, the language of Romans 5:12–21 can only be explained in more cosmic, spiritual terms.[30] There is something more than the environment of humans at work in the sinfulness of all humans.

Paul neither affirms nor denies *transmission of sin, a sinful nature, and death* by way of procreation and birth and a life lived before God. What became central in later theories of salvation—that each human sinned "in" Adam and that each human is born condemned and in need of salvation—no

matter how clear this is in logic, *cannot be found in Romans 5:12.*[31] The link
between Adam and all his descendants is as obvious as the manner of that
link is obscure. Put differently, we can offer explanations that make sense of
this obvious and yet obscure verse: perhaps Paul did believe and assume in
this verse that procreation and birth constitutionally put each human into
Adam's status as a condemned sinner, or one could argue—and I will do this
shortly—that each person is *Adamic in that each person sins in the way Adam
sinned.* One can argue then that one is born a sinner or that each person becomes a sinner, but *either theory is only an explanation of what is not stated
in this verse.* This, it must be noted, is *the only verse in the New Testament*
upon which this kind of theory can be constructed.

It is important to see that Paul stands between two poles here: not only did
Adam really unleash sin, but also each person sins, just as Adam unleashed
death, and each person exercises willful sin and so deserves his or her own
death. In Romans 8:19–22 Paul sees in creation itself a "futility" generated
by Adam and Eve's sin, and that creation awaits the redemption of humans
for its own redemption. There is, then, a "double death," a "physico-spiritual
death," or a "total death" at work in this passage. Paul is concerned not just
with Adam unleashing cosmic death but with each of us as an Adam or Eve
generating our own death.[32] N. T. Wright frames this double death in terms
of the exodus and cosmic war:

> In terms of his underlying new-exodus story, sin and death play the role of
> Pharaoh: Paul imagines them as alien powers, given access to God's world
> through the action of Adam. Once in, they had come to stay; staying, they
> seized royal power. Linked together as cause and effect, they now stride through
> their usurped domain, wreaking misery, decay, and corruption wherever they
> go. No one is exempt from their commanding authority.[33]

This double death is the Pauline balance beam, but it is a far cry from the
later developments connected to original sin and original guilt.

How then did we get to this belief in original sin, original sin nature, and
original guilt? Most likely it was a combination of what many early theologians
inferred from Romans 5:12's "because all sinned," how some early theologians
translated this into Latin (*in quo*—that is, "in whom" rather than "because"),
and the power of Augustine's theological mind—and he developed a theological anthropology in which all humans were guilty in Adam's original sin.
Of course we need to respect the power of the church tradition, but I am a
Protestant who believes in *prima scriptura*, and so we ask—with many others
who have similar questions today—if this verse can bear the weight of this

interpretation. The answer, I believe, is no. Behind what Ambrosiaster and Augustine translated as "in whom" and the NIV translates as "because" is the Greek expression *eph' hō*. This expression is found in Paul at these three references: 2 Corinthians 5:4; Philippians 3:12; 4:10. Here are the verses with the translation of *eph' hō* in italics:

> 2 Corinthians 5:4: "For while we are in this tent, we groan and are burdened, *because* we do not wish to be unclothed but to be clothed instead with our heavenly dwelling, so that what is mortal may be swallowed up by life."
>
> Philippians 3:12: "Not that I have already obtained all this, or have already arrived at my goal, but I press on to take hold of that *for which* Christ Jesus took hold of me." (The NRSV and CEB have "because.")
>
> Philippians 4:10: "I rejoiced greatly in the Lord that at last you renewed your concern for me. *Indeed*, you were concerned, but you had no opportunity to show it." (The NRSV has "Indeed," while the CEB has "Of course.")

In none of these cases does *eph' hō* mean "in whom," and in two of the three it means "because." The vast majority of scholars of Romans today agree that we should use this causal idea—thus leading to the translation "because all sinned."[34]

What needs to be observed and repeated for a generation with emphasis is what Paul is here saying: he is not saying that all have sinned in Adam and therefore die but instead *that each person, like Adam, sins and therefore dies because of that sinning*. Humans somehow inherit something from Adam, but they die not because of that inheritance but because they sin. Perhaps all Paul means when he says "so death spread to all" is that death spread *because, like Adam, everyone sins*. Yes, there is a sense of corporateness in Romans 5:18–19, which needs to be repeated here so that we can see that corporateness:

> Therefore just as one man's trespass led to condemnation for all, so one man's act of righteousness leads to justification and life for all. For just as by the one man's disobedience the many were made sinners, so by the one man's obedience the many will be made righteous. (NRSV)

All are condemned because of one's man trespass, just as all have life because of one man's obedience. Thus, in 5:12 we have an emphasis on the individual, while in 5:18–19 we have an emphasis on human solidarity. Which rules here, the individual or the solidarity?[35] Many think all sin "in and with"

Adam[36] or that Adam is our representative and what he did we did. No one
has stated the latter, federal theory more clearly than Tom Holland:

> Adam represents the human race. He is the father of mankind with an all-
> embracing headship. When he sinned and broke off his relationship with God,
> he took all of his offspring with him into darkness. Not only was Adam cut off
> from God, but so too was every one of his descendants. In biblical terms, the
> doctrine of original sin has nothing to do with an inherited, inherent distorted
> nature, but is about being in a condition of enmity towards God because of
> the sin of our father, Adam. Being born in sin is to be born into the rebellious
> human race. It is about being part of the kingdom of darkness that Adam's
> rejection of God has established. As children of Adam, all humankind shares
> in that same sin and, in so doing, has choosing [sic] to reject God. The root
> of Paul's doctrine of the sin of all mankind is rooted in Adam's disobedience
> and the covenantal relationship with Satan (Sin) that he, Adam, established. To
> be in sin is to be in Adam, and through him, to be in a covenant relationship
> with Sin (Satan).[37]

I'm unconvinced, though the logic and clarity of Holland's explanation
of Romans compel many to agree. He wants to emphasize solidarity all the
way down, but I'm not sure this can be grounded in what Paul actually says.
To begin with, notice that in Romans 5:18–19 the trespass is that of Adam
while the obedience is that of Christ—each passes on what each grants: death
or life. But, unless one is some kind of universalist, there's a profound hitch
in this passing on that breaks down all attempts to forge unbroken solidarity. I would contend that *just as one must act—believe—in order to benefit
from the one act of Christ's obedience in order to inherit eternal life, so we
need to act—sin or disobey—in order to accrue to ourselves death.* The big
picture is that Adam brings death and Christ brings life, but the *mechanism*
for each to become effective is the act of the human being: those who remain
in Adam's line perform the act of Adam—that is, they sin—while those who
enter into Christ's line perform the act of Christ—that is, they trust Christ.
This is what Paul actually says in Romans 5:12 when he says all die—not
because all are "Adamites" but "because all sinned." That is a difference with
dramatic implications.

Others prefer a more nuanced, balanced approach that combines some kind
of real unleashing of sin as a cosmic force and at the same time a pointing of
the accusing finger at the individual human for sin and accountability before
God. That is, humans have been impacted by Adam's sin, but individuals are
not accountable until they sin themselves. Once again, Dunn sheds light on
the text, this time by recalling the rebellion of Rhodesia (today's Zimbabwe)

to overthrow England's colonial powers. A baby born in Rhodesia was not a rebel until, as an adult, he or she chose to join the rebellion.[38] Again, we see the interplay of the themes of individuality and human solidarity in Adam. We are all Adam, and each of us becomes an Adam and an Eve. Fairness to Paul's own words requires both. N. T. Wright pulls this all together into a balanced view: "Paul's meaning must in any case be both that an entail of sinfulness has spread throughout the human race from its first beginnings and that each individual has contributed their own share to it. Paul offers no further clue as to how the first of these actually works or how the two interrelate."[39]

Such a conclusion does not undo Paul's ties to later Christian theology so much as it makes Paul like his Jewish forebears, as we sketched in the previous chapter. In Judaism Adam was the archetypal sinner who unleashed sin into the world. He was the moral archetype in his choice rather than the one depicted as responsible for the sin and death of others. We read Romans 5:12, then, in this typical Jewish manner. We agree with Paul Achtemeier, who sees Paul's mind clearly: "The universality of human mortality is Paul's empirical proof of the universality of human sin."[40] That is, Paul knows from Genesis that sin leads to death, and since all die, he knows all sin. Paul surely knew this also from experience:

> The folly, degradation, and hatred that are the chief characteristics of human history demand an explanation. Why do people so consistently turn from good to evil of all kinds? Paul affirms in this passage that human solidarity in the sin of Adam is the explanation—and whether we explain this solidarity in terms of sinning in and with Adam or because of a corrupt nature inherited from him does not matter at this point. On any view, this, the biblical, explanation for universal human sinfulness, appears to explain the data of history and experience as well as, or better than, any rival theory.[41]

We have now come to a crucial moment in this section of the book. What kind of Adam is found in Romans 5 (and 1 Cor. 15)? The answer is clear: Paul's Adam is the *literary* Adam of Genesis filtered through the Jewish tradition of interpreting Adam as the *archetypal, moral, and exemplary* Adam who both unleashes sin into the world by his own sin and at the same time forms a model for each human being: each human being stands condemned before God as a sinner because each human being sins as did Adam (and Eve). Adam is the precise counterpoint to Christ—what Adam did Christ undid; what Adam did not do Christ did. Hence, Paul cannot blame Adam; he blames each person for sinning like Adam. Notice, then, that Romans 5:12's mechanism for "sin came into the world through one man, and death came through sin" is explained by "because all sinned." This makes Romans 5:12 a dead-ringer parallel for Romans 3:23: "For all have sinned and fall short of the glory of God." Adam, the man formerly of glory, is the paradigmatic human who failed to live according to God's demand and so becomes the paradigmatic moral (or immoral) man, leaving the haunting question that runs right through the whole Bible: Will we follow Adam or will we follow Christ?

Thesis 5

The Adam of Paul was not the historical Adam.

Every substantial science-and-faith discussion I have been engaged in eventually comes down to one question on the part of some: "Do you believe in a *historical* Adam?" Lurking behind the second half of this book, this question has been waiting to jump up for discussion. For that question to be answered, we have plowed our way through how to read Genesis in the context of the ancient Near East and how Adam was understood in the Jewish world in which Paul was nurtured. We have seen time and time again that Adam is the literary-genealogical Adam of Genesis but that Adam and Eve have been used in various theological and philosophical contexts, which resulted in other interpretations of Adam. Of course, some will see slightly different nuances in both Genesis and the Jewish texts, and some will want to see hints that Jews really did believe in a "historical" Adam and Eve. In this book I have offered how I think about Adam and Eve, and this approach to Adam and Eve flows directly from the dialectic between what I've learned from science and what I've learned from Old Testament studies. It is unlikely that the debate about the historical Adam will go away any time soon, but this book has sought to bring to our attention what we mean by the adjective "historical" when attached to Adam and Eve.

While we find some kind of hinting at a historical Adam in the Bible's genealogical Adam and at times even more explicit statements in the Jewish literature, we have not found the fullness of what people really do mean when they ask about the historical Adam. So once again I want to repeat what it means to call Adam and Eve "historical":

1. two *actual* (and sometimes only two) persons named Adam and Eve existed suddenly as a result of God's creation;
2. those two persons have a *biological* relationship to all human beings that are alive today (biological Adam and Eve);

3. their *DNA* is our DNA (genetic Adam and Eve); and that often means

4. those two *sinned*, *died*, and *brought death into the world* (fallen Adam and Eve), and

5. those two *passed on their sin natures* (according to many) to all human beings (sin-nature Adam and Eve),[42] which means

6. without their sinning and passing on that sin nature to all human beings, *not all human beings would be in need of salvation*;

7. therefore, if one denies the *historical* Adam, one denies the gospel of salvation.

How much of this applies to what Paul says about Adam? It's clear that Paul is not thinking biologically or genetically. Like conservative types of Christians—young-earth creationists—Paul believed in the Bible; and not only did he believe in the Bible, but he also considered the Bible to be in some ways "scientific," as he thought of science. Unlike these same conservative types of Christians today, he *could* not have and therefore *did* not know better.

As I look over this list, I suspect Paul himself *may* have believed in meaning 1, but he never explicitly says anything quite like that.[43] I would contend that Paul, like the Jews of his day, would have thought that the *literary* Adam and Eve were also the *genealogical* Adam and Eve, and that as such they were persons in the history of Israel. But there are no explicit observations by Paul with respect to meanings 2, 3, or 5. Paul may have affirmed meaning 1; and he did affirm meaning 4 explicitly. But Paul does not anchor his gospel of redemption in the *historical* Adam, at least not as I have explained what "historical" means when attached to Adam and Eve. Rather, Paul believed that Genesis set up the category and a trajectory of disobedience leading to sin that leads to death; and, observing that all humans sin, Paul affirms what his fellow Jews affirmed: people die because they sin. Paul's gospel does not require that definition of "historical" Adam; what it requires is this:

- an Adam and Eve who were made in God's image
- an Adam and Eve who were commanded by God not to eat of the tree
- an Adam and Eve who chose to disobey
- an Adam and Eve who therefore were aimed toward death
- an Adam and Eve who passed on death to all humans

And it requires an Adam and Eve who are the paradigms of the condition of each and every human being: faced with the demand of God, each human in history chooses to disobey and therefore dies.

Among scholars of Paul, some argue that Paul believed in two real, actual human beings, while others are not so sure what Paul believed. I stand four-square with Joseph Fitzmyer: "Paul treats Adam as a historical human being, humanity's first parent, and contrasts him with the historical Jesus Christ. But in Genesis itself 'Adām is a symbolic figure, denoting humanity. . . . So Paul has historicized the symbolic Adam of Genesis." At this point one is not quite sure what Fitzmyer thinks, but he comes clean later when he reflects on what it would mean to speak of the *historical* Adam and Eve with respect to the first-century Jewish apostle:

> Paul, however, knew nothing about the Adam of history. What he knows about Adam, he has derived from Genesis and the Jewish tradition that developed from Genesis. "Adam" for Paul is *Adam in the Book of Genesis*; he is a literary individual, like Hamlet, but not symbolic, like Everyman. Adam is for Paul what Jonah was for the evangelist Matthew (12:40) and Melchizedek for the author of the Epistle to the Hebrews (7:3). All three have been used as foils for Christ. But they are literary figures who have or have not been historicized, as the case may be.[44]

Dunn presses this point as well, saying:

> In particular, it would not be true to say that Paul's theological point here depends on Adam being a "historical" individual or on his disobedience being a historical event as such. Such an implication does not necessarily follow from the fact that a parallel is drawn with Christ's single act: an act in mythic history can be paralleled to an act in living history without the point of comparison being lost. So long as the story of Adam as the initiator of the sad tale of human failure was well known, which we may assume (the brevity of Paul's presentation presupposes such a knowledge), such a comparison was meaningful.

I am not on board with Dunn's "mythic history," as is clear in our earlier chapter on Genesis. Precisely how Genesis's depiction of Adam and Eve relates to history is not something easily knowable from the text of Genesis itself, so assigning that powerful literary text to myth goes beyond what we know. Yet Dunn's point would be the same if we were to substitute "literary Adam and Eve" in place of "mythic history."

He continues with another important point, one that counters what I hear far too often from those who think that ancient Israelites were more than a little gullible, as if they could be easily duped into believing the impossible:

> Nor should modern interpretation encourage patronizing generalizations about the primitive mind naturally understanding the Adam stories as literally

historical. It is sufficiently clear, for example, from Plutarch's account of the ways in which the Osiris myth was understood at this period (*De Iside et Osiride* 32 ff.) that such tales told about the dawn of human history could be and were treated with a considerable degree of sophistication, with the literal meaning often largely discounted. Indeed, if anything, we should say that the effect of the comparison between the two epochal figures, Adam and Christ, is not so much to historicize the individual Adam as to bring out the more than individual significance of the historic Christ.[45]

If we are to read the Bible in context, to let the Bible be *prima scriptura*, and to do so with our eyes on students of science, we will need to give far more attention than we have in the past to the various sorts of Adams and Eves the Jewish world knew. One sort that Paul didn't know because it had not yet been created was what is known today as the *historical* Adam and Eve. Literary Adam and Eve, he knew; genealogical Adam and Eve, he knew; moral, exemplary, archetypal Adam and Eve, he knew. But the *historical* Adam and Eve came into the world well after Paul himself had gone to his eternal reward, where he would have come to know them as they really are.

AFTERWORD

I've been a church minister going on thirty years, a profession I entered partly because I was inept at science. God wired my brain more for metaphysics than for physics. Nevertheless, serving a university church in Boston for many years meant a lot of time spent with members of our congregation who were research scientists from some of the best schools in the world. While I wasn't good at doing science, I was fascinated with these scientists' research and its implications for Christian faith and practice. Seeing science through a theological lens, I marveled at nature's power as God's handiwork and the creativity of the Holy Spirit displayed in everything from quarks to quasars. Unfortunately, the scientists in our congregation didn't always enjoy the same perspective. One church member, a geneticist, concentrated her research on a particular disorder that targeting a gene switch might ameliorate. I asked whether, as a geneticist, she ever took time to consider the broader implications of her work, or even what might be its spiritual ramifications for human life. No, she said, her funding only permitted her to focus on her single gene.

Since the scientists and science graduate students in our church didn't have (or take) time to think about their work theologically, I started a small group to explore the intersection of science and theology, a discipline we whimsically called "theobiology." Each week we'd ponder and pray over various aspects of genetics, molecular biology, and evolution—or at least we'd try. Most scientists who attended our church and small group had resigned themselves to compartmentalizing their faith, in large part because of the issues raised by Dennis and Scot in this book. They weren't sure how to connect their personal faith and their research. Fidelity to Scripture and to a particular hermeneutical tradition made integration a challenge, as did the practice

193

of science itself. Science leaves little room for spiritual speculation, as the spirit is not something to be quantified, directly observed, or measured. We disbanded after just a few meetings, having failed to figure out how to have a productive conversation.

Most Sundays, people in churches don't concern themselves with science any more than they worry about theological controversies. The same goes for pastors and preachers. We have so much on our plates and little stomach for controversies of our own making. Still, every now and then, when the History Channel challenges the trustworthiness of the Bible, or when the National Geographic Channel or the Discovery Channel features reports on ancient hominids and civilizations, folks will question whether science and Scripture can abide together. I know enough church history to know that theologians and scientists over the centuries enjoyed significant cooperation that advanced the understanding of both Scripture and nature. So I decided to push past imposed demarcations and my own scientific ineptitude to try to learn a few things. I wanted to help my congregation better navigate the intensifying faith-versus-science conflict for the sake of their souls and the church.

Christians hold all truth to be God's truth, implying that faith and science, despite differences when it comes to explaining *why*, nevertheless should agree in regard to *what is*. Science informs the way we interact with our world; it is an indispensable aid in fighting disease, understanding organisms and growth, safeguarding the environment, and planning for the future. Science matters, regardless of whether we care about it or subscribe to its tenets. Because science matters, it warrants theological reflection. Christianity must remain faithful to the biblical narrative as its source for theological reflection. But at the same time, Christianity should herald scientific discovery as an accurate description of the universe on which theology reflects. As reliable witnesses of nature, we can only become more reliable witnesses to God. In congregations where science is not controversial, scientific discovery can be preached gladly as a source of beauty, wonder, and praise. Observing science and Scripture entwine is a powerful testimony to the God who creates and sustains his creation.

Among the lessons I've learned is the importance of stressing the necessary distinction between scientific *data* or findings (via observation, experiment, and the evidentiary outputs of the scientific process) and the *interpretation* of scientific data. Christians have wrongly attacked data instead of the interpretation of data and their misuse. Just because science can explain a phenomenon does not mean that God's involvement is negated. The universe hardly becomes less mysterious and spiritual the more we understand it. Science's demonstration of an old earth and evolved human beings does not necessarily presume an impersonal creation or creatures stranded on our planetary dust speck. As with the Bible, hermeneutics is everything.

I once gave a TEDx talk[1] in which I attempted to show how scientific data might be understood theologically and thus genuinely encourage faith in God. Interpreters of science customarily employ adjectives such as "simple," "elegant," "beautiful," and "wondrous" to describe scientific discoveries such as human consciousness, quantum indeterminacy, or the big bang. But in the next breath, these same people ascribe the emergence of these same "wonders" to processes they label "random," "wasteful," or "purposeless." But what if these same processes interpreted as random, wasteful, and purposeless were understood from another vantage point? For instance, what if what looks like *randomness* was instead understood as *freedom*? What if nature is creatively endowed with a liberty and capacity to self-assemble as it will? This is not to suggest that nature has a mind, but its free processes do allow for life to emerge in ways that result in organisms capable of exercising a freedom of will within limits we observe and experience. Or, what if wastefulness was instead understood as *sacrifice*? The universe and humanity come about at immense cost, a cost that ascribes to them immense value (cf. John 3:16). Or, what if purposelessness was understood as *fruitfulness* or, to borrow a fancy theological word, *telos* (from the Greek meaning "ultimate aim or end")? Like it or not, to view the evolution of life is to view a progression from simplicity to complexity and eventually to a humanity with unique capabilities of reason, empathy, cooperation, wonder, and worship.

Science does stretch biblical interpretation sometimes. In such times, we appeal to the "living and active" nature of Scripture (Heb. 4:12) for flexibility. As we know, Paul contrasts Adam and Jesus five times in Romans 5, critical material when it comes to preaching and teaching about Adam, origins, original sin, the fall, and the idea of our inherited sinful nature. As descended from Adam, we humans are natural-born sinners, wired for perversity and prone to do evil. Only a second Adam can rewrite human nature. Born in the likeness of Adam, we must be *born again* into the likeness of Christ. In Jesus we inherit a new nature. However, as you've read, science currently challenges what we mean by human origins, biological inheritance, the reality of Adam, and his genealogical connection to the person of Jesus.

Throughout church history, personalities who have shaped Christian doctrine had their own beliefs shaped by encounters with observable and measurable reality. I preached a recent sermon on *origins*, but the sermon was specifically about *Origen*, the early, influential (and to some heretical) church theologian. Origen was a guard dog of the gospel, deeply committed to Scripture and a passionate defender of doctrine. I preached my sermon on

Origen after hearing Dennis give a talk on the prehistoric Denisovans who
lived alongside Neanderthals and *Homo sapiens* of the same period. DNA
evidence gathered from fossils revealed the Denisovans to be not only our ancient neighbors but also ancestors to some of us. Sequence your own genome
(which you can do these days for less than a thousand dollars) and you may
find, due to prehistoric interbreeding, traces of Neanderthal or Denisovan
DNA inside your own body. A fellow in our congregation actually did this
and discovered his own inner Neanderthal (which, according to his wife,
explained quite a bit).

Again, what this means is that, scientifically and historically speaking,
there is not a solitary point in human history where a single pair of *Homo
sapiens* suddenly appeared as purely distinct from their hominin cousins.
Trace the human tree as far back as possible, given the current diversity of
the gene pool, and there seems to be no way, aside from God supernaturally
disrupting his own evident and elegant design, for a lone pair of people to
have ever existed and from whom the entire human race as we now know it
descended. This presents a titanic theological problem for some if God is to
be considered Creator of the natural world that science observes. If the science is right, was Paul's Adam-Christ typology based on a wrong premise?
Are people not so bad after all? And if Adam and Eve, the garden, the snake,
and the tree aren't historically real, what about Jesus and the cross and his
resurrection? This book has addressed these questions.

Many Christians still blame Charles Darwin for opening the can of worms.
Our faith would be fine had he not set foot on those Galápagos Islands and
come up with his theory. But interestingly, at least as far as Adam and Eve
are concerned, Darwin was something of a latecomer to the discussion.
Questions about the Genesis account of creation appeared some 1,650 years
earlier.

Writing in the second century, Origen posed the following questions:

Who that has understanding will suppose that the first, and second, and third
day, and the evening and the morning, existed without a sun, and moon, and
stars? And that the first day was, as it were, also without a sky? And who is so
foolish as to suppose that God, after the manner of a husbandman, planted
a paradise in Eden, towards the east, and placed in it a tree of life, visible and
palpable, so that one tasting of the fruit by the bodily teeth obtained life? And
again, that one was a partaker of good and evil by masticating what was taken
from the tree? And if God is said to walk in the paradise in the evening, and
Adam to hide himself under a tree, I do not suppose that any one doubts that
these things figuratively indicate certain mysteries, the history having taken
place *in appearance, and not literally.*[2]

Origen taught that Scripture, like human beings, has multiple layers of meaning. He believed Scripture operated at three levels: the literal, the moral, and the spiritual (corresponding to body, mind, and spirit). The spiritual or allegorical level of Scripture becomes accessible to believers as they ascend in holiness and righteousness in relationship to the Trinity. The closer you are to God, the more deeply you understand his Word. The moral reading reveals principles and ethics whereby anyone might govern their life for the good, whereas the literal reading is just the words on the page—the plainest, simplest understanding. Genesis may *literally* describe God "walking in the garden" (Gen. 3:8), but with Origen we do not presume God to be a physical person here, but rather abiding alongside Adam and Eve in faithful relationship. Morally speaking, "walking" denotes faithfulness throughout Scripture, a virtue toward which all people should aspire. Allegorically speaking, God's walking highlights his faithfulness despite Adam and Eve's disobedience. Rather than walk, they run and hide, a common response of shame whenever our sin exposes us as naked.

Origen's approach reminds me of the popular inductive Bible-study method on which I was weaned as a young Christian. It had me ask when I came to any verse, "What does it *say*, what does it *mean*, and what does it mean *to me*?" Origen would have recognized this method as akin to his own tripartite approach—the words as they appear to the eye or sound to the ear (literal), their meaning as it is understood by the mind (moral), and their power as the "word of God" as they affect the soul (spiritual).

Interpreting the Bible is not easy. As Scot demonstrates, taking into account the languages, contexts, and presumed intents from centuries ago is a lot like, well, paleontology. Again, when explaining the challenges science presents to Christian faith, I stress the important distinction between scientific findings (e.g., DNA in a Siberian cave) and the philosophical or theological interpretations of those findings (*Homo sapiens* therefore emerged by sheer luck of the genome, *or* God operates on a circuitous route not unlike wandering in the wilderness to get to the promised land).

Scientists agree on the genetic composition of an ancient bone or tooth, but they can diverge over its significance, especially when it comes to broader applications to modern humanity and its meaning and purpose. Similarly with theologians and biblical scholars: the Bible contains in its Hebrew, Aramaic, and Greek words the most dependable text in antiquity. We are very confident that the texts we have in our manuscript bank are very nearly what we would have if an archaeologist ever unearthed Mark's actual Gospel or a letter written with Paul's hand. But despite the consistent reliability of words on a papyrus, potsherd, or palimpsest, there is frequent inconsistency and disagreement over their meaning, as proliferating theologies and denominations attest. Theologians and preachers, like philosophers of science and doctors, have wrestled with interpretation and application for centuries. Data are data, findings are findings, texts are texts, but what these data and texts *mean* is where the arguments erupt. Humans care about meaning.

Origen wrote, "As the eye naturally seeks the light and vision, and our body naturally desires food and drink, so our mind is possessed with a becoming and natural desire to become acquainted with the truth of God and the causes of things."[3] As to the "causes" and "truth" pertaining to Adam and Eve, it is true that, like the apostle Paul before him, Origen likely considered the first parents to have been actual persons, despite his reservations about other aspects of Genesis. The first centuries AD had no access to DNA, biology, fossil evidence, or any theory of human evolution to call such a conviction into question. Like that of everyone else a century before Origen, Paul's likely understanding of Adam as the personal cause of all human sin reflected his first-century cultural assumptions. The good news—or honestly, the bad news—is that removing a specific, real person named Adam doesn't remove sin and death. Everyone still does wrong. Everyone certainly dies. All of us fail and cause harm to ourselves and to others, sometimes with horrific destruction and collateral damage. If a prehistoric Adam is not the first man and first cause of sin and death as Paul regarded him, Paul's theology is not diminished. Sin and death remain self-evident and irrefutable facts of human existence.

But what about the other side of the salvation equation? If geneticists, anthropologists, paleontologists, chemists, and biologists have it right about the unlikelihood of a living and breathing first *Homo sapiens* couple, what about Jesus as a real person? If an inspired Paul can't get Adam's biology straight, how do we know he's right about Jesus? Here's where the worries about slippery slopes, falling dominoes, and descending staircases emerge.

I've always appreciated that while Adam and Jesus are the two sides of Paul's salvation equation, they are not equal historically. Adam was known to Paul only through hundreds of years of religious and cultural transmission as a figure of Jewish theology and archetypal significance. But Jesus and his resurrection were recent realities and a personal experience for Paul, occurring in Jerusalem only twenty-five years or so before he wrote the Letter to the Romans. Admitting to historical and scientific problems with Paul's Adam does not undermine the gospel message. A specially selected representative Adam would work, as Scot has ably shown. Some make a literary Adam work too. But there's no need to worry about Jesus. Critics may take issue with his walking on water and rising from the dead, but no serious historian or scientist denies that Jesus lived as a flesh-and-blood human being.

At the academic meeting where Dennis gave his talk on the Denisovans, many in the room admitted that current theological debates would diminish if Christians would stop trying to run Scripture through a scientific grid and let the Bible do what the Bible does best. We could afford a little more Origen in our day, allowing our souls to be nourished by a broader and more deeply layered reading of the Word, which for Origen was Jesus himself speaking. Moreover, as anyone who's read Jesus's own words knows, you can't take everything he says literally. "Be born again," "Eat my flesh and drink my blood," "Cut off your hand if it causes you to sin"—we know that all these phrases and others like them figuratively bespeak potent truths for which preposterous obstetrics, cannibalism, vampires, or bodily dismemberment would be totally missing the point.

At the same time, there are plenty of areas of theological agreement among Christians—say, the ubiquity of sin (if not its causes) and the loving grace of God. Still, even where theological or doctrinal agreement occurs, circumstances and situations affect how doctrines are applied. Even if I hold that whoever believes in Jesus has eternal life (John 3:16), I'm not going to presume to know the heart of a deceased person who reportedly rejected Jesus and never darkened the door of a church if I'm asked to preach his funeral homily. I'll stress instead the all-knowing mercy and love of God. We ministers recognize space not only between text and interpretation but also between interpretation and application, between the theological and the pastoral. Genesis names Adam and Eve as real people in the creation account. Even if they aren't the first humans (or even real), as paleontology, genetics, and critical exegesis of Genesis purport, this doesn't mean I wouldn't appeal to Adam and Eve when preaching about sin and disobedience. It'd be the same as when I preach from Jesus's parables: the prodigal son and the good Samaritan don't have to be actual people for the parables to have their power.

Interestingly, the space that exists between text, interpretation, and application for Christians can be found in science between theory, experiment, and practice. Research data and their application by doctors are fraught with ambiguity. Because circumstances, situations, and individuals can differ widely, what applies in one case often does not automatically work in another. I awoke one morning to tingling in my face and fingers and fainted for the first time in my life. Though I came to immediately, I went to my doctor, who just as immediately rushed me to the hospital for an MRI—to the tune of $6,000. In the medical world, tingling equals stroke, even though I told my doctor I felt the sensation on both sides of my body instead of just one. The MRI came back clear, as did my cardiology workup (another $3,000). A $45 blood test later found the culprit: a vitamin B-12 deficiency, remedied by $4.99 in supplements from the drugstore. I'm feeling physically better, if economically poorer. It was much ado over something that should have been less.

Then again, when it comes to our faith, as with our health, what seems like nothing can mean everything. It's why we go see doctors. It's why people see pastors too. Years ago, after I gave a talk on science and faith, a young man approached and described his own loss of faith as a result of an encounter with biology. His theology and upbringing were not equipped to embrace what he heard as an onslaught of contrary scientific evidence. When push came to shove, he had to go with the science. As a pastor of a university church, I was accustomed to students getting slammed by biology and stumbling in wounded and needing reassurance that God still existed. I saw so much of this that I now insist on giving a talk on science and faith to our youth groups every year. It's one thing to assure people that God is still there, but it's more important to help them consider whether to understand God differently, and if so, how. And yet throughout Scripture, people are always coming up against a God who defies their expectations: from Moses atop Mount Sinai, to Jesus's own disciples, to Paul on the Damascus Road and Revelation's John on Patmos. God regularly revealed himself in ways that even the most faithful found hard to believe—and rightly so. Christianity is not fantasy fiction or a fairy tale. Our faith in God who creates and redeems is grounded in the reality of things as they truly are rather than in how we wish and want them to be.

Daniel Harrell
Senior Minister, Colonial Church
Edina, Minnesota

NOTES

Chapter 1 Evolution as a Scientific Theory

1. John Bohannon, "I Fooled Millions into Thinking Chocolate Helps Weight Loss. Here's How," *Gizmodo*, May 27, 2015, http://io9.gizmodo.com/i-fooled-millions-into-thinking -chocolate-helps-weight-1707251800.

2. Ibid.

3. Another notable example is Carl Zimmer, who writes for the *New York Times* and contributes to *National Geographic*, among other publications. Carl has also coauthored a highly respected textbook on evolutionary biology.

4. For an excellent discussion of the "two books" metaphor, I recommend Deborah B. Haarsma and Loren D. Haarsma, *Origins: Christian Perspectives on Creation, Evolution, and Intelligent Design* (Grand Rapids: Faith Alive Christian Resources, 2011).

5. Isaac Newton, *The Mathematical Principles of Natural Philosophy*, trans. Andrew Motte, 2 vols. (London: Printed for Benjamin Motte at the Middle-Temple-Gate in Fleetstreet, 1729), 2:388–89. Online at https://newtonprojectca.files.wordpress.com/2013/06/newton-general-scholium -1729-english-text-by-motte-letter-size.pdf.

6. John Edwards, *A Demonstration of the Existence and Providence of God from the Contemplation of the Visible Structure of the Greater and Lesser World* (London: Jonathan Robinson, 1696), 33–35. Note that John Edwards is not the same individual as the famous colonial American theologian Jonathan Edwards.

7. Ibid., 45–47.

8. The verse in question is 1 Tim. 6:20, which reads in the King James Version as follows: "O Timothy, keep that which is committed to thy trust, avoiding profane and vain babblings, and oppositions of science falsely so called." This, of course, has nothing to do with evolutionary biology, but it has commonly been employed in attempting to disparage it.

9. Those interested in reading about my "evolutionary conversion experience" can find my story, along with many others, in Kathryn Applegate and J. B. Stump, eds., *How I Changed My Mind about Evolution: Evangelicals Reflect on Faith and Science* (Downers Grove, IL: InterVarsity, 2016).

10. A famous example of a species with features that blur the distinction between "fish" and "amphibian" is *Tiktaalik roseae* (http://tiktaalik.uchicago.edu), though other, similar species are known.

11. For an engaging narrative of the search for and discovery of this species, *Tiktaalik roseae*, see Neil Shubin, *Your Inner Fish: A Journey into the 3.5-Billion-Year History of the Human Body* (New York: Pantheon, 2008).

12. This text is found in chap. 6 of the first edition of Charles Darwin's *On the Origin of Species by Means of Natural Selection* (London: John Murray, 1859), 184. It was subsequently reduced in later editions. See below.

13. Robert Benton Seeley, *Essays on the Bible* (London: Seeley, Jackson & Halliday, 1870), 231.

14. See "On the Origin of Species," Darwin Online, http://darwin-online.org.uk/Editorial Introductions/Freeman_OntheOriginofSpecies.html, for an excellent discussion of the various editions of Darwin's *Origin of Species*.

15. Richard Harlan, "Notice of Fossil Bones Found in the Tertiary Formation of the State of Louisiana," *Transactions of the American Philosophical Society* 4 (1834): 397–403.

16. Richard Owen, "Observations on the *Basilosaurus* of Dr. Harlan (*Zeuglodon cetoides*, Owen)," *Transactions of the Geological Society of London* 6 (1841): 69–79.

17. As we will see in chap. 4, intelligent-design proponent Michael Behe once used the lack of transitional whale fossils as an illustration of gaps in evolutionary science, gaps he still claims for other areas where less is known.

18. J. G. M. Thewissen, Lisa Noelle Cooper, John C. George, and Sunil Bajpai, "From Land to Water: The Origin of Whales, Dolphins, and Porpoises," *Evolution: Education and Outreach* 2 (2009): 272–88.

19. J. G. M. Thewissen, Lisa Noelle Cooper, Mark T. Clementz, Sunil Bajpai, and B. N. Tiwari, "Whales Originated from Aquatic Artiodactyls in the Eocene Epoch of India," *Nature* 450 (2007): 1190–94.

20. Thewissen et al., "From Land to Water." The YouTube video "Eagle vs. Water Chevrotain" shows the remarkable behavior of this species (https://www.youtube.com/watch?v=13GQb T2ljxs). This video remains available as of August 2016.

21. For an excellent review of cetacean evolution, see Thewissen et al., "From Land to Water."

22. J. G. M. Thewissen, M. J. Cohn, L. S. Stevens, S. Bajpai, J. Heyning, and W. E. Horton Jr., "Developmental Basis for Hind Limb Loss in Dolphins and the Origin of the Cetacean Body Plan," *Proceedings of the National Academy of Sciences of the United States of America* 103 (2006): 8414–18.

Chapter 2 Genomes as Language, Genomes as Books

1. The Chimpanzee Sequencing and Analysis Consortium, "Initial Sequence of the Chimpanzee Genome and Comparison with the Human Genome," *Nature* 437 (2005): 69–87.

2. Yoav Gilad, Orna Man, Svante Pääbo, and Doron Lancet, "Human Specific Loss of Olfactory Receptor Genes," *Proceedings of the National Academy of Sciences of the United States of America* 100 (2003): 3324–27.

3. Actually, we do expect them, but for reasons that we will not address until chap. 3. There we will discuss how such "incorrect pattern" mutations are useful for another purpose: estimating population sizes as lineages undergo speciation events.

4. Tom Mueller, "Valley of the Whales," *National Geographic*, August 2010, http://ngm .nationalgeographic.com/2010/08/whale-evolution/mueller-text (requires subscription).

5. See Dennis Venema, "Evolution Basics: Convergent Evolution and Deep Homology" (and references therein), *Letters to the Duchess* (blog), August 15, 2013, http://biologos.org /blogs/dennis-venema-letters-to-the-duchess/evolution-basics-convergent-evolution-and-deep -homology.

6. David Brawand, Walter Wahli, and Henrik Kaessmann, "Loss of Egg Yolk Genes in Mammals and the Origin of Lactation and Placentation," *PLOS Biology* 6 (2008): 507–17.

7. Ibid.

8. Ibid.

9. Todd, a geneticist, is quite up-front about the difficulties that comparative genomics pose for special creationism.

10. Todd C. Wood, "The Truth about Evolution," *Todd's Blog*, September 30, 2009, http://toddcwood.blogspot.ca/2009/09/truth-about-evolution.html.

11. Todd's approach is exemplified in his 2006 paper comparing the human and chimpanzee genomes. It is unique among the young-earth literature in that it is thoroughly accurate and does not misrepresent the data: Todd C. Wood, "The Chimpanzee Genome and the Problem of Biological Similarity," *Occasional Papers of the BSG* 7 (2006): 1–18.

Chapter 3 Adam's Last Stand?

1. I'm happy to report, some five years on, that the answer to these questions was an emphatic yes.

2. Richard N. Ostling, "The Search for the Historical Adam," *Christianity Today*, June 3, 2011, http://www.christianitytoday.com/ct/2011/june/historicaladam.html.

3. Dennis Venema, "Genesis and the Genome: Genomics Evidence for Human-Ape Common Ancestry and Ancestral Hominid Population Sizes," *Perspectives on Science and Christian Faith* 62 (2010): 166–78.

4. Dennis Venema and Darrel Falk, "Does Genetics Point to a Single Primal Couple?," *Letters to the Duchess* (blog), April 5, 2010, http://biologos.org/blogs/dennis-venema-letters-to-the-duchess/does-genetics-point-to-a-single-primal-couple.

5. Barbara Bradley Hagerty, "Evangelicals Question the Existence of Adam and Eve," National Public Radio, August 9, 2011, http://www.npr.org/2011/08/09/138957812/evangelicals-question-the-existence-of-adam-and-eve.

6. One of the quirks of being a biologist in the science-faith sphere is that often the questions one gets are theological, not scientific. I've often given a lengthy talk on evolutionary biology only to be faced with theological questions afterward. I hear from my theologian friends that the converse is often true for them.

7. Of course, this refers to sexually reproducing species that have two copies of every sequence, like humans do (i.e., one inherited from their mother and the other from their father). Such species are called "diploid." Species with only one copy of their DNA are called "haploid," and for these species any given member can hold only one variant of each sequence.

8. Katrina Morris, Jeremy J. Austin, and Katherine Belov, "Low Major Histocompatibility Complex Diversity in the Tasmanian Devil Predates European Settlement and May Explain Susceptibility to Disease Epidemics," *Biology Letters* 9 (2013), http://rsbl.royalsocietypublishing.org/content/roybiolett/9/1/20120900.full.pdf.

9. See, for example, Vern S. Poythress, "Adam versus Claims from Genetics," *Westminster Theological Journal* 75 (2013): 65–82. I have responded to Poythress (and others) on this issue at length in Dennis Venema, "Adam, Eve, and Human Population Genetics" (blog series), *Letters to the Duchess* (blog), November 12, 2014–December 14, 2015, http://biologos.org/blogs/dennis-venema-letters-to-the-duchess/series/adam-eve-and-human-population-genetics.

10. Those familiar with the young-earth creationist literature will see clear parallels here with their arguments for accelerated radioactive decay, or that the speed of light was once infinite just after creation 6,000–10,000 years ago.

11. Albert Tenesa, Pau Navarro, Ben J. Hayes, David L. Duffy, Geraldine M. Clarke, Mike E. Goddard, and Peter M. Visscher, "Recent Human Effective Population Size Estimated from Linkage Disequilibrium," *Genome Research* 17, no. 4 (2007): 520–26.

12. Ibid.

13. Heng Li and Richard Durbin, "Inference of Human Population History from Individual Whole-Genome Sequences," *Nature* 475 (2011): 493–96.

14. See Dennis Venema, "Evolution Basics: Incomplete Lineage Sorting and Ancestral Population Sizes" (and references therein), *Letters to the Duchess* (blog), August 1, 2013, http://

biologos.org/blogs/dennis-venema-letters-to-the-duchess/evolution-basics-incomplete-lineage
-sorting-and-ancestral-population-sizes.

15. Some readers might be familiar with Mitochondrial Eve, the most recent common female ancestor of all humans, who lived about 180,000 years ago in Africa. It is indeed true that all living humans have her as a common ancestor, *and* that we descend from a large population. Many Christian antievolutionary organizations attempt to portray Mitochondrial Eve as evidence that all humans descend from a single couple, but this is misleading. We will address the relevant science later in this chapter.

16. That said, so much effort has been expended to look for species closely related to humans that it is quite likely we have identified species that *are* our direct ancestors. Unless one can recover DNA from the remains, however, it is not possible to definitively identify direct ancestors.

17. Charles Darwin, *On the Origin of Species by Means of Natural Selection* (London: John Murray, 1859), 488.

18. See also Dennis Venema, "Evolution Basics: From Primate to Human, Part 2," *Letters to the Duchess* (blog), January 23, 2014, http://biologos.org/blogs/dennis-venema-letters-to-the-duchess /evolution-basics-from-primate-to-human-part-2.

19. Ibid.

20. See also Dennis Venema, "Evolution Basics: From Primate to Human, Part 4," *Letters to the Duchess* (blog), February 27, 2014, http://biologos.org/blogs/dennis-venema-letters-to-the-duchess /evolution-basics-from-primate-to-human-part-4.

21. C. Owen Lovejoy, "Reexamining Human Origins in Light of *Ardipithecus ramidus*," *Science* 326 (2009): 87–94.

22. Gen Suwa, Berhane Asfaw, Reiko T. Kono, Daisuke Kubo, C. Owen Lovejoy, and Tim D. White, "The *Ardipithecus ramidus* Skull and Its Implications for Hominid Origins," *Science* 326 (2009): 45–51.

23. William L. Jungers, "Lucy's Limbs: Skeletal Allometry and Locomotion in *Australopithecus afarensis*," *Nature* 297 (1982): 676–78.

24. Dean Falk, John C. Redmond Jr., John Guyer, Glenn C. Conroy, Wolfgang Recheis, Gerhard W. Weber, and Horst Seidler, "Early Hominid Brain Evolution: A New Look at Old Endocasts," *Journal of Human Evolution* 38 (2000): 695–717.

25. Venema, "Evolution Basics: From Primate to Human, Part 4"; see also Bernard Wood and Nicholas Lonergan, "The Hominin Fossil Record: Taxa, Grades and Clades," *Journal of Anatomy* 212 (2008): 354–76.

26. Wood and Lonergan, "Hominin Fossil Record."

27. Lee R. Berger et al., "*Homo naledi*, a New Species of the Genus *Homo* from the Dinaledi Chamber, South Africa," *eLife* 4 (2015), doi:10.7554/eLife.09560.

28. Craig D. Millar and David M. Lambert, "Ancient DNA: Towards a Million-Year-Old Genome," *Nature* 499 (2013): 34–35.

29. Richard E. Green et al., "A Draft Sequence of the Neandertal Genome," *Science* 328 (2010): 710–22.

30. Yes, lions and tigers can interbreed, even though all biologists hold them to be distinct species. Both "tiglons" (progeny of a male tiger mated with a female lion) and "ligers" (the converse) are out there, and pictures are only a short Google search away.

31. Matthias Meyer et al., "A High-Coverage Genome Sequence from an Archaic Denisovan Individual," *Science* 338 (2012): 222–26.

32. Ibid. See also Dennis Venema, "Neanderthals, Humans and Interbreeding: Old Bones, New Evidence" (and references therein), *Letters to the Duchess* (blog), July 3, 2015, http://biologos .org/blogs/dennis-venema-letters-to-the-duchess/neanderthals-humans-and-interbreeding-old -bones-new-evidence.

33. Venema, "Neanderthals, Humans and Interbreeding."

34. See also Dennis Venema, "Mitochondrial Eve, Y-chromosome Adam, and Reasons to Believe," *Letters to the Duchess* (blog), October 28, 2011, http://biologos.org/blogs/dennis-venema-letters-to-the-duchess/mitochondrial-eve-y-chromosome-adam-and-reasons-to-believe.

35. Interestingly, the mitochondrial genome uses its own ribosomes, which are slightly different from the ribosomes encoded in the nuclear genome. These ribosomes, however, are very similar to bacterial ribosomes. Other lines of DNA evidence similarly point to a bacterial origin for mitochondria in the very distant past (and a photosynthetic bacterial origin for chloroplasts in plants). These subcellular compartments with their own genomes seem to have once been free-living bacteria that were engulfed and incorporated into the single-celled ancestors of plant and animal life.

36. I work through an example with a much larger pedigree in "Mitochondrial Eve," showing the loss of several Y-chromosome and mitochondrial DNA variants over time.

37. For example, the old-earth creationist organization Reasons to Believe. See Venema, "Mitochondrial Eve."

38. The main problem is that, to date, no one in the creationist camp writing about these data seems to understand the evidence, much less has the ability to credibly undermine it. See Todd C. Wood, "Poythress on the Adam Debate," *Todd's Blog*, May 28, 2013, http://toddcwood.blogspot.ca/2013/05/poythress-on-adam-debate.html.

39. We will examine other claims from the intelligent-design movement in the next chapter.

40. The November 29, 2014, edition of *World* magazine ran a cover story entitled "Soft-Sell Slide" and cover art depicting people (one wearing a lab coat) pulling a church building down a slope with ropes. This quote comes from Daniel Levine's article "Interpretive Dance" in this issue. See https://world.wng.org/2014/11/interpretive_dance.

41. Wood, "Poythress on the Adam Debate."

Chapter 4 What about Intelligent Design?

1. Charles Darwin, *On the Origin of Species by Means of Natural Selection* (London: John Murray, 1859), 481–82.

2. Dietrich Bonhoeffer, *Letters and Papers from Prison*, enlarged ed., trans. Reginald Fuller et al. (New York: Macmillan, 1972), 311.

3. Though later I would realize that an understanding of evolutionary biology would have given me a deeper appreciation for what I was studying.

4. While all Christians believe that God is the designer (and creator) of all that is, and that he is (obviously) intelligent, this general view is not what is intended by the intelligent-design (ID) movement. The main claim of ID is that certain features in the natural world show the marks of design in the sense that they cannot be accounted for by "natural" mechanisms such as evolution. In this sense, ID has a high degree of similarity to standard Christian antievolutionary claims—indeed, there are no claims within ID that are not also made by overtly Christian, antievolutionary groups. Though the ID movement is not uniformly Christian, many of its leaders identify as such and name God as the designer.

5. Michael Behe, *Darwin's Black Box: The Biochemical Challenge to Evolution* (New York: Free Press, 1996), 39.

6. Ibid., 40.

7. Ibid., 193. Using the word "purposeful" may be begging the question somewhat, of course, since Behe is attempting to detect design (purpose) in biochemical structures.

8. Michael Behe, "Reply to My Critics: A Response to Reviews of *Darwin's Black Box: The Biochemical Challenge to Evolution*," *Biology and Philosophy* 16 (2001): 685–709.

9. Michael Behe, "Experimental Support for Regarding Functional Classes of Proteins to Be Highly Isolated from Each Other," in *Darwinism: Science or Philosophy*, Proceedings of a symposium entitled "Darwinism: Scientific Inference or Philosophical Preference?," ed. Jon

Buell and Virginia Hearn (Southern Methodist University, Dallas, Texas, March 26–28, 1992). Online at http://www.leaderu.com/orgs/fte/darwinism/chapter6.html.

10. Sidi Chen, Yong E. Zhang, and Manyuan Long, "New Genes in *Drosophila* Quickly Become Essential," *Science* 330 (2010): 1682–85. See also Dennis Venema, "The Evolutionary Origins of Irreducible Complexity, Part 2," *Letters to the Duchess* (blog), May 11, 2012, http://biologos.org/blogs /dennis-venema-letters-to-the-duchess/the-evolutionary-origins-of-irreducible-complexity-part-2.

11. Michael Behe, "At BioLogos, Confusion over the Meaning of 'Irreducibly Complex,'" *Evolution News*, July 9, 2012, http://www.evolutionnews.org/2012/07/at_biologos_con061851.html.

12. I suppose one could say that the designer chose to design organisms with the *appearance* of having evolved, but there is no way to test that hypothesis apart from testing for evidence of evolution.

13. Sarah P. Otto and Jeannette Whitton, "Polyploid Incidence and Evolution," *Annual Review of Genetics* 34 (2000): 401–37.

14. Paramvir Dehal and Jeffrey L. Boore, "Two Rounds of Whole Genome Duplication in the Ancestral Vertebrate," *PLOS Biology* 3, no. 10 (2005), doi:10.1371/journal.pbio.0030314.

15. Ibid.

16. Transcripts of the Kitzmiller case are archived at the National Center for Science Education, http://ncse.com/creationism/legal/kitzmiller-trial-transcripts.

17. See the trial transcript at The TalkOrigins Archive, http://www.talkorigins.org/faqs /dover/day12pm.html.

18. Justin R. Meyer, Devin T. Dobias, Joshua S. Weitz, Jeffrey E. Barrick, Ryan T. Quick, and Richard E. Lenski, "Repeatability and Contingency in the Evolution of a Key Innovation in Phage Lambda," *Science* 335 (2012): 428–32. Note that Justin Meyer is not ID proponent Stephen Meyer.

19. Meyer's two main books to date are *Signature in the Cell: DNA and the Evidence for Intelligent Design* (New York: HarperOne, 2009) and *Darwin's Doubt: The Explosive Origin of Animal Life and the Case for Intelligent Design* (New York: HarperOne, 2013).

20. Meyer, *Darwin's Doubt*, 221.

21. Ibid., 223.

22. Douglas D. Axe, "Estimating the Prevalence of Protein Sequences Adopting Functional Enzyme Folds," *Journal of Molecular Biology* 341, no. 5 (2004): 1295–315.

23. Meyer, *Darwin's Doubt*, 226.

24. For a discussion of these issues, see also Arthur Hunt, "Axe (2004) and the Evolution of Enzyme Function," *The Panda's Thumb* (blog), January 14, 2007, http://www.pandasthumb .org/archives/2007/01/92-second-st-fa.html.

25. Seiji Negoro, Tomoyasu Taniguchi, Masaharu Kanaoka, Hiroyuki Kimura, and Hirosuke Okada, "Plasmid-Determined Enzymatic Degradation of Nylon Oligomers," *Journal of Bacteriology* 155 (1983): 22–31.

26. Susumu Ohno, "Birth of a Unique Enzyme from an Alternative Reading Frame of the Preexisted, Internally Repetitious Coding Sequence," *Proceedings of the National Academy of Sciences of the United States of America* 81, no. 8 (1984): 2421–25. See also Dennis Venema, "Intelligent Design and Nylon-Eating Bacteria," *Letters to the Duchess* (blog), April 7, 2016, http://biologos .org/blogs/dennis-venema-letters-to-the-duchess/intelligent-design-and-nylon-eating-bacteria.

27. Ohno, "Birth of a Unique Enzyme." See also Seiji Negoro, Taku Ohki, Naoki Shibata, Nobuhiro Mizuno, Yoshiaki Wakitani, Junya Tsurukame, Keiji Matsumoto, Ichitaro Kawamoto, Masahiro Takeo, and Yoshiki Higuchi, "X-ray Crystallographic Analysis of 6-Aminohexanoate-Dimer Hydrolase: Molecular Basis for the Birth of a Nylon Oligomer-Degrading Enzyme," *Journal of Biological Chemistry* 47 (2005): 39644–52.

28. Negoro et al., "X-ray Crystallographic Analysis."

29. Readers closely following the ID conversation may recall that I pointed out this example to Meyer in 2010 when I reviewed his book *Signature in the Cell* (Venema, "Seeking a Signature: Essay Book Review of *Signature in the Cell: DNA and the Evidence for Intelligent Design* by

Stephen C. Meyer," *Perspectives on Science and Christian Faith* 62 [2010]: 276–83). To my knowledge Meyer has not addressed this evidence.

30. Meyer, *Darwin's Doubt*, 221. I admit I am unsure why Meyer thinks that "*de novo* origination" means "unexplained." As we will see, "de novo" genes do not arise out of thin air—they come from sequences that were very close to becoming transcribed and translated and became so with only a few small mutation events. Meyer either does not understand this (in which case one wonders why he is writing a book about it), or he does understand it (in which case he is misrepresenting the evidence to his readers). That Meyer also refers to de novo origination as "unexplained jumps" suggests that the former explanation is more likely.

31. Jorge Ruiz-Orera, Jessica Hernandez-Rodriguez, Cristina Chiva, Eduard Sabidó, Ivanela Kondova, Ronald Bontrop, Tomàs Marqués-Bonet, and M. Mar Albà, "Origins of *De Novo* Genes in Human and Chimpanzee," *PLOS Genetics* 11, no. 2 (2015), doi:10.1371/journal.pgen.1005721.

32. Qi Zhou, Guojie Zhang, Yue Zhang, Shiyu Xu, Ruoping Zhao, Zubing Zhan, Xin Li, Yun Ding, Shuang Yang, and Wen Wang, "On the Origin of New Genes in *Drosophila*," *Genome Research* 18 (2008): 1446–55.

33. Indeed, the major point of the whole "no new genes / folds" discussion in Meyer's *Darwin's Doubt* is to try to convince his readers that the innovation seen in the Cambrian fossil record requires divine input.

34. Indeed, Meyer strongly criticized me for apparently missing this point when I reviewed his *Signature in the Cell* in 2010. In that article, I critiqued his failure to address how evolutionary processes add information to genomes (Venema, "Seeking a Signature"). For Meyer's rebuttal, see Meyer, "Of Molecules and (Straw) Men: A Response to Dennis Venema's Review of *Signature in the Cell*," *Perspectives on Science and Christian Faith* 63 (2011): 171–82. For my response to his rebuttal, see Venema, "Intelligent Design, Abiogenesis, and Learning from History: A Reply to Meyer," *Perspectives on Science and Christian Faith* 63 (2011): 183–92.

35. Meyer, *Signature in the Cell*, 248.

36. Ibid., 247.

37. Michael Yarus, Jeremy Joseph Widmann, and Rob Knight, "RNA–Amino Acid Binding: A Stereochemical Era for the Genetic Code," *Journal of Molecular Evolution* 69 (2009): 406–29.

38. Meyer has attempted to refute the work of Yarus and his colleagues by claiming that the binding affinities observed between some amino acids and their codons or anticodons are merely an artifact of Yarus's experimental design. Meyer published this claim in the online, in-house ID journal *BIO-Complexity* in 2011. See Stephen Meyer and Paul Nelson, "Can the Origin of the Genetic Code Be Explained by Direct DNA Templating?," *BIO-Complexity* 2 (2011): 1–10, doi:10.5048/BIO-C.2011. This claim, however, is not supported by the evidence that Yarus and his colleagues present in their numerous publications. Moreover, since 2009 other independent research groups have built on the work of Yarus and his colleagues, confirming that the observed binding affinities are indeed real and not spurious. One notable example is the discovery that within the ribosome, which is a complex of RNA and proteins, amino acids in the protein component are preferentially located close to their anticodons on the RNA component. This observation supports the hypothesis that the ribosome complex comes from a time in biological history when such binding affinities were important. See David Johnson and Lei Wang, "Imprints of the Genetic Code in the Ribosome," *Proceedings of the National Academy of Sciences of the United States of America* 107 (2013): 8298–303. Meyer and Nelson do not address or mention this research in their attempted rebuttal.

39. Ard Louis used this example in an interview with *Socrates in the City* (https://vimeo.com/153015977).

40. Darwin, *Origin of Species*, 490.

41. See Venema, "Intelligent Design, Abiogenesis, and Learning from History." The ID movement has progressively shifted away from arguments as new evidence comes in, forcing a retreat into areas where less is known.

Chapter 5 Adam, Eve, and the Genome: Four Principles for Reading the Bible after the Human Genome Project

1. For the history of this encounter, a story told often and by many and one that far too often has degenerated into hardened extremes (we believe in God, we believe in science) and plenty of name-calling (heretic, Darwinist, etc.), I recommend Ronald Hendel, *The Book of "Genesis": A Biography*, Lives of Great Religious Books (Princeton: Princeton University Press, 2012). For more extensive description, I recommend these scholarly treatments: David N. Livingstone, *Adam's Ancestors: Race, Religion, and the Politics of Human Origins* (Baltimore: Johns Hopkins University Press, 2011); Livingstone, *Dealing with Darwin: Place, Politics, and Rhetoric in Religious Engagements with Evolution*, Medicine, Science, and Religion in Historical Context (Baltimore: Johns Hopkins University Press, 2014); Bradley J. Gundlach, *Process and Providence: The Evolution Question at Princeton, 1845–1929* (Grand Rapids: Eerdmans, 2013); Monte Harrell Hampton, *Storm of Words: Science, Religion, and Evolution in the Civil War Era* (Tuscaloosa: University of Alabama Press, 2014).

2. All three quotations are from Luther's *Lectures on Genesis* (1.125, 123, 131), as quoted in Hendel, *Book of "Genesis,"* 126. It is well known that St. Augustine (Luther himself was an Augustinian monk) took the opposite tack across the rough seas of science conflicting with the Bible. See Augustine, *The Literal Meaning of Genesis*, 2 vols., trans. J. H. Taylor (New York: Paulist Press, 1982), 1:42–43.

3. Quoted in Hendel, *Book of "Genesis,"* 162.

4. For a wonderful collection of approaches, see S. C. Barton and David Wilkinson, eds., *Reading Genesis after Darwin* (New York: Oxford University Press, 2009).

5. For what it's worth, and I am not a scientist, I line up most comfortably with the view Gerald Rau calls "planned evolution." See Gerald Rau, *Mapping the Origins Debate: Six Models of the Beginning of Everything* (Downers Grove, IL: IVP Academic, 2013), 45–46. For scientists, see Simon Conway Morris, *Life's Solution: Inevitable Humans in a Lonely Universe* (New York: Cambridge University Press, 2004); Francis S. Collins, *The Language of God: A Scientist Presents Evidence for Belief* (New York: Free Press, 2007); Denis Alexander, *Creation or Evolution: Do We Have to Choose?*, rev. ed. (Oxford: Monarch Books, 2014). See also Denis O. Lamoureux, "No Historical Adam: Evolutionary Creation View," in *Four Views on the Historical Adam*, ed. Matthew Barrett and Ardel Caneday (Grand Rapids: Zondervan, 2013), 37–65, with the response by John Walton on pp. 66–71.

6. In what follows, I use Gen. 1–2 for the creation stories, Gen. 1–3 for the story of Adam and Eve through the so-called fall, and Gen. 1–11 for the "prologue" to Gen. 12–50, the larger narrative into which it is placed.

7. L. Duane Thurman, *How to Think about Evolution and Other Bible-Science Controversies*, 2nd ed. (Downers Grove, IL: InterVarsity, 1978); Adrian Desmond and James Moore, *Darwin: The Life of a Tormented Evolutionist* (New York: W. W. Norton, 1994).

8. Dennis R. Venema, "Genesis and the Genome: Genomics Evidence for Human-Ape Common Ancestry and Ancestral Hominid Population Sizes," *Perspectives on Science and Christian Faith* 62, no. 3 (2010): 166–78; Daniel C. Harlow, "After Adam: Reading Genesis in an Age of Evolutionary Science," *Perspectives on Science and Christian Faith* 62 (2010): 179–95.

9. My go-to book for nonscientists like me is Edward J. Larson, *Evolution: The Remarkable History of a Scientific Theory* (New York: Modern Library, 2006).

10. For the translation of the names Cain and Abel, see Matthew Richard Schlimm, *This Strange and Sacred Scripture: Wrestling with the Old Testament and Its Oddities* (Grand Rapids: Baker Academic, 2015), 19.

11. Genesis 1–11 is some kind of "theological history" when it comes to genre, here history and there theology, and that theological history is directly engaged with other sorts of theological histories in the ancient Near East. For an exceptional introduction to the genre of the opening chapters of Genesis, see ibid., 12–27. For a recent book addressing different views of

the genre of Gen. 1–11, see James K. Hoffmeier, Gordon John Wenham, and Kenton Sparks, *Genesis: History, Fiction, or Neither? Three Views on the Bible's Earliest Chapters*, ed. Charles Halton, Counterpoints (Grand Rapids: Zondervan, 2015). I side at times with Wenham and at other times with Sparks in this discussion.

12. Hendel, *Book of "Genesis,"* 6.

13. Ibid., 11.

14. Two important resources for the ancient Near Eastern evidence are Richard J. Clifford, ed., *Creation Accounts in the Ancient Near East and in the Bible* (Washington, DC: Catholic Biblical Association of America, 1994); John H. Walton, *Genesis 1 as Ancient Cosmology* (Winona Lake, IN: Eisenbrauns, 2011). For an innovative and pastoral approach to Gen. 1 as well as to Gen. 2–3 in light of the ancient Near Eastern context, I recommend John H. Walton, *The Lost World of Genesis One: Ancient Cosmology and the Origins Debate* (Downers Grove, IL: InterVarsity, 2009); Walton, *The Lost World of Adam and Eve: Genesis 2–3 and the Human Origins Debate* (Downers Grove, IL: IVP Academic, 2015).

15. For solid expositions of God as Creator, see the recent studies of David Fergusson, *Creation* (Grand Rapids: Eerdmans, 2014); Ron Highfield, *The Faithful Creator: Affirming Creation and Providence in an Age of Anxiety* (Downers Grove, IL: IVP Academic, 2015).

16. My favorite book on this theme is Alan Jacobs, *A Theology of Reading: The Hermeneutics of Love* (Boulder, CO: Westview, 2001).

17. Terence E. Fretheim, "The Book of Genesis: Introduction, Commentary, and Reflections," in *The New Interpreter's Bible*, ed. Leander E. Keck et al. (Nashville: Abingdon, 1994), 1:335.

18. For a brilliant book on this topic, see Jon D. Levenson, *Creation and the Persistence of Evil* (Princeton: Princeton University Press, 1994).

19. That question is answered decisively in Ronald E. Osborn, *Death before the Fall: Biblical Literalism and the Problem of Animal Suffering* (Downers Grove, IL: IVP Academic, 2014). For a sensitive examination of the ethical issues, see Nicola Hoggard Creegan, *Animal Suffering and the Problem of Evil* (Oxford: Oxford University Press, 2013).

20. Debates about the authorship and date of Genesis, Gen. 1–11, and the Pentateuch have been occurring for centuries. Just for the record, Gen. 1–3 has been dated to the time of Moses (the traditional view), to the time of the monarchy, and to the time of the exile in Babylon. A standard critical view is that Gen. 2–3 is from the monarchic period (the Yahwist source), while Gen. 1 is from the Priestly source and dates from the period of the exile. Most think the two accounts were brought together by the final editor of Genesis.

In addition, there are debates about how to relate Gen. 1 to Gen. 2. Some think the sixth day of Gen. 1 is given fuller treatment in Gen. 2. John Walton contends that Gen. 2 is not the clarification of the sixth day but is instead the election by God of two of the large population of humans originally created in Gen. 1 and now in need of two representative humans to carry on the mission of God. Thus, Gen. 2 is a sequel to Gen. 1. See John Walton, "A Historical Adam: Archetypal Creation View," in Barrett and Caneday, *Four Views on the Historical Adam*, 109–13.

For sketches of the history of the interpretation of Gen. 1–3, see Peter C. Bouteneff, *Beginnings: Ancient Christian Readings of the Biblical Creation Narratives* (Grand Rapids: Baker Academic, 2008); Seth D. Postell, *Adam as Israel: Genesis 1–3 as the Introduction to the Torah and Tanakh* (Eugene, OR: Wipf & Stock, 2011), 5–42. Bouteneff, in particular, examines how the post–New Testament era (the fathers of the church) read Scripture theologically through trinitarian and christological lenses. Adam is depicted as the first sinner, but some blame is shifted by such theologians toward the serpent, and at times Cain's sin in Gen. 4 is understood as much worse than Adam's. This shifting of blame will be countered by Augustine's heavy emphasis on the fall of Adam. For our purposes it is enough to observe that at times the earliest interpreters of the creation narrative were willing to diminish the historicity of the accounts in favor of theology and allegory.

21. Joseph Blenkinsopp, *Creation, Un-Creation, Re-Creation: A Discursive Commentary on Genesis 1–11* (New York: Bloomsbury T&T Clark, 2011), 16.

22. Severian of Gabala and Venerable Bede, *Commentaries on Genesis 1–3*, ed. Michael Glerup, trans. Robert C. Hill and Carmen S. Hardin (Downers Grove, IL: IVP Academic, 2010), 44–45. For an anthology that places side by side many early Christian observations about creation, science, and the text of Genesis, see Andrew Louth, ed., *Genesis 1–11*, Ancient Christian Commentary on Scripture 1 (Downers Grove, IL: IVP Academic, 2001). For the Reformation era, see John L. Thompson, ed., *Genesis 1–11*, Reformation Commentary on Scripture 1 (Downers Grove, IL: IVP Academic, 2012).

23. On this topic, see Kyle Greenwood, *Scripture and Cosmology: Reading the Bible between the Ancient World and Modern Science* (Downers Grove, IL: IVP Academic, 2015).

24. For discussion of a wide-ranging set of issues, problems, and solutions, see Blenkinsopp, *Creation, Un-Creation, Re-Creation*.

25. Osborn, *Death before the Fall*, 177.

26. Ibid., 177–78. For a recent book assessing the problem of unbiased research, see Alice Dreger, *Galileo's Middle Finger: Heretics, Activists, and the Search for Justice in Science* (New York: Penguin, 2015).

27. For a defense of the view just sketched, see Claude F. Mariottini, *Rereading the Biblical Text: Searching for Meaning and Understanding* (Eugene, OR: Wipf & Stock, 2013), 3–6. Mariottini is supported by nearly all interpreters, conservative and liberal.

28. For a book sensitive to students but that covers the spectrum of theories, see Tim Stafford, *The Adam Quest: Eleven Scientists Who Held on to a Strong Faith while Wrestling with the Mystery of Human Origins* (Nashville: Thomas Nelson, 2014).

29. Joseph Epstein, *Alexis de Tocqueville: Democracy's Guide*, Eminent Lives (New York: HarperCollins, 2006), 18.

30. Ibid.

31. Ibid., 193.

32. I have a chapter on why people walk away from the faith in Scot McKnight and Hauna Ondrey, *Finding Faith, Losing Faith: Stories of Conversion and Apostasy* (Waco: Baylor University Press, 2008), 7–61.

33. We need perhaps to ponder that the apostle Peter struggled to comprehend the apostle Paul's theology, as can be seen in 2 Pet. 3:16.

34. Russell Kirk, *The Conservative Mind: From Burke to Eliot*, 7th ed. (Washington, DC: Regnery, 1985), 38.

35. This has been a passionate concern for Karl Giberson. See Karl W. Giberson, *Saving the Original Sinner: How Christians Have Used the Bible's First Man to Oppress, Inspire, and Make Sense of the World* (Boston: Beacon, 2015), 27–43.

36. For a good defense of "archetypal" Adam (and Eve), see Walton, "Historical Adam," 89–118. Walton thinks the Bible focuses far more on the archetypal than the "real" Adam and Eve, though he also believes the archetypal Adam and Eve of Genesis were two real, historical people. Walton is one of the few who care about Eve in this discussion.

37. In using the word "literary," I do not mean "fictional" or "mythical," nor do I mean their opposite: "historical," "actual," or "real." I mean to say that the Adam and Eve of Genesis are persons in a literary product—Genesis—designed by the author to speak into and against various ancient Near Eastern ideas and literary texts. In this sense, "literary" is chosen because it is neutral and avoids what has become a problem in today's discussion—the so-called "historical" Adam. One of the great words in the history of literature—the literary world—is the word "myth," but that term has been put onto the shelf of suspicion by those who are more concerned with history. To have any awareness of what myths do is to be in contact with dimensions of life more real than real and deeper in history than the historical. But, again, by "literary" I don't mean "mythical."

38. Walton, "Historical Adam," 107.

Chapter 6 Adam and Eve of Genesis in Their Context: Twelve Theses

1. John Walton has pointed me to an exceptional study on this topic: Marc van de Mieroop, *Philosophy before the Greeks: The Pursuit of Truth in Ancient Babylonia* (Princeton: Princeton University Press, 2016).

2. For an introductory sketch defining science, see Gerald Rau, *Mapping the Origins Debate: Six Models of the Beginning of Everything* (Downers Grove, IL: IVP Academic, 2013), 23–27.

3. Bill T. Arnold, *Genesis*, New Cambridge Bible Commentary (Cambridge: Cambridge University Press, 2009), 29n3.

4. Walter Brueggemann, *Genesis*, Interpretation (Louisville: Westminster John Knox, 2010), 12.

5. For extensive lists of parallels between Genesis and ancient Near Eastern stories, see Peter Enns, *The Evolution of Adam: What the Bible Does and Doesn't Say about Human Origins* (Grand Rapids: Brazos, 2012), 54–56; Daniel C. Harlow, "After Adam: Reading Genesis in an Age of Evolutionary Science," *Perspectives on Science and Christian Faith* 62, no. 3 (2010): 179–95.

6. For a readable comparison of Genesis with this text, see Enns, *Evolution of Adam*, 38–43.

7. Gen. 1:2 uses the word "deep" in "darkness was over the surface of the deep." The Hebrew word translated as "deep" is *tehom*, a word that many think echoes and criticizes belief in Tiamat in the *Enuma Elish*. My colleague Claude Mariottini reminded me of this association.

8. I use the translation of W. G. Lambert, *Babylonian Creation Myths* (Winona Lake, IN: Eisenbrauns, 2013). One can also find a translation and summary in Victor Harold Matthews, *Old Testament Parallels: Laws and Stories from the Ancient Near East*, 3rd ed. (New York: Paulist Press, 2007), 11–20.

9. For an introduction and translation, see Andrew George, ed., *The Epic of Gilgamesh* (New York: Penguin, 2003).

10. Again, a good introductory comparison of *Atrahasis* with Genesis can be found in Enns, *Evolution of Adam*, 53–56.

11. Quotations of *Atrahasis* come from W. G. Lambert, A. R. Millard, and Miguel Civil, eds., *Atra-Hasis: The Babylonian Story of the Flood* (Winona Lake, IN: Eisenbrauns, 1999).

12. John Walton notes that in the Sumerian *Song of the Hoe*, humans sprout from the earth/ground on the basis of divine insemination or planting of seeds in the ground. See John H. Walton, *Genesis 1 as Ancient Cosmology* (Winona Lake, IN: Eisenbrauns, 2011), 74.

13. Quotations are taken from Richard J. Clifford, ed., *Creation Accounts in the Ancient Near East and in the Bible* (Washington, DC: Catholic Biblical Association of America, 1994), 49–51.

14. For a complementary listing, see John Walton, "A Historical Adam: Archetypal Creation View," in *Four Views on the Historical Adam*, ed. Matthew Barrett and Ardel Caneday (Grand Rapids: Zondervan, 2013), 102–4.

15. An important book on this topic, recommended by my colleague Jason Gile, is Nathan MacDonald, *Deuteronomy and the Meaning of "Monotheism,"* Forschungen zur Religion und Literatur des Alten und Neuen Testaments 2.1 (Tübingen: Mohr Siebeck, 2012).

16. Arnold, *Genesis*, 29.

17. Ibid., 46.

18. A very typical interpretation in the church; e.g., Johannes Brenz, John Calvin, and others in John L. Thompson, ed., *Genesis 1–11*, Reformation Commentary on Scripture 1 (Downers Grove, IL: IVP Academic, 2012), 41.

19. E.g., Arnold, *Genesis*, 44; C. John Collins, *Genesis 1–4: A Linguistic, Literary, and Theological Commentary* (Phillipsburg, NJ: P&R, 2005), 59–61.

20. J. Richard Middleton, *The Liberating Image: The* Imago Dei *in Genesis 1* (Grand Rapids: Brazos, 2005), 55–60. See also Donald Gowan, *From Eden to Babel: A Commentary on the Book of Genesis 1–11*, International Theological Commentary (Grand Rapids: Eerdmans, 1988), 27–28; Nahum M. Sarna, *Genesis*, JPS Torah Commentary (Philadelphia: The Jewish Publication Society, 2001), 12; Gordon John Wenham, *Genesis 1–15*, Word Biblical Commentary 1 (Grand Rapids: Zondervan, 2014), 28. This view was popular in the rabbinic tradition

as well. See Rabbi Nosson Scherman, *The Chumash: The Torah, Haftaros, and Five Megillos*, The Stone Edition (Brooklyn, NY: Mesorah Publications, 2000), 8.

21. Walton, *Genesis 1 as Ancient Cosmology*, 68–69.

22. For other combat texts, see Job 26:7–14; Ps. 89:5–14. For discussion, see Joseph Blenkinsopp, *Creation, Un-Creation, Re-Creation: A Discursive Commentary on Genesis 1–11* (New York: Bloomsbury T&T Clark, 2011), 35–39; Enns, *Evolution of Adam*, 62–65.

23. Walton, *Genesis 1 as Ancient Cosmology*, 69, 70–72; Middleton, *Liberating Image*, 263–69.

24. Middleton, *Liberating Image*, 74–77.

25. Ibid., 77–88; Walton, *Genesis 1 as Ancient Cosmology*; Walton, *The Lost World of Genesis One: Ancient Cosmology and the Origins Debate* (Downers Grove, IL: InterVarsity, 2009); Walton, *The Lost World of Adam and Eve: Genesis 2–3 and the Human Origins Debate* (Downers Grove, IL: IVP Academic, 2015). See also Jon D. Levenson, *Creation and the Persistence of Evil* (Princeton: Princeton University Press, 1994), 53–127; Enns, *Evolution of Adam*, 70–73.

26. A distinction now made by John Walton throughout *Genesis 1 as Ancient Cosmology*, *The Lost World of Genesis One*, and *The Lost World of Adam and Eve*.

27. Levenson, *Creation*, 47.

28. See also Edwin M. Good, *Genesis 1–11: Tales of the Earliest World* (Stanford, CA: Stanford University Press, 2011), 11–12.

29. Walton, *Lost World of Adam and Eve*, 48.

30. Arnold, *Genesis*, 48.

31. Leslie Stevenson, David L. Haberman, and Peter Matthews Wright, *Twelve Theories of Human Nature*, 6th ed. (New York: Oxford University Press, 2012).

32. Walton, *Genesis 1 as Ancient Cosmology*, 78.

33. Ryan S. Peterson, *Imago Dei as Human Identity*, Journal of Theological Interpretation Supplement 14 (Winona Lake, IN: Eisenbrauns, 2016), 1–2 (emphasis added). For an anthology of how theologians of the Reformation era understood "image," see Thompson, *Genesis 1–11*, 43–55.

34. See also Sarna, *Genesis*, 12; Wenham, *Genesis 1–15*, 31–32; Arnold, *Genesis*, 44–45. C. John Collins arrives at a similar though much thinner conclusion by ignoring the ancient Near Eastern context (*Genesis 1–4*, 61–67).

35. Middleton, *Liberating Image*, 25.

36. Ibid., 27.

37. Ibid., 109.

38. Peterson, *Imago Dei as Human Identity*, 3.

39. This polemic against idolatry is perfected in Isa. 40–48. See the brief notes in Blenkinsopp, *Creation, Un-Creation, Re-Creation*, 28.

40. One might infer that this indicates that creation was not, in fact, originally perfect, that it was perfect in potentiality only, and that death could well have been already present, and so Genesis and science can be more concordant—so Ronald E. Osborn, *Death before the Fall: Biblical Literalism and the Problem of Animal Suffering* (Downers Grove, IL: IVP Academic, 2014), 31 (and elsewhere).

41. I line up most closely with Roger Scruton, *How to Be a Conservative* (London: Continuum, 2014), 93–103.

42. Blenkinsopp, *Creation, Un-Creation, Re-Creation*, 70.

43. Notice how Paul goes back and forth on this in 1 Cor. 11:1–16. Man is from woman and woman is from man. Paul knows his Bible and he knows how human reproduction works.

44. It is necessary here to state that I am not hereby offering support for same-sex marriage but instead am speaking of common mutual relations of humans with one another.

45. I discuss this understanding of love in Scot McKnight, *A Fellowship of Differents: Showing the World God's Design for Life Together* (Grand Rapids: Zondervan, 2015), 51–63.

46. An excellent book on work is Göran Agrell, *Work, Toil and Sustenance* (Lund: Håkan Ohlssons, 1976).

47. *Enuma Elish* 1:1–2: "When on high, no heaven had been named, / When no earth had been called, / When there were no divine elders . . . / When there was nothing . . . / Nothing but . . . / Godfather Apsu and Mummu-Tiamat, Godmother of All Living, / Two bodies of water becoming one, / When no reed hut was erected, / When no marsh land was drained, / When there were no divine warriors, / When no names had been called, / When no tasks had been assigned . . ." (Matthews, *Old Testament Parallels*, 12).

48. The Hebrew word for "earth" is *adamah*, and the word used for the first human, a male, is *adam*. At this point (Gen. 2:7) *adam* is not a name but a generic classification: human, male, man. Only in Gen. 4 does "Adam" become his personal name. *Adam* is thus at times "human(kind)" (1:26–27; 2:5; 3:22–24; 5:1–2; 6:1–7), a male (2:7–4:1), or a proper name for the first male (4:25–5:5).

49. Church history has been filled with attempts to find the location of the original garden of Eden; this story has been told with abundant illustrations in Alessandro Scafi, *Maps of Paradise* (Chicago: University of Chicago Press, 2013).

50. There are remote parallels to the tree in the *Gilgamesh Epic*'s depiction of the giant tree in tablet 5.

51. Walton, *Lost World of Adam and Eve*, 77–81. Walton contends that being put to sleep refers to a dream vision of Adam's and that therefore this is not divine surgery but instead a visionary reality.

52. I would use the term "complement," but that term has been hijacked in modern conservative evangelical discussions to mean patriarchal hierarchy. There is a rabbinic tradition that sees in *kenegdo* a woman who will offer both support and resistance when the man needs to be brought in line or opposed. See Scherman, *Chumash*, 13.

53. E.g., Ps. 121:1–2.

54. Victor P. Hamilton, *The Book of Genesis: Chapters 1–17*, New International Commentary on the Old Testament (Grand Rapids: Eerdmans, 1990), 175–76.

55. Tremper Longman III, *Genesis*, Story of God Bible Commentary (Grand Rapids: Zondervan, 2016), 50. Very important on the meaning of *ezer* are the several works of Carolyn Custis James, and I mention but one: *Half the Church: Recapturing God's Global Vision for Women* (Grand Rapids: Zondervan, 2015).

56. Augustine, in his typical derogation of women, sees the *ezer* reduced to bearing children. See, e.g., Andrew Louth, ed., *Genesis 1–11*, Ancient Christian Commentary on Scripture 1 (Downers Grove, IL: IVP Academic, 2001), 68–69. Wolfgang Musculus (sixteenth century) sexualizes the woman as an *ezer*; see Thompson, *Genesis 1–11*, 105. But on p. 107 we read this far more important (deriving from others and oft-quoted) statement about the woman by Musculus: "[She was taken] . . . not from Adam's head, lest the woman grow haughty on account of her origin; nor from his feet, lest she seem to be demoted to the worthlessness and insignificance of a slave; but rather from Adam's side, so that he would know she was made to be his partner and the inseparable companion of his life, and so that she might legitimately cleave to his side, whence she was taken."

57. See, e.g., Brueggemann, *Genesis*, 41. To be sure, in both 1 Cor. 15 and Rom. 5 Paul opens the door to reading at least some themes in the Bible beginning with Adam, but that does not mean everyone (or anyone) else does the same.

58. See a brief defense of this view in Longman, *Genesis*, 70–73. We will discuss this in chap. 8.

59. The word "death" here raises questions: Does this mean they were immortal until they chose to eat of the tree and then became mortal (subject to death)? Does it mean capital punishment? Does it mean death in a more pervasive sense—the dust of death infiltrating the earthling's existence? Why, the reader asks, did God not put them to death, instead preserving them and locking them out of the garden of Eden? These questions, and others, are not answered in Genesis. Nor are any of the answers compelling to me.

60. For a defense of this view, see Claude F. Mariottini, *Rereading the Biblical Text: Searching for Meaning and Understanding* (Eugene, OR: Wipf & Stock, 2013), 7–10.

61. Terence E. Fretheim, "The Book of Genesis: Introduction, Commentary, and Reflections," in *The New Interpreter's Bible*, ed. Leander E. Keck et al. (Nashville: Abingdon, 1994), 1:361.

62. Severian of Gabala and Venerable Bede, *Commentaries on Genesis 1–3*, ed. Michael Glerup, trans. Robert C. Hill and Carmen S. Hardin (Downers Grove, IL: IVP Academic, 2010), 154.

63. We cannot chase down the interesting implications, but a good parallel to the serpent in the garden of Eden can be found in Ezek. 28:11–19, where instead of the serpent we find the haughty and fallen king of Tyre.

64. "Desire" in Gen. 3:16 is understood in the rabbinic tradition often as sexual desire, which also then will return the woman to the pain of childbearing; see Sarna, *Genesis*, 28.

65. This view is common in the church; see John Chrysostom in Louth, *Genesis 1–11*, 92–93. Importantly, Chrysostom thought that male and female were originally created as equals, but that this equality was undone by Eve's sin, and so subordination became her station in life. So too among others, Luther in Thompson, *Genesis 1–11*, 162. Calvin disastrously calls her station now "servitude" (ibid., 163).

66. For the descriptive view, see Arnold, *Genesis*, 70. Nahum Sarna sees male dominance coming from the fall, though it is not clear if he thinks it is merely descriptive (*Genesis*, 28). For the war of wills, see Susan T. Foh, "What Is the Woman's Desire?," *Westminster Theological Journal* 37 (1975): 376–83; Collins, *Genesis 1–4*, 159–60; Longman, *Genesis*, 67. See also Phyllis Trible, "Depatriarchalizing in Biblical Interpretation," *Journal for the American Academy of Religion* 41 (1973): 30–48. For a statement of the prescriptive view, though the author is clearly critical of what the Bible says, see Good, *Genesis 1–11*, 41.

67. Brueggemann, *Genesis*, 51 (emphasis original).

68. Notice they are *both* called Adam, showing that Adam in Gen. 1:26–27 was not just the male but both the male and female. "Adam," then, is a term of equality. Also, as my colleague Claude Mariottini pointed out to me, the KJV of Gen. 5:2 has a noteworthy, if literal, translation (emphasis added): "Male and female created he *them* . . . and called *their* name Adam." Instead of "Adam," the ESV has "Man" in uppercase to denote "humanity."

69. This has been worked out in a variety of ways. One can begin with Enns, *Evolution of Adam*, 65–70. Then turn to the midrashic approach of John H. Sailhamer, *The Pentateuch as Narrative: A Biblical-Theological Commentary* (Grand Rapids: Zondervan, 1995). His student Seth Postell has developed his midrashic theory in more detail; see Postell, *Adam as Israel: Genesis 1–3 as the Introduction to the Torah and Tanakh* (Eugene, OR: Wipf & Stock, 2011). Their choice not to read Gen. 1–3 in the ancient Near Eastern context seriously hampers their studies. On this, I think the wiser course is the way of Peter Enns's and John Walton's studies.

70. Enns, *Evolution of Adam*, 66.

71. See Christopher J. H. Wright, *The Mission of God: Unlocking the Bible's Grand Narrative* (Downers Grove, IL: IVP Academic, 2006); N. T. Wright, *The New Testament and the People of God*, Christian Origins and the Question of God 1 (Minneapolis: Fortress, 1992). For the most recent statement by N. T. Wright, see his excursus in Walton, *Lost World of Adam and Eve*, 170–80.

72. For a brief discussion, see Enns, *Evolution of Adam*, 88–92.

73. Walton, *Lost World of Adam and Eve*, 82–91.

74. N. T. Wright, "Do We Need a Historical Adam?," in *Surprised by Scripture: Engaging Contemporary Issues* (New York: HarperOne, 2014), 26–40. This chapter was Tom Wright's response at the BioLogos event in Manhattan after hearing papers on theistic evolution.

75. For sure, some might say there were something like 10,000 hominins from whom Adam and Eve were chosen by God; that they were chosen to represent all of those hominins; and the flood itself was not as global as it sounds—and this kind of explanation then permits a

concordist reading of Genesis. I don't dispute this as a possible reading; I do think such a reading is determined more by concordism than by historical readings of Genesis in context.

76. Concordism refers to a way of reading/interpreting Genesis that is in concord with science as we know it now, thereby granting to the Bible knowledge of science transcending its historical context.

Chapter 7 The Variety of Adams and Eves in the Jewish World

1. Notice these tensions at work in Alan Jacobs, *Original Sin: A Cultural History* (New York: HarperOne, 2008). One also observes the distinctiveness of the Christian understanding when one sees it in comparison with other religious and philosophical conceptions of human nature, as in Leslie Stevenson, David L. Haberman, and Peter Matthews Wright, *Twelve Theories of Human Nature*, 6th ed. (New York: Oxford University Press, 2012); Leslie Stevenson, ed., *The Study of Human Nature: A Reader*, 2nd ed. (New York: Oxford University Press, 2000).

In what follows, texts are referred to and cited from the Loeb Classical Library, the Old Testament Apocrypha from the New Revised Standard Bible, and from J. H. Charlesworth, ed., *The Old Testament Pseudepigrapha*, 2 vols. (Garden City, NY: Doubleday, 1985).

2. I am not satisfied with the book, but a good place to start is Matthew Barrett and Ardel Caneday, eds., *Four Views on the Historical Adam* (Grand Rapids: Zondervan, 2013). See also the controversial, fearless, and well-informed piece by Daniel C. Harlow, "After Adam: Reading Genesis in an Age of Evolutionary Science," *Perspectives on Science and Christian Faith* 62, no. 3 (2010): 179–95.

3. Prize of all books on this subject is John R. Levison, *Portraits of Adam in Early Judaism: From Sirach to 2 Baruch*, Journal for the Study of the Pseudepigrapha Supplement Series 1 (Sheffield: JSOT Press, 1988). My sketch here could not have been done without Levison's careful work. See also Levison, "Adam and Eve," in *The Eerdmans Dictionary of Early Judaism*, ed. J. J. Collins and Daniel C. Harlow (Grand Rapids: Eerdmans, 2010), 300–302. An older but useful study is W. D. Davies, *Paul and Rabbinic Judaism: Some Rabbinic Elements in Pauline Theology*, 4th ed. (Philadelphia: Fortress, 1980), 36–57. The most recent account can be found in Felipe de Jesús Legarreta-Castillo, *The Figure of Adam in Romans 5 and 1 Corinthians 15: The New Creation and Its Ethical and Social Reconfiguration*, Emerging Scholars (Minneapolis: Fortress, 2014). For a more wide-ranging study, see Gary A. Anderson, *The Genesis of Perfection: Adam and Eve in Jewish and Christian Imagination* (Louisville: Westminster John Knox, 2001). A brief sketch can be found in Peter Enns, *The Evolution of Adam: What the Bible Does and Doesn't Say about Human Origins* (Grand Rapids: Brazos, 2012), 99–103.

4. Sirach/Ecclesiasticus, Wisdom of Solomon, works by Philo of Alexandria.

5. *Jubilees*, works by Josephus, Pseudo-Philo's *Biblical Antiquities*, *Sibylline Oracles*, Greek *Life of Adam and Eve* (also called the *Apocalypse of Moses*).

6. *4 Ezra, 2 Baruch*.

7. Legarreta-Castillo, *Figure of Adam*, 38.

8. Ibid., 65–66.

9. Ibid., 96.

10. Quotations from Sirach are taken from the NRSV.

11. The Greek word translated here as "free choice" (*diaboulia*) refers to the inner deliberation and choice of Eve and then Adam (see a good Greek-English lexicon). Importantly, Levison connects this to the *yetser* theology—that is, to the human power of will (good will vs. bad will); see Levison, *Portraits of Adam*, 34.

12. Sirach 15:14 reads, "It was he who created humankind in the beginning," but the Greek text here is *ek* (from) and not *en* (in), and the Hebrew is *min* (from) and not *be* (in). Thus, Ben Sira sees God's creative work as continuous, and this puts the onus on each human as God's creation to respond to God. See Levison, *Portraits of Adam*, 35.

13. It is customary from Augustine through the Reformers, and all their faithful expositors, to think this text disconnects from a proper response to God's covenant, which is by faith, not works; but the language here is not unlike the language of Jesus (Matt. 16:27) or Paul (2 Cor. 5:10) or any of the other New Testament authors.

14. The order of the verses changes in various texts so that in this text v. 9 appears after v. 10. On this, see Patrick W. Skehan and Alexander A. Di Lella, *The Wisdom of Ben Sira*, Anchor Bible 39 (New York: Doubleday, 1987), 279.

15. This can be taken as a reference to Lev. 19:18, a theme Jesus will bring to the fore in Mark 12:28–34.

16. Skehan and Di Lella, *Wisdom of Ben Sira*, 399–401.

17. In Greek, *hyper pan zōon en tē ktisei*, "above every living thing in creation."

18. Skehan and Di Lella, *Wisdom of Ben Sira*, 545.

19. Levison, *Portraits of Adam*, 46–47. Thus, one needs to consider here that Ps. 8:6–7 gave to the author the idea of glory.

20. There is debate over whether Sir. 25:24 ("From a woman sin had its beginning, and because of her we all die") refers to Eve or to the wicked wife. For the former, see Legarreta-Castillo, *Figure of Adam*, 45–46. For the latter, see John R. Levison, "Is Eve to Blame? A Contextual Analysis of Sirach 25:24," *Catholic Biblical Quarterly* 47 (1985): 617–23.

21. Unless indicated otherwise, quotations from Wisdom of Solomon are from the NRSV.

22. David Winston, *The Wisdom of Solomon: A New Translation with Introduction and Commentary*, Anchor Bible 43 (Garden City, NY: Doubleday, 1979), 121.

23. The Greek reads, *kai ton empneusanta autō psychēn energousan kai emphysēsanta pneuma zōtikon*.

24. The Greek reads, *eikona tēs idias aidiotētos*. See Levison, *Portraits of Adam*, 49–62; J. Richard Middleton, *The Liberating Image: The* Imago Dei *in Genesis 1* (Grand Rapids: Brazos, 2005).

25. J. Edward Wright, *The Early History of Heaven* (New York: Oxford University Press, 2000); Colleen McDannell and Bernhard Lang, *Heaven: A History* (New Haven: Yale University Press, 1988); Jeffrey Burton Russell, *A History of Heaven* (Princeton: Princeton University Press, 1997); N. T. Wright, *The Resurrection of the Son of God*, The New Testament and the Question of God 3 (Minneapolis: Fortress, 2003).

26. Levison, *Portraits of Adam*, 51.

27. Ibid., 56.

28. In Greek, *gēgenous apogonos prōtoplastou*. See the brief listing of parallels in Winston, *Wisdom of Solomon*, 163.

29. For an introduction with important bibliography, see Everett Ferguson, *Backgrounds of Early Christianity*, 3rd ed. (Grand Rapids: Eerdmans, 2003), 478–85.

30. Translations of Philo are those of F. H. Colson and Ralph Marcus in the Loeb Classical Library.

31. *Pace* Legarreta-Castillo, *Figure of Adam*.

32. Levison, *Portraits of Adam*, 63–88. Philo is emphasized more in Legarreta-Castillo, *Figure of Adam*, 51–65. This figures more into his view of Paul in 1 Corinthians and Romans as his thesis unfolds.

33. Greek, *mimēma theias eikonos*.

34. This theme is also found in Philo, *Questions and Answers on Genesis* 1.4, 8, 51; 2.56.

35. See Plato, *Timaeus* 41–42.

36. For the one who has read Aristophanes's fantastical theory of human origins and the origins of the sexes in Plato (*Symposium* 189C–193D), Philo's observation that the two were "divided halves, as it were, of a single living creature" connects to Plato. As Levison observes, in *On the Contemplative Life* 63 Philo denies this view of Aristophanes.

37. Levison, *Portraits of Adam*, 71.

38. Ibid., 89–97.

39. The text of *Jubilees* can be found in Charlesworth, *Old Testament Pseudepigrapha*, 2:35–142.

40. Levison, *Portraits of Adam*, 96.

41. Legarreta-Castillo, *Figure of Adam*, 77–83. For the text, see Charlesworth, *Old Testament Pseudepigrapha*, 2:297–377, here 322.

42. For Adam in Josephus, see Levison, *Portraits of Adam*, 99–111. For an exceptional introduction by one of America's finest Josephus scholars, see L. H. Feldman, "Josephus," in *Dictionary of New Testament Background*, ed. C. A. Evans and S. E. Porter (Downers Grove, IL: InterVarsity, 2000), 590–96. For another view, see S. Mason, "Josephus," in Collins and Harlow, *Eerdmans Dictionary of Early Judaism*, 828–32.

43. The terms are palatable to a Greek-reading Roman audience: *kai physiologein Mōysēs . . . peri tēs tou anthrōpou kataskeuēs*. The verb *physiologein* speaks of examining natural causes and origins. Translations of Josephus's *Jewish Antiquities* are those of H. St. J. Thackeray in the Loeb Classical Library.

44. Greek: *ouk echonta koinōnian pros to thēly kai syndiaitēsin.*

45. See Levison, *Portraits of Adam*, 113–27.

46. Translations of *4 Ezra* are from Charlesworth, *Old Testament Pseudepigrapha*, 1:517–60, here 541.

47. Levison is less inclined to see inherited sinfulness or a fall in the traditional sense; see *Portraits of Adam*, 123.

48. Ibid., 129–44.

49. Translations of *2 Baruch* are from Charlesworth, *Old Testament Pseudepigrapha*, 1:615–52, here 640.

50. For brief commentary, see Levison, *Portraits of Adam*, 139–42.

Chapter 8 Adam, the Genome, and the Apostle Paul

1. As discussed in Scot McKnight and Hauna Ondrey, *Finding Faith, Losing Faith: Stories of Conversion and Apostasy* (Waco: Baylor University Press, 2008), 7–8.

2. Mary McCarthy, "My Confession," in *The Art of the Personal Essay: An Anthology from the Classical Era to the Present*, ed. Phillip Lopate (New York: Anchor Doubleday, 1994), 573.

3. From McKnight and Ondrey, *Finding Faith, Losing Faith*, 25.

4. Marilynne Robinson, *Gilead* (New York: Farrar, Straus & Giroux, 2004), 24.

5. See Augustine, *Against Two Epistles of the Pelagians* 4.4.7.

6. Once again, notice Sirach 25:15–26.

7. See the new study by Gary G. Hoag, appealing especially to Xenophon of Ephesus's novel *The Story of Anthia and Habrocomes* (otherwise known as *Ephesiaca*), *Wealth in Ancient Ephesus and the First Letter to Timothy: Fresh Insights from "Ephesiaca" by Xenophon of Ephesus*, Bulletin for Biblical Research Supplements 11 (Winona Lake, IN: Eisenbrauns, 2015).

8. I date 1 Corinthians before Romans. But Rom. 5:12–21 is more extensively concerned with the themes of this book, so my focus will be on Romans.

9. In the context of Romans, which is concerned with the relations between Jewish and gentile Christians in the churches of Rome, our passage forms a pivot, moving us from chapters 1–5 into the more ethical implications of Rom. 6–8. Hence, establishing new life in Christ, a theme in Rom. 5:12–21, will lead Paul to exhort the Romans to live a life pleasing to Christ.

10. Robert Jewett, *Romans: A Commentary*, Hermeneia (Minneapolis: Fortress, 2006), 370.

11. N. T. Wright, "The Letter to the Romans," in *The New Interpreter's Bible*, ed. Leander E. Keck et al. (Nashville: Abingdon, 2002), 10:523.

12. James D. G. Dunn, *The Theology of Paul the Apostle* (Grand Rapids: Eerdmans, 1998), 90–91.

13. For a brief sketch of the connections between Paul and the Jewish traditions, see Felipe de Jesús Legarreta-Castillo, *The Figure of Adam in Romans 5 and 1 Corinthians 15: The New Creation and Its Ethical and Social Reconfiguration*, Emerging Scholars (Minneapolis: Fortress, 2014), 154–56.

14. Plato, *Symposium*, trans. T. Griffith (Berkeley: University of California Press, n.d.), 189C–194E.

15. Translations of the *Apocalypse of Moses / Life of Adam and Eve* are from *The Old Testament Pseudepigrapha*, ed. J. H. Charlesworth (Garden City, NY: Doubleday, 1985), 2:249–96, here 281.

16. See Dunn, *Theology*, 98–100.

17. There were other options in Judaism, but Paul chose *epithymia*. For others, see Jewett, *Romans*, 374.

18. See John H. Walton, *The Lost World of Adam and Eve: Genesis 2–3 and the Human Origins Debate* (Downers Grove, IL: IVP Academic, 2015), 92–95.

19. See James D. G. Dunn, *Romans*, Word Biblical Commentary 38 (Grand Rapids: Zondervan, 2015), 1:288.

20. That much of what Paul says about Adam is not found in the Old Testament has been emphasized by Peter Enns, *The Evolution of Adam: What the Bible Does and Doesn't Say about Human Origins* (Grand Rapids: Brazos, 2012), 82–88.

21. A major emphasis on beginning with Christ can be seen in ibid., 131–35.

22. This theme has been emphasized time and again by N. T. Wright. For one of his most recent statements, see Wright, *Pauline Perspectives: Essays on Paul, 1978–2013* (Minneapolis: Fortress, 2013), 510–46, esp. 533–44.

23. For the former, see Dunn, *Romans*, 1:283. For the second meaning, see Wright, "Romans," 529.

24. Some have tripped over "all" as if Paul could somehow reverse the direction of all his missionary work and think that all would be saved. What Paul means by "all" is found in texts like Gal. 3:28 and Col. 3:11—namely, that in Christ redemption is expanded beyond Israel to include gentiles. The "all" is the "everyone may come" rather than "every single one will be saved." See, e.g., Dunn, *Romans*, 1:285.

25. Discussed in Wright's excursus in Walton, *Lost World of Adam and Eve*, 173–76.

26. Dunn, *Theology*, 94.

27. Douglas J. Moo, *The Epistle to the Romans*, New International Commentary on the New Testament (Grand Rapids: Eerdmans, 1996), 319.

28. Paul knows this, as is clear from 2 Cor. 11:3; 1 Tim. 2:14.

29. The translation of Rom. 5:12 is that of the NIV except for "spread," which is the NRSV translation of *dielthen* (aorist of *dierchomai*).

30. Thus, Robert Jewett: "Paul depicts Adam's act as decisively determining the behavior of his descendants." But he explains this not as original sin but in terms of society: "A social theory of sin appears to be implied here in which the actions of forebears determine those of their descendants" (*Romans*, 375).

31. For an extensive discussion of the Augustinian line of thinking, see S. Lewis Johnson, "Romans 5:12—An Exercise in Exegesis and Theology," in *New Dimensions in New Testament Study*, ed. Richard N. Longenecker and Merrill C. Tenney (Grand Rapids: Zondervan, 1974), 298–316.

32. Dunn, *Theology*, 96. For "physico-spiritual" and "total death," see Moo, *Romans*, 320.

33. Wright, "Romans," 525.

34. The Greek tense of *hēmarton* is aorist (thus, "sinned") and not perfect ("have sinned"). The latter props up a sinning of all *in Adam*, while the former presses responsibility more upon each person. Joseph Fitzmyer thinks *eph' hō* means "with the result that," but that makes death an act that provokes sin when in this passage it is sin that provokes death; see Fitzmyer, *Romans*, Anchor Bible 33 (New Haven: Yale University Press, 1993), 413–17.

35. Some emphasize the solidarity and see the solidarity clarifying what "because all have sinned" (in Adam) means. Two who do so are Moo, *Romans*, 321–29; Henri Blocher, *Original Sin: Illuminating the Riddle*, 2nd ed. (Downers Grove, IL: IVP Academic, 2000), 63–81.

36. The language of "in and with" comes from Moo's attempt to be more like Augustine than not, though he does not fully identify with him either; see Moo, *Romans*, 326.

37. Tom Holland, *Romans: The Divine Marriage; A Biblical Theological Commentary* (Eugene, OR: Wipf & Stock, 2011), 159. Blocher's paraphrase of Rom. 5:12 buries the grammar of Paul under some federal representation when he writes: "Just as through one man, Adam, sin entered the world and the sin-death connection was established, and so death could be inflicted on all as the penalty of their sins" (*Original Sin*, 78). It is clearer than that: they die because they sin. With slightly more emphasis on each person's responsibility, see Michael F. Bird, *Romans*, Story of God Bible Commentary (Grand Rapids: Zondervan, 2016), 178–80.

38. Dunn, *Theology*, 97n82.

39. Wright, "Romans," 527.

40. Paul J. Achtemeier, *Romans*, Interpretation (Atlanta: John Knox, 1986), 97.

41. Moo, *Romans*, 329; see also Wright, "Romans," 531–32.

42. Significant theological debate has taken place regarding the manner of transmission (realism, biological, seminal) and the more representative or federal headship theory of the relationship between Adam (and Eve) and the rest of the human race. But my perception of the belief in the historical Adam has as much to do with the biological and genetic connection as it does with the representative theory.

43. One could point to genealogies as an indicator leading toward some kind of biological and eventually historical Adam and Eve; for this argument, see Walton, *Lost World of Adam and Eve*, 96–103.

44. Fitzmyer, *Romans*, 407–8, 410.

45. Dunn, *Romans*, 1:289–90.

Afterword

1. Daniel Harrell, "Nature's Witness: How Science Inspires Faith," TEDx Talks, December 28, 2015, https://www.youtube.com/watch?v=4txYvRf-r_I.

2. Origen, *De Principiis* 4.16, in *Ante-Nicene Fathers*, ed. Alexander Roberts, James Donaldson, and A. Cleveland Coxe, trans. Frederick Crombie (repr., Grand Rapids: Eerdmans, 1979), 4:365 (emphasis added).

3. Origen, *De Principiis* 2.11.4, in *Ante-Nicene Fathers*, 4:298.

INDEX